THE NEW MIDDLE AGES

BONNIE WHEELER, *Series Editor*

The New Middle Ages is a series dedicated to pluridisciplinary studies of medieval cultures, with particular emphasis on recuperating women's history and on feminist and gender analyses. This peer-reviewed series includes both scholarly monographs and essay collections.

PUBLISHED BY PALGRAVE:

Women in the Medieval Islamic World: Power, Patronage, and Piety
  edited by Gavin R. G. Hambly

The Ethics of Nature in the Middle Ages: On Boccaccio's Poetaphysics
  by Gregory B. Stone

Presence and Presentation: Women in the Chinese Literati Tradition
  edited by Sherry J. Mou

The Lost Love Letters of Heloise and Abelard: Perceptions of Dialogue in Twelfth-Century France
  by Constant J. Mews

Understanding Scholastic Thought with Foucault
  by Philipp W. Rosemann

For Her Good Estate: The Life of Elizabeth de Burgh
  by Frances A. Underhill

Constructions of Widowhood and Virginity in the Middle Ages
  edited by Cindy L. Carlson and Angela Jane Weisl

Motherhood and Mothering in Anglo-Saxon England
  by Mary Dockray-Miller

Listening to Heloise: The Voice of a Twelfth-Century Woman
  edited by Bonnie Wheeler

The Postcolonial Middle Ages
  edited by Jeffrey Jerome Cohen

Chaucer's Pardoner and Gender Theory: Bodies of Discourse
  by Robert S. Sturges

Crossing the Bridge: Comparative Essays on Medieval European and Heian Japanese Women Writers
  edited by Barbara Stevenson and Cynthia Ho

Engaging Words: The Culture of Reading in the Later Middle Ages
  by Laurel Amtower

Robes and Honor: The Medieval World of Investiture
  edited by Stewart Gordon

Representing Rape in Medieval and Early Modern Literature
  edited by Elizabeth Robertson and Christine M. Rose

Same Sex Love and Desire among Women in the Middle Ages
  edited by Francesca Canadé Sautman and Pamela Sheingorn

Sight and Embodiment in the Middle Ages: Ocular Desires
  by Suzannah Biernoff

Listen, Daughter: The Speculum Virginum *and the Formation of Religious Women in the Middle Ages*
  edited by Constant J. Mews

Science, the Singular, and the Question of Theology
  by Richard A. Lee, Jr.

Gender in Debate from the Early Middle Ages to the Renaissance
  edited by Thelma S. Fenster and Clare A. Lees

Malory's Morte D'Arthur: *Remaking Arthurian Tradition*
  by Catherine Batt

The Vernacular Spirit: Essays on Medieval Religious Literature
  edited by Renate Blumenfeld-Kosinski, Duncan Robertson, and Nancy Warren

Popular Piety and Art in the Late Middle Ages: Image Worship and Idolatry in England 1350–1500
  by Kathleen Kamerick

Absent Narratives, Manuscript Textuality, and Literary Structure in Late Medieval England
  by Elizabeth Scala

Creating Community with Food and Drink in Merovingian Gaul
  by Bonnie Effros

Representations of Early Byzantine Empresses: Image and Empire
  by Anne McClanan

Encountering Medieval Textiles and Dress: Objects, Texts, Images
  edited by Désirée G. Koslin and Janet Snyder

Eleanor of Aquitaine: Lord and Lady
  edited by Bonnie Wheeler and John Carmi Parsons

Isabel La Católica, Queen of Castile: Critical Essays
  edited by David A. Boruchoff

Homoeroticism and Chivalry: Discourses of Male Same-Sex Desire in the Fourteenth Century
  by Richard E. Zeikowitz

Portraits of Medieval Women: Family, Marriage, and Politics in England 1225–1350
  by Linda E. Mitchell

Eloquent Virgins: From Thecla to Joan of Arc
  by Maud Burnett McInerney

The Persistence of Medievalism: Narrative Adventures in Contemporary Culture
  by Angela Jane Weisl

Capetian Women
  edited by Kathleen D. Nolan

Joan of Arc and Spirituality
  edited by Ann W. Astell and Bonnie Wheeler

The Texture of Society: Medieval Women in the Southern Low Countries
  edited by Ellen E. Kittell and Mary A. Suydam

Charlemagne's Mustache: And Other Cultural Clusters of a Dark Age
  by Paul Edward Dutton

Troubled Vision: Gender, Sexuality, and Sight in Medieval Text and Image
  edited by Emma Campbell and Robert Mills

Queering Medieval Genres
  by Tison Pugh

Sacred Place in Early Medieval Neoplatonism
  by L. Michael Harrington

The Middle Ages at Work
  edited by Kellie Robertson and Michael Uebel

Chaucer's Jobs
  by David R. Carlson

Medievalism and Orientalism: Three Essays on Literature, Architecture and Cultural Identity
  by John M. Ganim

Queer Love in the Middle Ages
  by Anna Klosowska

Performing Women in the Middle Ages: Sex, Gender, and the Iberian Lyric
  by Denise K. Filios

Necessary Conjunctions: The Social Self in Medieval England
  by David Gary Shaw

Visual Culture and the German Middle Ages
  edited by Kathryn Starkey and Horst Wenzel

Medieval Paradigms: Essays in Honor of Jeremy duQuesnay Adams, Volumes 1 and 2
  edited by Stephanie Hayes-Healy

False Fables and Exemplary Truth in Later Middle English Literature
  by Elizabeth Allen

Ecstatic Transformation: On the Uses of Alterity in the Middle Ages
  by Michael Uebel

Sacred and Secular in Medieval and Early Modern Cultures: New Essays
   edited by Lawrence Besserman

Tolkien's Modern Middle Ages
   edited by Jane Chance and Alfred K. Siewers

Representing Righteous Heathens in Late Medieval England
   by Frank Grady

Byzantine Dress: Representations of Secular Dress in Eighth-to-Twelfth Century Painting
   by Jennifer L. Ball

The Laborer's Two Bodies: Labor and the "Work" of the Text in Medieval Britain, 1350–1500
   by Kellie Robertson

The Dogaressa of Venice, 1250–1500: Wife and Icon
   by Holly S. Hurlburt

Logic, Theology, and Poetry in Boethius, Abelard, and Alan of Lille: Words in the Absence of Things
   by Eileen C. Sweeney

The Theology of Work: Peter Damian and the Medieval Religious Renewal Movement
   by Patricia Ranft

On the Purification of Women: Churching in Northern France, 1100–1500
   by Paula M. Rieder

Writers of the Reign of Henry II: Twelve Essays
   edited by Ruth Kennedy and Simon Meecham-Jones

Lonesome Words: The Vocal Poetics of the Old English Lament and the African-American Blues Song
   by M.G. McGeachy

Performing Piety: Musical Culture in Medieval English Nunneries
   by Anne Bagnell Yardley

The Flight from Desire: Augustine and Ovid to Chaucer
   by Robert R. Edwards

Mindful Spirit in Late Medieval Literature: Essays in Honor of Elizabeth D. Kirk
   edited by Bonnie Wheeler

Medieval Fabrications: Dress, Textiles, Clothwork, and Other Cultural Imaginings
   edited by E. Jane Burns

Was the Bayeux Tapestry Made in France?: The Case for St. Florent of Saumur
   by George Beech

Women, Power, and Religious Patronage in the Middle Ages
   by Erin L. Jordan

Hybridity, Identity, and Monstrosity in Medieval Britain: On Difficult Middles
   by Jeffrey Jerome Cohen

Medieval Go-betweens and Chaucer's Pandarus
   by Gretchen Mieszkowski

The Surgeon in Medieval English Literature
   by Jeremy J. Citrome

Temporal Circumstances: Form and History in the Canterbury Tales
   by Lee Patterson

Erotic Discourse and Early English Religious Writing
   by Lara Farina

Odd Bodies and Visible Ends in Medieval Literature
   by Sachi Shimomura

On Farting: Language and Laughter in the Middle Ages
   by Valerie Allen

Women and Medieval Epic: Gender, Genre, and the Limits of Epic Masculinity
   edited by Sara S. Poor and Jana K. Schulman

Race, Class, and Gender in "Medieval" Cinema
   edited by Lynn T. Ramey and Tison Pugh

Allegory and Sexual Ethics in the High Middle Ages
   by Noah D. Guynn

England and Iberia in the Middle Ages, 12th-15th Century: Cultural, Literary, and Political Exchanges
  edited by María Bullón-Fernández

The Medieval Chastity Belt: A Myth-Making Process
  by Albrecht Classen

Claustrophilia: The Erotics of Enclosure in Medieval Literature
  by Cary Howie

Cannibalism in High Medieval English Literature
  by Heather Blurton

The Drama of Masculinity and Medieval English Guild Culture
  by Christina M. Fitzgerald

Chaucer's Visions of Manhood
  by Holly A. Crocker

The Literary Subversions of Medieval Women
  by Jane Chance

Manmade Marvels in Medieval Culture and Literature
  by Scott Lightsey

American Chaucers
  by Candace Barrington

Representing Others in Medieval Iberian Literature
  by Michelle M. Hamilton

Paradigms and Methods in Early Medieval Studies
  edited by Celia Chazelle and Felice Lifshitz

King and the Whore: King Roderick and La Cava
  by Elizabeth Drayson

Langland's Early Modern Identities
  by Sarah A. Kelen

Cultural Studies of the Modern Middle Ages
  edited by Eileen A. Joy, Myra J. Seaman, Kimberly K. Bell, and Mary K. Ramsey

Hildegard of Bingen's Unknown Language: An Edition, Translation, and Discussion
  by Sarah L. Higley

Medieval Romance and the Construction of Heterosexuality
  by Louise M. Sylvester

Communal Discord, Child Abduction, and Rape in the Later Middle Ages
  by Jeremy Goldberg

Lydgate Matters: Poetry and Material Culture in the Fifteenth Century
  edited by Lisa H. Cooper and Andrea Denny-Brown

Sexuality and Its Queer Discontents in Middle English Literature
  by Tison Pugh

Sex, Scandal, and Sermon in Fourteenth-Century Spain: Juan Ruiz's Libro de Buen Amor
  by Louise M. Haywood

The Erotics of Consolation: Desire and Distance in the Late Middle Ages
  edited by Catherine E. Léglu and Stephen J. Milner

Battlefronts Real and Imagined: War, Border, and Identity in the Chinese Middle Period
  edited by Don J. Wyatt

Wisdom and Her Lovers in Medieval and Early Modern Hispanic Literature
  by Emily C. Francomano

Power, Piety, and Patronage in Late Medieval Queenship: Maria de Luna
  by Nuria Silleras-Fernandez

In the Light of Medieval Spain: Islam, the West, and the Relevance of the Past
  edited by Simon R. Doubleday and David Coleman, foreword by Giles Tremlett

Chaucerian Aesthetics
  by Peggy A. Knapp

Memory, Images, and the English Corpus Christi Drama
  by Theodore K. Lerud

Cultural Diversity in the British Middle Ages: Archipelago, Island, England
  edited by Jeffrey Jerome Cohen

Excrement in the Late Middle Ages: Sacred Filth and Chaucer's Fecopoetics
   by Susan Signe Morrison

Authority and Subjugation in Writing of Medieval Wales
   edited by Ruth Kennedy and Simon Meecham-Jones

The Medieval Poetics of the Reliquary: Enshrinement, Inscription, Performance
   by Seeta Chaganti

The Legend of Charlemagne in the Middle Ages: Power, Faith, and Crusade
   edited by Matthew Gabriele and Jace Stuckey

The Poems of Oswald von Wolkenstein: An English Translation of the Complete Works (1376/77–1445)
   by Albrecht Classen

Women and Experience in Later Medieval Writing: Reading the Book of Life
   edited by Anneke B. Mulder-Bakker and Liz Herbert McAvoy

WOMEN AND EXPERIENCE IN LATER MEDIEVAL WRITING

READING THE BOOK OF LIFE

Edited by
Anneke B. Mulder-Bakker and
Liz Herbert McAvoy

Publication of this work in English has been made possible by grants from the Royal Dutch Academy of Sciences (KNAW) and the Groningen Institute for Research in the Humanities (ICOG)

WOMEN AND EXPERIENCE IN LATER MEDIEVAL WRITING
Copyright © Anneke B. Mulder-Bakker and Liz Herbert McAvoy, 2009.

All rights reserved.

First published in 2009 by
PALGRAVE MACMILLAN®
in the United States—a division of St. Martin's Press LLC,
175 Fifth Avenue, New York, NY 10010.

Where this book is distributed in the UK, Europe and the rest of the world, this is by Palgrave Macmillan, a division of Macmillan Publishers Limited, registered in England, company number 785998, of Houndmills, Basingstoke, Hampshire RG21 6XS.

Palgrave Macmillan is the global academic imprint of the above companies and has companies and representatives throughout the world.

Palgrave® and Macmillan® are registered trademarks in the United States, the United Kingdom, Europe and other countries.

ISBN-13: 978–0–230–60287–8
ISBN-10: 0–230–60287–8

Library of Congress Cataloging-in-Publication Data

    Women and experience in later medieval writing : reading the book of life / edited by Anneke B. Mulder-Bakker and Liz Herbert McAvoy.
       p. cm.—(New Middle Ages)
    Includes bibliographical references and index.
    ISBN 0–230–60287–8
    1. Literature, Medieval—History and criticism. 2. Women in literature. 3. Literature, Medieval—Women authors—History and criticism. I. Mulder-Bakker, Anneke B. II. McAvoy, Liz Herbert.

PN682.W6W65 2009
809'.9335220902—dc22   2008040403

A catalogue record of the book is available from the British Library.

Design by Newgen Imaging Systems (P) Ltd., Chennai, India.

First edition: May 2009
10 9 8 7 6 5 4 3 2 1

Printed in the United States of America.

CONTENTS

Acknowledgments   xi

List of Abbreviations   xiii

1. *Experientia* and the Construction of Experience in Medieval Writing: An Introduction   1
   Anneke B. Mulder-Bakker and Liz Herbert McAvoy

2. The New Devout and their Women of Authority   25
   Koen Goudriaan

3. Partners in Profession: Inwardness, Experience, and Understanding in Heloise and Abelard   47
   Ineke van 't Spijker

4. Communities of Discourse: Religious Authority and the Role of Holy Women in the Later Middle Ages   65
   Carolyn Muessig

5. Two Women of Experience, Two Men of Letters, and the Book of Life   83
   Anneke B. Mulder-Bakker

6. "[A]n awngel al clothyd in white": Rereading the Book of Life as *The Book of Margery Kempe*   103
   Liz Herbert McAvoy

7. *Die Gheestelicke Melody*: A Program for the Spiritual Life in a Middle Dutch Song Cycle   123
   Thom Mertens

8. Handing on Wisdom and Knowledge in Hadewijch of Brabant's *Book of Visions*   149
   Veerle Fraeters

9	Afterword *Diane Watt*	169

Notes on Contributors   177
General Index   179
Index of Modern Authors   191

ACKNOWLEDGMENTS

This volume can be read in terms of its being the "Book of Life" of an international community of medieval scholars, sometimes friends, who have been meeting over the years at conferences in order to discuss the contribution of urban women and men—the so-called laity—to religious culture in medieval Europe.

It was, however, a workshop in Groningen, The Netherlands, in 2005, organized by the Groningen colleagues Catrien Santing and Karl Heidecker and devoted to the *Book of Life: The Transmission of Knowledge and the Problems of Gender*, that first induced us to use *experientia* as the theme of our research and to make an attempt to provide a better qualified understanding of the gender and power dynamics in the community of the faithful in Northern Europe in the Later Middle Ages. We are grateful to Bonnie Wheeler and Palgrave Macmillan, USA, for facilitating the publication of our findings.

As the initial Dutch équipe, we received considerable support, both material and otherwise, in The Netherlands and abroad. The Royal Dutch Academy of Sciences (KNAW) and the Groningen Institute for Research in the Humanities (ICOG) endowed the costs of the 2005 workshop. They also subsidized translation costs and editorial assistance. We are also grateful to Robert Olson who undertook the translations and to Evelien Timperer for her assistance with the editing process.

Great thanks are also due to Diane Watt, author of the recently published *Medieval Women's Writing* (Polity, 2007), for her acceptance of a late invitation to write an afterword evaluating the results of our research and for setting out a firm research agenda for the coming years.

My chief debt is to Liz Herbert McAvoy, a pivotal contributor from the start, for being amenable to my appeal to join the editorial team by scrutinizing the texts of the second-language contributors and focusing the theoretical reflection.

ABBREVIATIONS

AASS	*Acta Sanctorum* (quoted from the new edition, Brussels 1868–1925, which has a continuous numbering of all volumes)
CCCM	Corpus Christianorum, Continuatio mediaevalis
CCSL	Corpus Christianorum, Series Latina
EETS	Early English Text Society
PL	J.-P. Migne, *Patrologia cursus completus: Series Latina*. 221 vols. Paris: Migne, 1861–1864

CHAPTER 1

EXPERIENTIA AND THE CONSTRUCTION OF EXPERIENCE IN MEDIEVAL WRITING: AN INTRODUCTION

Anneke B. Mulder-Bakker and Liz Herbert McAvoy

In her essay entitled "The Power of Discourse," feminist commentator Luce Irigaray demands: "How, then, are we to try to redefine this language work that would leave space for the feminine? Let us say that every dichotomizing—and at the same time redoubling—break, including the one between enunciation and utterance has to be disrupted."[1] Recognizing the "work" undertaken by language as traditionally a male and masculinist enterprise, Irigaray posits a position of disruptive potential lying within the hegemonic realm between thought–conception and speech–act. If women were to take up a position within this realm between the dichotomies, their own disruptive enterprises "would thus attempt to thwart any manipulation of discourse that would also leave discourse intact." Moreover, this disruption would come about not through utterance itself, but in "its *autological presupposition*."[2]

By *autological presupposition* Irigaray refers to the default position of male thought and assumptions that have traditionally been brought to bear upon the world as interpretive mechanisms. Men were considered the ones who produced and read the written word; they were also the ones schooled and qualified as *litterati* [men of letters]; they became teachers and instructors. Women, on the other hand, were not traditionally schooled in literate matters, nor were they ever considered to be *litteratae*. Women did not read, they learned from the "book of experience." They were experts in nonintellectual, experiential ways of knowing. Women were not teachers or writers, but devouts awash with mystical raptures.

These types of suppositions embody the fundamental dichotomy between attitudes toward male and female intellectual endeavor during the Middle Ages. Reliant on the type of gender distinctions generally widespread during the period, this dichotomy, as Irigaray clearly demonstrates, continues to have repercussions on our contemporary views of male and female learning activities and potential. Thus, it is exactly these types of suppositions that will be strongly contested in this volume of essays, all of which focus on the fabric of experience as woven into the writings by, for, and about women in the later Middle Ages. Under particular scrutiny will be the issue of women who, supposedly restricted to learning only from the book of experience because of the "limitations" of their gender, move on and embrace fully the desire to become writers themselves, taking up a position within the Irigarayan realm of disruptive potential between the accepted male and female intellectual positions.

Women's Life Experiences

Medieval texts often speak of *experientia* and *experimento docta* [learning by trial and error] in their discussions of women. Typical in this respect is the saint's Life written by the Premonstratensian monk Hugh of Floreffe about the anchoress Yvette of Huy.[3] Speaking of the budding saint, he observes that she "had not yet learned from experience" [*nondum experimento didicerat* and that "she was still reliant upon learning by trial and error" [*experimento discere cogebatur*]. Further on, Hugh notes that Yvette "came to know by experience" [*experimento cognovit*] and concludes even more explicitly: "rebus potius, quam verbis edocta, prout in libro experientiae didicerat" [events taught her rather than words as she learned from the book of experience].[4] Modern scholarship interprets Hugh's words here as self-explanatory, reading them within the paradigm of the aforementioned dichotomy of bookish learning vis à vis experiential training. It has long been taken for granted that a woman such as Yvette was devoid of any school education and was probably illiterate, unable to read and write. She was understood to have had no choice but to learn by hands-on training, pointing again toward the type of "autological presupposition" identified by Irigaray. This presupposition is clearly configured within the text: Hugh takes pains to recount that Yvette married young at the age of thirteen and had already borne three children by the time she reached eighteen. Having then been widowed, she bore the responsibility for her family and a fairly substantial property all on her own. Obviously enough, the young Yvette would most likely have been completely occupied by her children and the running of her household at that time. Her experience and learning referred to by Hugh was therefore considered to be the result of such life experience and the type of practical wisdom acquired by Yvette within the domestic sphere. In this case, *experientia* can certainly be interpreted as "the method or process of acquiring knowledge or understanding by observation, especially through sensory perception, as opposed to gaining knowledge through logical inference" or by studying books.[5] And, as we have seen, *experimentum*, the learning by trial and error, is also equated with the experiential accumulation of knowledge.

Such an interpretation of Hugh's text not only complies with medieval usage of the terms *experientia* and *experimentum*, but also with modern notions of experience as being a practical acquaintance with knowledge obtained from "hands-on" training rather than from bookish learning practices.[6] There are several reasons, however, not to trust this prima facie understanding of *experientia* and to reevaluate it in ways that allow for a rather different, far more nuanced understanding of the term. The *Middle English Dictionary*, cited earlier, offers several other meanings for *experientia*, including: "knowledge, information, 'know-how,'...understanding, or wisdom." Here it can be inferred that the person acquiring the experience has already been able to gain knowledge in other ways, that there is some kind of teleology at play. However, the ability to see with one's own eyes and hear with one's own ears gives this previously acquired knowledge an extra dimension that is clearly predicated on personal experience.[7]

A careful reading of women's life stories from the Middle Ages shows that a significant number of the women concerned evidently possessed a great deal of knowledge about matters that were far beyond the reach of the simple and uneducated women that traditional gender ideologies have claimed them to be. Yvette, for instance, taught her son the basics of sacred learning and expounded Bible passages to young monks. She also "understood the virtues of the gemstones and the names of the angels and their distinct orders...and knew them though as a simple unlearned woman she had never studied such things before." All things considered, Yvette reveals that she possesses fivefold knowledge: she had accumulated life experience in her daily affairs, including marriage and motherhood;[8] she possessed clear insight into the human soul, identified by Hugh as *sapientia* [sapiential knowledge or wisdom];[9] she was granted, what he terms prophetic knowledge about people's salvation;[10] she also possessed bookish learning, as described earlier; and even speculative, divine knowledge. As Hugh indicates: although she never "wished to know more than she ought to know,...her mind sometimes was rapt to contemplation of the eternal and the individuals of the Trinity." In fact, Yvette actually appears to have had similar knowledge to what clerics might have expected to acquire in schools. Yet, her own education, schooled or otherwise, is typified as life experience or as wisdom by her biographer Hugh of Floreffe. In this way he constructs her formation and keeps her attitude toward it firmly dressed up within accepted gender parameters: it was neither presumptuous nor "more than she ought to know." Thus we can clearly see in operation here the archetypical male construction of female learning practices based on what I will argue is a false dichotomy. As readers and scholars, we need to be alert to this type of autological construction, rethink the relationship between medieval women and learning, and be sensitive to the alternatives that lie beneath the surface of the texts. In truth, Hugh's concept of *experientia* would seem also to include types of school-based learning. This, however, is not to say that it simply equates with school learning itself, since it may refer to a much wider-ranging concept of knowing than the term "learning" would suggest, as we will see presently.

The same thing can be said of other holy women of the time.[11] Mary of Oignies, for example, is sometimes said to have been "adequately instructed in Holy Scripture." However, she simultaneously "belched forth [in rapture] many and wondrous readings from a wondrous and unheard of fullness and...read to us from the book of life, suddenly changing from a disciple into a master."[12] Similarly, Juliana of Cornillon, a scholarly young woman from Liège, was, according to her hagiographer, taken up into heaven during a vision where she received "thorough insight into all the articles pertaining to the catholic faith," an insight that is balanced against the factual knowledge of the masters, or even surpasses it (see chapter five).

We can go even further. While frequently associated with female religious experience, this "miraculous" type of divine learning is not limited to women, however, but is also encountered in reports of and about male clerics and monks. In a sermon, the learned monk Helinand of Froidmont (d. after 1229) told his audience of masters:

> Real knowledge is not found by studying the liberal arts at Paris, the classical writers at Orléans, the legal codices at Bologna, the medicine chests at Salerno, or the spirits of astrology at Toledo but only in the book of life, which is also the book of knowledge [liber scientiae], that means the wisdom of God [Dei sapientia] in which all treasures of sapiential knowledge and learning [thesauri sapientiae et scientiae] are hidden.[13]

Experientia as practical know-how, as sapiential knowledge, as a source of wisdom, divine learning, and scholastic theology is thus a much richer and more complicated concept than suggested by the aforementioned—and somewhat simplistically configured—dichotomy between female experience and male learning. It is for this reason that the ways in which that experience is constructed need to be thoroughly revisited and reinterpreted in each individual text by, about, or for women of the period. Nor should we neglect the experience of men either, as I have suggested: was there ever as clearly marked a dichotomy between male and female learning experiences as we have been led to believe, particularly among the laity? And what conclusions about the literacies of men and women can we derive from the use of *experientia* as a category of analysis in medieval texts, or about the relationship of women to learning? More generally, how did the clergy and other groups in society view the various forms of experience? All of the chapters collected together in this present volume will focus on aspects of these issues and, in particular, will examine how women's experience was viewed when taken in conjunction with spiritual issues. Most medieval women's writing was deeply religious in content[14] and interpretation of these texts and the amount of learning or literacy that lay behind them continues to cause far and away the greatest number of difficulties for the contemporary scholar. It is hoped, therefore, that the essays included here will go some way to resolving some of the more intransigent of those difficulties.

While each of the essays represents an exploratory probing by its contributor into a specific case concerning female learning practices and/or literary production, in this introduction I aim to focus first upon what we know about the actual school-training of the devout women mentioned in the sources, and second on what we know about the "communities of discourse" in which these women were engaged with clerics, friars, and the common faithful. Additionally, I aim to address the religious culture in which they all lived, the ways of knowing and the ways of writing practiced there. After pondering these questions, I will return to the concept of *experientia* as it is addressed by each of the individual contributors to this collection.

School Education

At the time before universities and other *studia generalia* had begun to widen the educational gender division within society by profiling themselves as the standard institution for higher education and consistently excluding females, girls often seem to have enjoyed considerable education.[15] For example, they received schooling at home, were educated in beguine houses, or even attended chapter schools in the cities.[16] As a result, Mary of Oignies (d. 1213) regularly read devotional texts with other women in her beguinage and was able to read the psalter (in Latin).[17] Ida of Nivelles (d. 1231), who fled to beguines as a child clasping her psalter to her breast, had some familiarity with Latin when she entered the cloister at the age of sixteen.[18] Margaret of Ypres (d. 1234) studied the Bible and Christian doctrine in the home of her uncle, who was a priest.[19] Christina the Astonishing (d. 1224) must have received an excellent education despite her itinerant existence, for in her old age she demonstrated a knowledge of Latin and an ability to interpret Scripture.[20] The recluse with whom Thomas of Cantimpré maintained a spiritual friendship told him that as a child she had been too poor for ordinary schooling but that pious women in the town had given her a psalter and arranged for her to attend Sunday school.[21] Juliana of Cornillon (d. 1259), the studious maiden from Liège, read the Bible in both Latin and the vernacular, and studied the Church Fathers. At a young age, she was brought into contact with theological masters from the diocese and may have even attended a chapter school in Liège. Her younger friend Eve (d. after 1264), the recluse of Saint-Martin in Liège, was well educated, even learned, and the circle of spiritual friends that formed around her came to speak with her and Juliana about matters of faith (see chapter five). In addition, Hadewijch, the thirteenth-century or perhaps early-fourteenth-century mystic and author, must have also been well schooled in the theological developments of her age, as Fraeters (chapter eight) reveals. Furthermore, we simply do not know if the academic education of Heloise (d. 1164, see chapter three) made her an exception in the twelfth century or just another case of a highly educated "civil-servant" daughter, as Yvette of Huy must also have been.

These, of course, were all women from the Low Countries and Northern France in the twelfth and thirteenth centuries. However, Angela of Foligno (d. 1309) and Margaret of Faenza (d. 1330) lived in Italy, and well into the fourteenth century. As Muessig notes (chapter four), Margaret stunned her Latin teacher with the language knowledge she possessed, while Agnes Blannbekin (d. 1315) who lived in Vienna, also knew Latin and studied religious authors (chapter five). In the later Middle Ages, schools had been established in most of the towns and cities, at least in Northern Europe. The elementary schools were usually coeducational and, as a result, girls received a school education just like their male counterparts. As far as the sources reveal anything on this subject, the women of authority mentioned in Goudriaan's essay (chapter two) appear to have had a good education. In fact, during the fifteenth century about half of the urban population, both male and female, seems to have received some kind of basic schooling. Nevertheless, in matters divine women's views continued to be presented as insights from above, infused by Mary or the Holy Spirit, and very little to do with a formal acquisition of knowledge. The same remains true of England during the same period. The one-time recluse and later prioress Christina of Markyate (d. after 1155) appears to have had reading abilities in English, French, and Latin, although her learning is frequently depicted in her *Life* as having been obtained from a divine or angelic source. The later mystic and recluse Julian of Norwich (d. after 1416) demonstrates a sophisticated understanding of mystical theology and Christocentric devotion, while professing to be both unlettered and unlearned. And Margery Kempe (see chapter six), a near contemporary of Julian, again professes illiteracy and divine inspiration while demonstrating a more than passing familiarity with the writings of Walter Hilton, pseudo-Bonaventura, and Richard Rolle.[22] Close scrutiny, therefore, of such women and their learning practices, points toward a much less clearly defined dichotomy than has previously been considered. Of course, the educational level of these women is extraordinary, but so is the level of contemporary learned men such as Abelard or Bernard of Clairvaux. As John Van Engen notes: "They become intelligible only if we presume, as they did, hundreds of cleric-students and monks around them, doing what they did, in less brilliant, even entirely unknown, ways." Something similar holds true for the women we encounter in the sources.[23]

Community of Discourse

It is important to remember that in the Middle Ages, far from occupying separate spheres, people of all backgrounds met and interacted within an informal, community-based public arena, as opposed to the deeply gendered institutional environments of the schools, universities, and monasteries. Here, in what can be termed communities of discourse—to borrow a felicitous concept from Bernard McGinn[24]—they discussed their ideas and enriched each other. This interchange involved discursive interaction among various individuals in all kinds of informal settings: between couples in the bedroom and within the family context, between devout men and women talking with beguines in the beguinage, in informal reading groups in the city, or with recluses instructing the faithful from the windows of their anchorholds. Nor were such interactions necessarily gender-specific, giving rise to an unofficial "discursive economy" that lay closer to the grey area between the traditionally allocated poles of male–female interactions than has generally been acknowledged.[25]

For instance, the laywoman Margery Kempe (chapter six) paid a visit at the beginning of her spiritual career in 1413 to the celebrated recluse Julian of Norwich and remained "many days" with her while they engaged in spiritual matters. Kempe was overtly placing herself here within a circle of male and female disciples who formed "an authorizing community" around the anchoress who was evidently of some renown within Norwich and its environs. The "sweet thyngys and good cownsel" given by Julian during this encounter were to lead Kempe on to her own spiritual path and contribute in no small way to the eventual production of her own book.[26] As Muessig also demonstrates in her appraisal of the *Memorial* by Angela of Foligno and her Brother A. (chapter four), this text encapsulates perfectly the nature of the community of discourse as a mutual endeavor to comprehend one's soul and God through conversation with others. In his monograph devoted to the mystical chaplain and hermit Ruusbroec (d. 1381), Geert Warnar writes about the "intellectual clerical middle class" in Brussels and the circles of God-fearing men and women to whom we owe the flowering of Middle Dutch literature,[27] and it is clear that medieval East Anglia was similarly endowed with such circles of intellectual activity, possibly influenced by its Dutch neighbors.[28] In Brussels, prosperous citizens commissioned translations of the Bible, as Jan Taye did in 1360; mendicants mediated scholastic learning from Paris, informal reading groups of clergy and laymen read spiritual texts. Widows and beguines residing in the vicinity of these clerics were in contact with them, and perhaps the literary idiom of Hadewijch (chapter eight) reached Ruusbroec through them. Ruusbroec was in fact not university-educated and even possessed a certain disdain for scholastic hair-splitting. For him, divine experience, which is after all another form of experience, was much more essential than theological astuteness: "Dies noeyt en ghevoelde, hi en saelt niet wel verstaen" [He who has not experienced this will not understand it].[29] Devout laypeople of both sexes and spiritual leaders from elsewhere, as exemplified by the New Devout Geert Grote, came to him in order to "ghecrighen experiencie van gewariger wijsheit" [receive experience of true wisdom].[30] It was therefore here in this type of colorful company that *experientia*, the affective experience of faith, the lived religion of men and women, took shape. And thanks to the increasing literacy and growing self-confidence of city dwellers, the writing of new texts was encouraged and new forms of vernacular literature created in which experience was given its due place.[31]

This community of the faithful provided far more leeway for equal and open interaction between all kinds of believers than was the case within the patriarchal, hierarchical system of the more formal learning environments that had a vested interest in maintaining its own gendered hegemony. Such was certainly the case for women who were *experimento doctae* and who had a strong sense of their own identity. Historians and literary scholars alike tend to forget about this community, this "informal" grouping that was not part of an official "public"—that is to say "institutional"—life and that, as a result, was deemed "marginal" and irrelevant as a subject for historical research. Traditionally, researchers have tended to overlook the fact that the public or official in medieval times was not the same as institutional. The public and the official were not (yet) contained in formal structures but housed within the oral community, not (yet) in the institution but in what we can term the "public orality" and the community of discourse within which public opinion would be formed and disseminated.

In many ways medieval society can be regarded in terms of a woven cloth, a fabric made up of warp and weft. Each society needs standing threads, the warp threads of laws and institutions, but also requires the connecting threads of conventions and traditions, which are not mandated by coercive power but acted out by individuals with *poid* and *presence*, relying on their persuasive power. Without warp threads society has no solidity, without weft it has no social dignity. Scholastic theology and Church doctrine belong to the warp threads of political and ecclesiastical institutions. No women participated in this activity; they had no access to cathedral schools or to leading positions within the Church. The only ecclesiastical status open to them was that belonging to vowed nuns, cloistered sisters secluded from the outside world in convents. But in the world of conventions and traditions, there were certainly opportunities for women and it is clear that many women took full advantage of them in a way that enabled them to do more than, to coin Irigaray's words, "rival...men in constructing a logic of the feminine that would still take onto-theo-logic as its model." Instead, it allowed them a personal idiom based on their own ways of accumulating knowledge, which would allow them an attempt to "wrest this question away from the economy of the logos"[32] and make a contribution to matters divine on their own terms.

It is noteworthy, therefore, that the women of experience we encounter in the sources are never nuns.[33] Often, they are independent holy women, members of the urban community and actively engaged in urban religious life. In this capacity Margery Kempe is again a case in point, as is Angela of Foligno (chapters six and four). There are also many beguines among them—and we should remember that beguine houses and beguinages were urban institutions not ecclesiastical ones. Hadewijch (chapter eight) was such a beguine, as was Agnes Blannbekin in Vienna (chapter five). We additionally come across anchoresses—also predominantly lay women—living in cells attached to parish churches or in well-frequented chapels, as illustrated by Juliana and Eve of Liège (chapter five). Finally, there are a few abbesses and mothers of religious houses, authoritative figures who venture out of their convents and have an immediate impact on people in the towns and beyond. Margaret of Faenza and Clare of Montefalco (chapter four) were such abbesses, and Aleid Willem Buser's widow and her daughter Aechte the respective maters of a convent, the latter two being included among the women of authority discussed in chapter two. In the case of Clare of Montefalco, almost five hundred people witnessed her saintly miracles after her death, attesting to her widespread influence upon the community beyond the nunnery walls.

In addition, many of these authoritative women began their careers as married women and mothers living within the urban elite who, after playing their roles in the cultural and religious life of the city, emerged at later stages of their lives as religious leaders and mothers of the devout. This group of women certainly includes Heloise, the lover of Abelard and mother of his son (chapter three). It also numbers Katrijn Wouters in Leyden, Katrijn Jacob's daughter also in Leyden, Machteld Cosijn's widow in Gouda, as well as Aleid Cluten in Utrecht, four of the eight women of authority examined in chapter two. These women were all urban matrons of some considerable standing who assembled followers around them and became founders of tertiary convents.

Aechte Eernstes from Utrecht was a distinguished woman who gained renown as the "*mater* and *procuratrix* of clerics, monks and devout women." Aleid and her daughter Aechte were *matres* of the tertiaries of St. Agatha in Delft. These women all became authority figures in their convent and in the city, women of experience, bearers of sapiential wisdom, who helped their disciples and fellow citizens reach spiritual perfection.

Ways of Knowing

Notwithstanding the urban schools and universities, medieval society was still a predominantly oral world and knowledge was mostly acquired in the personal exchange between an older voice of experience and a younger audience (and again the interchange between Julian of Norwich, then in her seventies, and the younger Margery Kempe, probably in her early forties, is a case in point). Hands-on training was not a mode of inferior instruction for the uneducated, but the primordial way of obtaining a proper "schooling". Most youngsters learned on the job: the young priest was trained by assisting the old one, the journeyman by laboring in the workshop of his master, the housemaid by serving her lady. By observing the example of their older compeers, they were presented with what they should know: learning was effected by imitation.

In matters of faith too, people primarily drew their examples from the individuals around them, such as the holy women and the living saints of their own times, while still having recourse to the type of cultural memory embedded in the Bible stories and saints' Lives, which provided their main ballast. In this context, Bernard of Clairvaux, writing in the twelfth century, was the first churchman to speak of "reading in the book of experience" [hodie legimus in libro experientiae].[34] Here Bernard was thinking primarily of the reading of his fellow brothers, of course, but it also applied to women who were *experimento doctae* in spite of the fact that they were barred from the schools. They were even the primary participants who, as ladies of the house, assumed a central role in transmitting knowledge and became, in Irigarayan terms, the alternative "force of its cohesion."[35]

The faithful were thus raised in a religious culture with a strongly experiential spirituality tied to physical objects and the bodily experience of faith. They eagerly attended the parish church, where they experienced their love of God. In the course of the ecclesiastical year they recreated the entire history of salvation. They lived through all the important events in the life of Christ, as well as his Mother. Kneeling in front of paintings and sculptures, mumbling prayers, participating in liturgical celebrations, and especially ingesting the Eucharistic bread—by all these actions their eyes of faith were opened and they were instantly drawn to experience what the symbols represented. The faithful became personally involved in the story of salvation as they saw holiness enacted before their inner eyes. In this sense, they became eyewitnesses: raised to the biblical level, they even became actors themselves in sacred history and instructors of their fellow believers using these same images, figurative language, and visions.[36]

Devout eyes looked through surface appearances to what lay hidden beneath them. As McAvoy demonstrates in chapter six, Margery Kempe "was present" at the birth of Christ when she visited the stable in Bethlehem. And she expressed her theological views by means of anecdotes concerning actual, personal encounters: meeting a mother breastfeeding her small son, for example. The faithful, especially women of holy experience, thus embodied salvation; they experienced it in their bodies and radiated it out to their fellow believers by means of those same bodies. Clare of Montefalco (chapter four) had the symbols of the

Passion imprinted on her heart. Angela of Foligno refused to open her missal and read the written words: in a vision, she understood the passage with perfection. It is in this context that we have to place the dreams and visions in which the chosen ones—individuals such as Ruusbroec and Hadewijch but also Kempe and other ordinary women—beheld God's hidden truths. Their way of seeing and knowing was a powerful stimulus to new kinds of spirituality; it gave believers, and particularly lay believers, direct access to the divine.

We can conclude then that, within a religious context, *experientia* was clearly seen as salvational wisdom gathered from the written word *and* the lived experience within the public community of the faithful. It was salvation incarnate, shared equally by men and women, clerics, and laypeople. It only became a problem once a woman moved on and embraced the desire to explain these things herself in writing, on her attempts to occupy a position within the "break between what is perceptible and what is intelligible."[37] Suddenly, the equation became much more complicated.

Ways of Writing

As has frequently been noted, women were barred from higher education and Latin learning in scholastic theology and Church doctrine after the Gregorian Reform and the Fourth Lateran Council of 1215. This was a result of the compulsion within the ecclesiastic hierarchy to define its own group—the *sacerdotium*—as a separate body differentiated from the community of the faithful. As markers of this difference, they started to adopt different attire, embrace the ideal of celibacy, and claim for themselves the prerogatives of administering salvation. Such a discursive and epistemological shift—in Irigarayan terms, part of a perpetual "reappropriation of the various productions of history"[38]— meant that, with the coming of the universities, clerics started to train their youngsters in formal classroom settings, taught them from well-established Latin textbooks, and educated them in the androcentric Liberal Arts. Thus, in a highly gendered move that set in place a new "systematicity," they claimed their Latin learning as the prerogative of their group: they were *litterati*, all others were not. This resulted in "the creation of a new and cosmopolitan clerical elite, formally defined by ordination but distinguished and united above all by its common Latin culture."[39]

Women who were inspired to write about matters of faith but wished to remain within the bounds of orthodoxy had to seek out forms of writing and an idiom that would not bring them into difficulty with this new system. It is often argued in studies on prophecy and female mysticism that creative women did so by having visions and mystical raptures and writing prophetic or visionary texts. They employed the inspirational and the experiential as their method of writing and set it up in opposition to scholastic reason.[40] Within this paradigm, Hadewijch thus wrote her visions in which she incorporated theological knowledge and insights of a high intellectual order (chapter eight). Juliana expressed her criticism of the Church in the form of a vision concerning an imperfectly full moon and composed a liturgy for the celebration of Corpus Christi (chapter five). Angela of Foligno "read" her theological insights through her spiritual eye (chapter four). Dominican nuns in south Germany wrote their *Sister books*, which are to be read as forms of narrative theology.[41] As John Coakley notes, the visions of women gave them "access to the divine that was parallel to that of preachers."[42] Their revelations were quickly recognized as prophecies in line with the female prophets of the Old Testament and a fulfillment of the authority granted them by Peter in the New Testament: "yea, and on my menservants and my maidservants in those days I will pour out my Spirit; and they shall prophesy" (Acts 2.16–18). The texts they wrote are not composed in the form of scholastic treatises. They did not refer to Latin authors and package their new ideas as commentaries on them. They did not derive their authority from the Ancients but from living beings who received inspiration directly from Christ or the Holy Spirit. They wrote exempla and life stories full of visionary experiences and mystical raptures. Mostly, their works were written in the vernacular. As a result, they lack, as has often been remonstrated by their critics both past and present, the reasoning and depth of Latinate models.[43]

All this may indeed be true; however, these types of explanations, along with their condescending discriminatory undertones are unsatisfactory, particularly in the light of the analyses presented by the contributors to this collection. For this reason, I wish to venture the following hypothesis, one that must, of course, be tested in subsequent research.

The emergence of a Church hierarchy with its monopolistic and "autological presuppositional" claims to *sacerdotium* belongs to a much more fundamental process of change in medieval society during and following the Gregorian Reform. As historian Robert I. Moore demonstrates in his seminal study, *The First European Revolution*, in the course of the Investiture Contest and the rise of national states to be distinguished from the body of the Church, a transformation occurred that domesticated the holy, the charismatic, the sacred—which is to say the experiential—and placed these elements in separately structured realms of control.[44] Salvation was allocated to the consecrated priesthood, the *sacerdotium*, with a professional organization, the clergy, who had at their disposal the instruments of redemption, namely, the seven sacraments that were to be employed only by them. Charismatically inspired believers were no longer officially part of the salvific equation. Personal holiness was housed in cloisters and prefigured the hereafter, where canonized saints found their place of work. So-called living saints were not longer recognized—at least in theory. Everything was given its place in the new religious structure, its position comprising one of the standing threads in the social fabric. Experience had no place within the hierarchy of this "tightly woven systematicity," to coin Irigaray's terminology, becoming instead a "re-source ... rejected as the waste product of reflection, cast outside."[45] The *sacerdotium* perpetrated rational scholarship; *experientia* was situated outside the structure—and found shelter in the community of the faithful, the connecting threads of conventions and traditions.[46]

This could be effectuated because the fellowship of believers, the common faithful, the networks of the devout, the communities of discourse and the informal, community-based public arena, as outlined earlier, remained in existence. People continued to shape and express their belief in an experiential religious culture and they did not allow salvation and salvatory experience to be taken from them. Parallel to and amidst the institutional structure, they further emancipated and cultivated the old conventions and traditions. The charismatic, the experiential, was lived out in the community and, where necessary, cast in new forms. The community in question may have been that of the parish church (as, e.g., in the new feast of Corpus Christi), but it may also have been the community of discourse such as that formed by Angela of Foligno and Brother A.

In the still partly oral, vernacular culture, these cultural features also insured—and this is the point we are most concerned with here—that texts were produced in which this *experientia* was recorded, enabling experiential believers to instruct, inspire, or even to entertain others, if called upon to do so (and some examples of these genres will be further examined in the studies assembled in this collection). Moreover, what often remains unsaid is that scholastically trained theologians or clerics such as Ruusbroec and the brethren of the New Devout also felt rather dissatisfied by the new structure. As a result, they also wrote new texts in which *experientia* had a place, or they produced such writings in collaboration with the women of experience themselves. Again, this point is made clear in various contributions included here.[47]

The Contributions

The collection is opened by Koen Goudriaan's study based on traditional historical sources, documentary evidence, letters, and chronicles, in which he offers the practical example of eight wealthy matrons belonging to the well-to-do middle class in Holland. Each woman was responsible for founding one or more female convents or leading them in their initial phases. In their management, their pastoral leadership (sometimes acting as confessors), and their negotiations with the civic administration, they demonstrated great practical wisdom and spiritual knowledge. Three of them also had prophetic or para-mystical gifts and one was an author. Most noteworthy, perhaps, is their companionship—and formation of a community of discourse—with a rector or a priest.

Focusing on the example of Abelard and Heloise and based on Latin letters and commentaries, Ineke Van 't Spijker demonstrates how the experiential quality of thinking itself and the reciprocal influence of thought and feeling can function in the bulwark of Latinate learning. Both Heloise and Abelard were concerned with the *homo interior*, the inner person in relation to the outer, and therefore with interiority as a mode of experience.

Following on from this appraisal, Carolynn Muessig presents us with a dialogue of love between theologians schooled in Paris and women who directly experienced the divine. Basing her study on the hagiographic texts, the *Arbor Vitae Crucifixe Jesu* by Ubertino of Casale, and the *Memorial* of Angela of Foligno and Brother A. as a product of authorial collaboration, she concludes that these educational ideologies clearly privileged *experientia* over a pedagogy based on the written word. She continues with the examples of Clare of Montefalco and Margaret of Faenza whose roles indicate alternative modes of theological conversation.

Anneke Mulder-Bakker's contribution turns to Latin hagiography, Juliana's liturgy *Animarum Cibus* and Agnes' *Vita et Revelationes*, in order to argue that Juliana of Cornillon and Agnes Blannbekin received spiritual and doctrinal insights in the form of revelations or visions that confirmed (or reiterated?) what they had already read in divine Scripture. Both women proceeded to further elaborate upon the details in subsequent inner dialogues with Christ. They studied Latin and vernacular works; their texts were transcribed and validated by clerical assistants. These texts, "books of life," enabled the readers and listeners to reexperience the *religion vécue* of the authorial personae.

Liz Herbert McAvoy's essay takes as its focus the *Book of Margery Kempe* written in the English vernacular. Here she examines how

Margery Kempe, as a woman within a male-sculpted ideological system, and not versed in Latin culture herself, struggled to find a personally conceived linguistic idiom to describe her journey to religious perfection. She draws heavily on her own life experiences as a wife and a mother to develop a language suitable for expressing the mystical. By inserting her own living and culturally situated body into the sacred text, that same sacred text itself becomes, in effect, the book of her own life, the one eventually becoming interchangeable with the other.

Introducing the new genre of the song cycle, Thom Mertens' essay discusses a fortnightly cycle that sings about the ascension of the soul and that is intended for sisters in an informal convent (they do not pray the Latin hours, e.g.). A female lyrical, first-person "I" takes her fellow sisters in a strong fellowship up a spiral of hope, ascension, regression, and spiritual growth. The cycle has a profound effect despite its deceptive simplicity. Mertens bases his study on three manuscripts with various forms and versions of the songs and their prose introductions. He consequently reveals the *mouvance* [fluidity] within versions of the cycle, as well as the transition from oral to written, from private to communal, from lay existence to life within the cloister.

Just like Angela, Juliana, and Agnes, Hadewijch of Brabant received spiritual insights in the form of revelations and visions that provide hermeneutics of divine Scripture. Her book of life enabled her spiritual daughter(s) to reexperience the *religion vécue* of the authorial persona. Just like Margaret, Juliana, and Agnes, Hadewijch was Latin-literate and well-educated. Unlike them, she snatched up the pen and herself became a writer. Also unlike them, she did not receive clerical assistance as far we know.

Veerle Fraeters studies the transfer of experiential and intellectual knowledge in Hadewijch's *Book of Visions*. Analysis of the structure and the communicative context of the Book as a whole reveals that Hadewijch composed it in such a way that it reflects her personal growth toward spiritual perfection while, at the same time, providing an example for her female disciple of how to become perfect like Hadewijch herself "through" Hadewijch—not just by example but by herself experiencing Hadewijch's own experiences. Detailed analysis of one vision from the Book, Vision 9, shows how the visionary imagery is woven from a wide range of intertextual associations that must have lit up in the memory of Hadewijch by the liturgical text that triggered the rapture. Hadewijch's visions can therefore be seen as experiential hermeneutics. By grounding her visions in text, Hadewijch offered her visual exegesis of liturgical text to her female disciple(s).

Experientia and the Book of Life

This book is not an attempt to recapture the voices and experiences of subordinate groups that may not have left sufficient traces in official history in the line of what Dominick LaCapra terms the "experiential turn." Historical studies on experience mostly follow that trajectory and try to ascribe experiences to people in order to situate them in the past and give them a history. Nor is this book concerned with the simple and emotional souls of neglected females.[48]

This book is also not an appraisal of the experiences of sainted women as recounted by their male confessors, men who were not privy to direct divine experience themselves but who held a deep fascination for those ecstatic women ascribed with a "privileged subjective experience of the divine." Indeed, it was this type of male cleric who created in their hagiographies the very dichotomy between themselves as the products of rational learning possessing institutional power and the experiential holy women with their informal, charismatic power that I alluded to at the start of this introduction.[49]

This book is even less concerned with the bodily experience of suffering pious women such as described by Caroline Walker Bynum—notwithstanding the fact that Anglo-American scholarship is greatly indebted to her (and going back through her to German scholars such as Grundmann) for the current upsurge in interest in the vernacular texts of mystical women.[50]

This book will also not study female authors and male–female authorship pairs who, through a detour of prophecy and mystical experiences, sought out means to participate in the theological debates current within the Church. Indeed, that has been done to great effect elsewhere and almost to the point of exhaustion.

Instead, this book seeks to unpick the construction of *experientia* within the new cultural turn within Western Christianity in the later Middle Ages. Now that we are beginning to know more about lay culture in urban communities; about the self-awareness of the citizens and their inquisitiveness; about the holy women "claiming an authority of their own to speak and be heard and to affect the lives of others";[51] about the collaboration and community of the clergy and laity, men and women, it is time to investigate them with regard to the construction of experience in cultural practice. The starting point is therefore not the church fortifications and the holy women outside the gate; the research begins at the center of popular religion and moves out from there. The starting point, therefore, is found in the (primarily urban) populace and the book will examine theology and scholasticism from that perspective. Indeed, having abandoned the misleading binarism of nineteenth-century Neo-Thomism with its rational and dichotomous construction of medieval theology, the ground is far more fruitful and varied. Using experience as the theme of our research, we will attempt to provide a better qualified understanding of the gender and power dynamics in the community of the faithful. Casting our gaze first upon texts, it should then be extended to the relationship between those texts and their readers and finally to the interaction between learning, literature, and the community. This will prove to be an experience governing both the head and the heart: the conceiving and embodying of salvation incarnate.

Finally, all of the studies presented in this volume aim to provide only initial soundings into the inquiry—but immediately make surprising discoveries. They very quickly unearth partnerships and communities of discourse. They frequently discover new genres and modes of writing. They consistently identify new concepts of authorship and authorial persona. They unearth new ideas about the authority of a text and its author. They reveal new ways of reading and reexperiencing texts. They delve into the collaboration of female author, male assistant, and an empathizing audience.[52] They uncover the "specular make-up of discourse"[53] and the locus of its disruption.

Thus, the book of life is a term that encompasses all of these new discoveries and captures both the life experiences of medieval women *and* men, as well as the written books that articulate them.[54] The book of life operates from a perspective of producing a general religious account of one's life before God and one's fellow human-beings and points toward the pivotal role of experience within that relationship. The notion therefore serves as an apt and primary emblem for this book that, in turn, becomes the book of the lives of those medieval subjects included within it.

Notes

The translation of this chapter has been done by Robert Olsen.

1. Luce Irigaray, "The Power of Discourse and the Subordination of the Feminine," in *Literary Theory: An Anthology*, ed. Julie Rivkin and Michael Ryan (Oxford: Blackwell, 1998, repr. 2004), p. 797 [795–798].
2. Ibid. Italics in the original.
3. Yvette (1158–1228) lived in Huy, a commercial center near Liège in present-day Belgium. Her (saint's) Life is written by Hugh of Floreffe, a relative and intimate friend of hers, and a regular canon of Floreffe: *Vita Beatae Juettae sive Juttae, viduae reclusae* [*Vita Juettae*], in *Acta Sanctorum* [*AASS*], 13 January: vol. 2, cols. 145–169; *Hugh of Floreffe, The Life of Yvette of Huy by Hugh of Floreffe*, trans. Jo Ann McNamara (Toronto: Peregrina, 2000; Turnhout: Brepols, forthcoming). See also Anneke B. Mulder-Bakker,

Lives of the Anchoresses: The Rise of the Urban Recluse in Medieval Europe (Philadelphia: University of Pennsylvania Press, 2005), chapter 3, pp. 51–77.
4. *Vita Juettae* 2.9, trans. 40; 2.10, trans. 41; 2.12, trans. 43; 2.14, trans. 44.
5. This is the first meaning given in the *Middle English Dictionary*, ed. Hans Kurath (Ann Arbor, MI: University of Michigan Press, 1952), E, p. 337. Other definitions are: demonstration or proof; observation or investigation; what is observed or experienced; knowledge and understanding; see later.
6. Dominick LaCapra, *History in Transit: Experience, Identity, Critical Theory* (Ithaca, NY: Cornell, 2004) provides an outstanding survey, especially in the introduction and chapter one. Of great importance are the theoretical reflections of Joan Wallach Scott, "The Evidence of Experience," *Critical Inquiry* 17 (1991): 773–797.
7. Bernard McGinn, "The Language of Inner Experience in Christian Mysticism," *Spiritus* 1 (2001): 162 [156–171], writes about the "experiential confirmation of the message found in the *liber scripturae* and a heightened concern for the analysis of states of inner experience" from the twelfth century onward. Bernard of Clairvaux introduced the concept of *liber experientiae* for this.
8. *Vita Juettae* 2.9: "nondum experimento didicerat grave jugum legem esse matrimonii, fastidiosa onera ventris, pericula partus, educationes liberorum."
9. Ibid., 2.89: "sapientissima materfamilias."
10. Ibid., 2.38: "spiritum prophetiae frequenter habuit a Domino."
11. Walter Simons, "Staining the Speech of Things Divine: The Uses of Literacy in Medieval Beguine Communities," in *The Voice of Silence: Women's Literacy in a Men's World*, ed. Thérèse de Hemptinne and Maria Eugenia Góngora (Turnhout: Brepols, 2004), pp. 85–110; see also Simons, *Cities of Ladies: Beguine Communities in the Medieval Low Countries, 1200–1565* (Philadelphia: University of Pennsylvania Press, 2001), pp. 80–85 on Beguines, and Mulder-Bakker, *Lives of the Anchoresses*, pp. 60–62 on recluses. Both groups of non-monastic religious women must have received their education in an urban context.
12. *Vita Mariae* 2.68, in *AASS*, 23 Junii, vol. 25, cols. 542–72; trans. Margot King in: *Mary of Oignies: Mother of Salvation [Vita Mariae]*, ed. Anneke B. Mulder-Bakker (Turnhout: Brepols, 2006), p. 98 and *Vita Mariae* 2.48, p. 84. Intriguing in this regard is the fact that the hagiographer, the curate James of Vitry, describes the process involving the mystical acquisition of knowledge as "reading in a book." See later for Mary and the book of life.
13. Helinand of Froidmont, *Sermo* 15, in *PL* 212, col. 603B-D; quoted by Giles Constable, *The Reformation of the Twelfth Century* (Cambridge, UK: Cambridge University Press, 1996), p. 215.
14. Diane Watt, *Medieval Women's Writing: Works by and for Women in England, 1100–1500* (Cambridge, UK: Polity Press, 2007), p. 1. Three-quarters of the transmitted manuscripts containing Middle Dutch texts concern religious content! See Thom Mertens in his introduction to *Boeken voor de Eeuwigheid: Nederlands geestelijk proza*, ed. Thom Mertens

(Amsterdam: Prometheus, 1993), p. 8, n. 3. The same holds true for German-speaking countries; in England, this percentage is much lower but vernacular texts in this country also frequently have religious content.
15. References are given in note 11.
16. Gate Gunn, *Ancrene Wisse: From Pastoral Literature to Vernacular Spirituality* (Cardiff: University of Wales Press, 2008), in particular pp. 110–118, has recently argued for the influence of sermons, written in Paris for the edification of beguines during the thirteenth century, as having a marked effect upon the rise of what she terms "vernacular spirituality" in the later Middle Ages, both in insular and continental contexts.
17. *Vita Mariae* 2.102, p. 122.
18. *Vita Idae*, 1, in *Quinque prudentes virgines*, ed. Chrysostomos Henriquez (Antwerp: Joannes Cnobbaert, 1630), p. 203.
19. Thomas of Cantimpré, *Vita Margarethae Yprensis* 5, in G. Meersseman, "Les Frères Prêcheurs et le mouvement devôt en Flandre au xiiie siècle," *Archivum Fratrum Predicatorum* 18 (1948): 108 and 112–113 [106–130], trans. Margot King in: *Thomas of Cantimpré: The Collected Saints' Lives*, ed. Barbara Newman (Turnhout: Brepols, 2008), p. 167 [161–213].
20. Thomas of Cantimpré, *Vita S. Christinae Mirabilis* 4.37–40, ed. *AASS*, 24 July, vol. 32: 657 [637–660], trans. Margot King in: *Thomas of Cantimpré: The Collected Saints' Lives*, ed. Newman, pp. 146–148.
21. Thomas of Cantimpré, *Der Byen Boeck: De Middelnederlandse vertalingen van Bonum Universale de Apibus van Thomas van Cantimpré*, ed. Christina M. Stutvoet-Joanknecht (Amsterdam: VU Uitgeverij, 1990), pp. 45–46.
22. Again, see Watt, *Medieval Women Writers*, pp. 91–135, for a nuanced appraisal of the various literacies of these women and their relation to writing and collaboration with male spiritual authority.
23. John Van Engen, "The Voices of Women in Twelfth-Century Europe," in *Voices in Dialogue: Reading Women in the Middle Ages*, ed. Linda Olson and Kathryn Kerby-Fulton (Notre Dame: University of Notre Dame Press, 2005), p. 204 [199–212].
24. Bernard McGinn, ed., *Meister Eckhart and the Beguine Mystics* (New York: Continuum, 1997), p. 4; Niklaus Largier, "Von Hadewijch, Mechthild und Dietrich zu Eckhart und Seuse?" in *Deutsche Mystik im abendländischen Zusammenhang: Neu erschlossene Texte, neue methodische Ansätze, neue theoretische Konzepte*, ed. Walter Haug and Wolfram Schneider-Lastin (Tübingen: Niemeyer, 2000), pp. 93–117.
25. Irigaray, "The Power of Discourse," p. 797.
26. Nicholas Watson, "Julian of Norwich," in *Medieval Women's Writing*, ed. Carolyn Dinshaw and David Wallace (Cambridge, UK: Cambridge University Press, 2003), p. 211 [210–221]; Felicity Riddy, "Julian of Norwich and Self-Textualization," in *Editing Women*, ed. Ann M. Hutchison (Toronto: Toronto Press, 1998), pp. 101–124. McAvoy and Watt demonstrate in their contributions to this collection how the *Visions* and *Revelations* of Julian and the *Book* by Kempe belong to

the oldest vernacular literature in English in which experience has a prominent place.
27. Geert Warnar, *Ruusbroec: Literature and Mysticism in the Fourteenth Century* (Leiden: Brill, 2007), pp. 137–145.
28. Cf. Mary C. Erler, *Women, Reading, and Piety in Late Medieval England* (Cambridge, UK: Cambridge University Press, 2002), p. 106, who states for the same Norwich around 1500: "the lively exchange between male and female devout persons whether lay or religious, the high number of parishes, the strong local identity, the influence of continental religious developments, seems to have produced an atmosphere especially stimulating to religious life..."
29. Warnar, *Ruusbroec*, p. 106.
30. Ibid., p. 232.
31. German scholars such as Niklaus Largier refer to the groups of Friends of God, *Gottesfreunde*, in the Upper Rhine region and the interaction between mendicants and mystic women in Lower Germany; see Largier, "Von Hadewijch, Mechthild und Dietrich zu Eckhart und Seuse?" (see note 24 earlier), p. 99 [93–117]: "wo sich die Texte aus aktuellen Diskussionen heraus konstituieren und in ein gegenseitiges Reflexionsverhältnis treten."
32. Irigaray, "The Power of Discourse," p. 796.
33. See, for female learning in a monastic context, Fiona J. Griffiths, *The Garden of Delights: Reform and Renaissance for Women in the Twelfth Century* (Philadelphia: University of Pennsylvania Press, 2007).
34. Bernard of Clairvaux, *Sermo* 3, in Bernard of Clairvaux, *S. Bernardi Opera*, ed. Jean Leclercq, C.H. Talbot, and H.M. Rochais, 8 vols (Rome: Editiones Cistercienses, 1957–77), 1:14 [14–17].
35. Irigaray, "The Power of Discourse," p. 795.
36. More on this in chapter five.
37. Irigaray, "The Power of Discourse," p. 797.
38. Ibid., p. 795.
39. Robert I. Moore, "Heresy, Repression, and Social Change in the Age of Gregorian Reform," in *Christendom and Its Discontents. Exclusion, Persecution, and Rebellion, 1000–1500*, ed. Scott L. Waugh and Peter D. Diehl (Cambridge, UK: Cambridge University Press, 1996), p. 39 [19–46].
40. A seminal study for this is Amy Hollywood, *The Soul as Virgin Wife: Mechthild of Magdeburg, Marguerite Porete, and Meister Eckhart* (Notre Dame: University of Notre Dame Press, 1995). A recent survey with references to previous studies: Bernard McGinn, "'Trumpets of the Mysteries of God': Prophetesses in Late Medieval Christianity," in *Propheten und Prophezeiungen—Prophets and Prophecies*, ed. Matthias Riedl and Tilo Schabert (Würzburg: Königshausen & Neumann, 2005), pp. 125–141; McGinn, "Inner Experience," pp. 162, 164: "since women could not be scriptural commentators *ex officio*," they stress "the need for experiential confirmation of the message found in the *liber scripturae*."

41. See, among others, Susanne Bürkle, *Literatur im Kloster: Historische Funktion und rhetorische Legitimation frauenmystischer Texte des 14. Jahrhunderts* (Tübingen and Basel: Francke, 1999) and studies mentioned there.
42. John W. Coakley, *Women, Men, and Spiritual Power: Female Saints and their Male Collaborators* (New York: Columbia University Press, 2006), p. 78.
43. Martina Wehrli-Johns, "Voraussetzungen und Perspektiven mittelalterlicher Laienfrömmigkeit seit Innozenz III: Eine Auseinandersetzung mit Herbert Grundmanns 'Religiöse Bewegungen,'" *Mitteilungen des Instituts für Österreichische Geschichtsforschung* 104 (1996): 286–309.
44. Robert I. Moore, *The First European Revolution, c. 970–1215* (Oxford: Blackwell, 2000).
45. Irigaray, "Power of Discourse," p. 796.
46. On the two alternative modes of social existence (structure and community), see the challenging study by Lior Barshack, "The Communal Body, the Corporate Body, and the Clerical Body: An Anthropological Reading of the Gregorian Reform," in *Sacred and Secular in Medieval and Early Modern Cultures*, ed. Lawrence Basserman (New York: Palgrave Macmillan, 2006), pp. 102–104 [101–121].
47. See Hendrik Mande, *Vanden licht der waerheit*, ed. Thom Mertens (1984), ll. 390–393, 431–438. Thom Mertens alerted me to this author. For the English situation, Nicole R. Rice, "Devotional Literature and Lay Spiritual Authority: *Imitatio Clerici* in *Book to a Mother*," *Journal of Medieval and Early Modern Studies* 35 (2005): 187–217, notes that English scholarship up till recently mostly focused attention on authors in the margin and actual heretics. Now interest has shifted to the negotiations of orthodox lay believers and clerics at the center.
48. LaCapra, *History in Transit*, p. 3.
49. Coakley, *Women, Men*, p. 9; see also 1–24, 211–227.
50. First in Caroline Walker Bynum, *Holy Feast and Holy Fast: The Religious Significance of Food to Medieval Women* (Berkeley: University of California Press, 1987), but see also her "The Female Body and Religious Practice in the Later Middle Ages," in *Fragmentation and Redemption: Essays on Gender and the Human Body in Medieval Religion*, ed. Caroline Walker Bynum (New York: Zone Books, 1992), pp. 181–238, 365–393.
51. Coakley, *Women, Men*, in the conclusion, pp. 213–215: clerics discovered "something legitimately beyond them...and explored the relationship between the authority of office and what lay beyond it."
52. Jennifer Summit, "Women and Authorship," in *Medieval Women's Writing*, eds. Dinshaw and Wallace (see note 26 earlier), pp. 91–108. A large number of the characteristics of women's writing runs parallel to the character traits of general English literature from this time; see *The Cambridge History of literary Criticism,* vol 2: *The Middle Ages*, ed. Alistair J. Minnis and Jan Johnson (Cambridge, UK: Cambridge University Press, 2005), in which, for example, Alistair Minnis, "Medieval imagination and memory," pp. 239–274.

53. Irigaray, "Power of Discourse," p. 797.
54. In Rev. 5.1 (Douay Rheims translation) the book of life is "in the right hand of him that sat on the throne, a book, written within and without, sealed with seven seals." And Rev. 20: 12 has "the dead, great and small, standing in the presence of the throne. And the books were opened: and another book was opened, which was the book of life. And the dead were judged by those things which were written in the books, according to their works." In the Middle Ages the term refers to this sealed book, but it was more often applied to the personal book of life, the book that each Christian had on his person as he died and that contained his/her life experiences. It evolves into the equivalent of a spiritual vademecum.

CHAPTER 2

THE NEW DEVOUT AND THEIR WOMEN OF AUTHORITY

Koen Goudriaan

In the early phases of the Modern Devotion women played a leading role: this contribution investigates the way their authority was construed and expressed itself.

This contribution focuses on a group of eight women in the region now known as the Netherlands who were conspicuous for the recognition they received as a result of their experience in religious matters. This experience united several components, ranging from managerial qualities acquired in connection with their social background in the urban elite, to religious knowledge proper, comprising ascetic experience, expertise based on studying and teaching, and supernatural revelation. The women together shared a supra-local women's network, but each one of them was also a member of what Mulder-Bakker has identified in the Introduction as the "community of discourse" functioning within their respective home city. With one exception, their religious experience did not find expression in any writing of their own, however (unlike some of the women focused on elsewhere in this volume). Instead, it manifested itself through agency, which was expressed primarily in their founding of a number of congregations of women who had recently been converted to a new type of religious life. Although the wisdom of these eight women was clearly pivotal to the role they were allowed to play, their agency was reinforced by two additional factors: their previous status in society (which was also central to their managerial skills) and the specific setting in which they operated. This setting typically coupled them to priests who had an affinity with the religious choices the women had made.

Interestingly, such an association affected the traditional gender-based role division between clergy and female laity—part of the ideological "dichotomy" again identified by Mulder-Bakker in the Introduction. In the process of forming such an alliance, both players reached and even stretched the limits of what was possible in terms of male–female collaboration, causing an occasional strain but in the end reconciling both parties to their place within religious life.

As already mentioned, the eight women under scrutiny here were interconnected and operated closely in terms of time and space—that is to say in or around the year 1400 in Holland and the neighboring episcopal city of Utrecht. Their activities thus occurred at a particular juncture in time that saw the rapid development of a religious movement that would later become known by the catchphrase "Modern Devotion." In the western Netherlands, this movement's new adherents, known as The New Devout and among whom women were overwhelmingly predominant, assembled in unconventional congregations, which soon, however, adopted the status of tertiaries and joined the so-called Chapter of Utrecht.[1] Typically, their convents were situated in the many fast growing cities of this region. The eight women upon whom this contribution will focus, have already received some recent attention.[2] However, an analysis of the way female authority was construed among these western New Devout and of the types of religious experience involved is still lacking. The primary reason for this is that, with the exception of a few letters, no personal writings were left behind by these women and thus their agency has to be approached in a more circumventory way by turning to traditional historiographical sources as well as those of legal documents—both of which have unexpected relevance for the subject being focused on here. This essay will, therefore, first introduce the women individually and then review the sources. Next, it will analyze the agency of the women from four perspectives: their status and age; their managerial qualities; "natural" and "supernatural" varieties of religious knowledge they may have possessed; and the settings in which they operated.

Eight Women

The type of agency with which we are dealing is exemplified by an event that occurred in the city of Leiden in 1428. In this year a new hospital was founded for poor and sick women under the patronage of St. Elisabeth. The founders, a rich couple, had long hesitated about whom they would ask to take care of the hospital, whether the city authorities or a confraternity. Finally they turned for advice to Katrijn Wouter's daughter,[3] who was the *ministra* (superior) of St. Margaret's, the oldest convent of tertiaries in town. She came up with the solution of handing over the hospital jointly to the city magistracy and to her own convent. As a corollary to the foundation, an extensive ordinance was formulated. Christina Ligtenberg, who published a fine study on the Leiden hospitals a century ago, suggested that Katrijn may herself have been the author of this ordinance.[4]

Katrijn Wouters is known in at least two other instances to have operated with authority in cases not directly dealing with her own convent. In 1410 she was the recipient of a piece of land near the parish church of Warmond, a few miles north of Leiden, a transaction sealed by a couple of legal deeds.[5] The donor, the local lord Jan van der Woude, asked Katrijn to instigate the foundation of a new women's convent for which he was providing material support. Seven years later, Katrijn was one of the "fathers and mothers," the authorities within the Chapter of Utrecht who assisted at the election of a successor to the deceased Aechte Willems, mater of St. Agatha's convent in Delft. The choice, though formally free and democratic, was in actual practice directed from above. Before dying, Aechte had mentioned the name of the sister she thought most fit to succeed. The fathers and mothers recommended Aechte's choice to the assembled sisters, who accepted it "as if this word had come to us from heaven."[6]

In Leiden, already in 1386 another strong woman, Katrijn Jacob's daughter, had taken action with some authority on behalf of a congregation of devout women that she herself had assembled. In front of the aldermen she surrendered her house for the benefit of this congregation. The deed drafted on that occasion—our only source—contains the rules according to which this community would have to live in future and which transformed it into a house of sisters of the common life. Clearly, these rules express Katrijn's own ideas.[7]

Also within the group of eight women are two *matres* or *ministrae* of the tertiaries of St. Agatha in Delft, whose lives are documented by the chronicle of this convent.[8] These are Aechte Willem's daughter, whose death occasioned the election procedure mentioned earlier, and her predecessor, who was also her biological mother, Aleid, Willem Buser's widow. Aleid Buser was not the first leader of the convent, which had been founded in 1380, but had experienced much adversity during the first fifteen years of its existence. It was thanks to the improvements introduced by Aleid Buser, however, that the convent began to flourish in the middle of the 1390s. The way she had been elected as its leader resembles the 1417 procedure already described, but in this earlier instance the outside authorities who recommended Aleid were exclusively male. When the convent adopted the Third Rule of St. Francis in 1400, Aleid became its first *ministra*. She died in 1409, to be succeeded by her biological daughter, Aechte, who had accompanied her when she first entered the convent.

Another woman of authority was Machteld Cosijn's widow from Gouda. In fact, Cosijn was still alive when Machteld first started to exercise leadership. As early as 1386, she assembled a group of religious women in a house in the Hofstrate. Later, when the group had become too large, she arranged its transfer to a greater house across the street and, in order to cater for their material needs, she gave them whatever she could save from her own resources. Machteld achieved great success in 1396, when both the count of Blois (Lord of the city) and the city government itself granted the convent an extensive privilege. The municipal privilege also contained a set of rules of conduct to be followed by Machteld's community. When shortly afterward Cosijn died, Machteld was free to apply herself entirely to the well-being of her convent, which in due time came to be called St. Margaret's. She guided it through a series of metamorphoses, including the adoption of the Third Rule of St. Francis, enclosure, the transition to the Rule of St. Augustine, and the adherence to the small Congregation of Holland that rivaled the Congregation of Windesheim. Our source of information on all this is the chronicle of St. Margaret's, in which several important privileges have been inserted.[9] In 1426, tired by old age, Machteld resigned from the office of prioress and during her last years she was entirely free to live for God and for herself. She died in 1439.

In Gorinchem, the tertiary convent of St. Agnes was founded in 1401 but began to flourish only from the moment enclosure was imposed in 1411. This coincided with the beginning of the rule of Machteld, master Willem's daughter, as *mater*. She is the first in a series of *matres* who are given a short biography in a Dutch chronicle, written around 1475.[10] The reign of Machteld Willems lasted from 1411 to 1416 only, but her burning love for the sacrament and her frequent ecstasies made her period of office all the more memorable.

The pride of place within this group of women is taken by Aleid Cluten. She was a widow originating from Kampen, and her first recorded activity was the visitation of a congregation of religious women in Zwolle (ca. 1387). But the center of her activities was the city of Utrecht, where—together with her male counterpart, Wermboud van Boskoop—she founded St. Caecile's convent, the "headquarters" of the tertiary movement within the Modern Devotion. She and Wermboud were inseparable in the dissemination and organization of the chaste life. The beguinage of St. Nicholas, which led a waning existence, was revitalized by turning it into a house of sisters of the common life, the inmates "submitting wholly to the lord Wermboud and to the mother of

St. Caecile's convent in order to follow their advice in all things."[11] In Delft, together with Katrijn Wouters, Aleid Cluten was one of the persons taking part decisively in the 1417 election of a new *ministra*. But Aleid is best known for the fact that she and her convents attracted the attention of the Dominican inquisitor Eylard Schoneveld, as is made clear by a couple of documents originating from this inquisitor. Understandably, they shed an unfavorable light on the role played by Aleid: the accusations, revolving around the monastic lifestyle of her communities, implied that they transgressed the ban on *novae religiones* (new orders) and promoted the suspicion that Aleid and her followers belonged to the *swestriones*, a type of semi-religious women outlawed by the recent papal bull *Sedis apostolicae providentia* (1395). But in the eyes of the inquisitor, Aleid's case was worsened by the unprecedented competences she vindicated for herself by exerting a kind of supra-local authority over a whole series of convents. The intervention of the inquisitor was triggered by complaints concerning Aleid's interference with a convent in Rhenen, a small city in the south-eastern part of the prince-bishopric of Utrecht.[12]

The series is completed by Aechte Eernstes from Utrecht. As was the case with Aleid Cluten, Aechte Eernstes' activity is documented by a variety of sources.[13] Already during the lifetime of her husband, Eernst, she had made the vow to remain chaste for the rest of her life, a promise she kept during the thirty years she survived him. The vow was made in the presence of Wermboud van Boskoop, whose death in 1413 provides a *terminus ad quem*. Aechte gained renown all over the country as a friend of the devout, as "mother and *procuratrix* of all religious people,"[14] especially of the canons regular and the tertiaries. On one occasion, the noble family of Heenvliet (on the border of Holland and Zeeland) undertook the long journey to the monastery of Diepenveen, where their niece, Catharine van Naaldwijk, was to receive the habit. Young Elisabeth van Heenvliet was part of the company, but she fell severely ill on the road, apparently not far from Utrecht. At that point, her mother and her aunt remembered Aechte Eernstes as the "spiritual woman" [geestelike vrouwe][15] and entrusted Elisabeth to her care. Aechte persuaded many a maiden to leave the vanities of the world and to enter religion, among whom were two of her own daughters. She was also the driving force behind the foundation of at least two monasteries. The first one was Bethlehem near Utrecht, a convent of enclosed tertiaries, in which her biological sister took the lead and in which Aechte Eernstes herself would spend the last years of her life. The other was called Jerusalem and was founded on an existing chapel on the outskirts of Utrecht and harbored regular canonesses. It was told that the location for the foundation of the monastery had been indicated to Aechte Eernstes in a vision.

The Sources: Narrative and Legal

The sources we have that testify to the agency of these eight women are narrative, legal, or epistolary. The narrative sources fall into two main categories: the sister books, which are built on a biographical pattern, and the chronicles, which are not. The chronicles range from the all-embracing Latin work by John Busch on the origin of the Modern Devotion, which is incorporated in his *Chronicon Windeshemense*,[16] to a variety of small-scale chronicles devoted to the origin and progress of individual convents. The typical sister book is written in the vernacular and contains a series of sisters' lives, composed according to hagiographical models. It retains the collective memory of a convent, with the double intention of reinforcing its cohesion and of guiding the lives of younger sisters by presenting them with the examples of their predecessors. The finest representatives of this genre are the sister books from Diepenveen near Deventer, which are also relevant to the devout women in the western part of the country;[17] three women from our sample are assigned a biography in the "chronicles" of St. Agatha in Delft and of St. Agnes in Gorinchem, which, despite their titles, belong more or less to the sister book type.[18]

Among the legal documents figure privileges emanating from various authorities as well as transaction deeds involving movable and immovable goods. They are couched in formulaic language that—apart from a casual reference to the salvation of souls—reveals nothing in particular about the motives of the donors or vendors, nor of the recipients, among whom are several of the women in my sample, acting on behalf of their convents. Occasionally, however, the nature of their agency materializes indirectly. Jan van der Woude's gift of a piece of land to Katrijn Wouters was accompanied by his request that she should instigate the foundation of a new convent, as I have mentioned.[19] Evidently, Katrijn's reputation had spread outside the city walls of Leiden so as to impress this noble lord of a neighboring village.

Transactions such as these seem to be unaffected by the question of whether or not women were entitled to appear in court without male accompaniment. The picture that emerges from the sources is not uniform, however. The privilege granted in 1396 by the city of Gouda to the sisters of St. Margaret's stipulates that, as women, they are unacquainted with secular law and, as a result, they are enjoined to choose a guardian who, if necessary, may act on their behalf to defend legal claims or to receive donations.[20] In fact, however, we see Machteld Cosijns act personally in her capacity as head of the convent.[21] Practice, therefore, may have varied according to the type of legal action and also according to local custom. It can also be argued that even if a woman was not allowed to appear in court without a guardian, this did not impair her ability to promote her own wishes.

More directly reflecting the intentions of the women involved are those documents that contain regulations or ordinances for the inner life of a convent or a hospital. From a formal perspective, they belong to the categories already mentioned, taking the shape of either a privilege or of a transaction, for example, a *donatio inter vivos* [gift between living persons] but, unlike the documents examined so far, they contain a large proportion of material that is not formulaic.

The institutional character of this type of evidence should not necessarily be played off against the experience of "real" life. The juridical apparatus created for channeling a religious movement may be expected to contain a great deal of practical wisdom: otherwise it would not function adequately. While it is true that the written documents have the disadvantage of representing only the tip of the iceberg, with the main body of oral discourse lying hidden beneath the surface, nevertheless on close analysis these documents reveal good common sense as well as glimpses of the value system that lies at the base of the arrangements that they aim to consolidate. And, of course, both common sense and value systems belong to the type of *experientia* that circulates in a specific community and its discourse.

The Sources: Epistolography

The sources discussed so far cannot be ascribed directly to one of the eight women under scrutiny, as I intimated earlier. They report on their actions and, at best, they reflect their influence, as was the case with the ordinances. There is a unique source, however, for which one of the eight women may be claimed as author with some plausibility. A series of three *Devout Letters*, which were written during the foundation process of the aforementioned monastery of Jerusalem near Utrecht, has been preserved.[22] In the early years of this monastery, three, and later two more, sisters were sent from Utrecht to Diepenveen in order to be taught the monastic way of life under the direction of Salome Sticken. When they returned to their own monastery, the Diepenveen nun Elisabeth van Delft accompanied them and in due time would become its first prioress.[23] The *Devout Letters* are addressed to the sisters who had been sent from Jerusalem to Diepenveen.[24] Traditionally, this has been interpreted to mean that they were sent by an anonymous author connected with Jerusalem to the sisters abroad in Diepenveen. Recently, Wybren Scheepsma has argued that they must have been sent in the opposite direction, by a person in Diepenveen who wished to provide a follow-up to the schooling of the Jerusalem sisters after their return to their own convent. His main argument is that a newly inaugurated monastery such as Jerusalem could not be expected to produce a female writer of the maturity apparent from the *Devout Letters*, whereas Diepenveen could boast no less a person than Salome Sticken, authoress of the *Vivendi formula*.[25] The presumed affinity between the *Vivendi formula* and the *Devout Letters* is an additional argument, and Scheepsma quite logically suggests that Salome Sticken was responsible for the *Devout Letters* too.

This argument is not convincing, however. A passage in the first letter clearly enjoins the addressees to obey "their superiors and all those where you are" and so confirms that they still reside in a convent that was not their own.[26] Nor is there any evidence for a kinship with the *Vivendi formula*. While this is an eminently practical rule governing daily monastic routine, the content of the *Devout Letters* is devotional and in some passages even strikes a mystical note, reflecting the particular sources which have been used.[27] The dialect of the main manuscript of the *Devout Letters* is an eastern type of Dutch, suggesting that it was copied from an exemplar kept in the IJssel region, which is just what one would expect in the case of letters sent to a monastery in Diepenveen near Deventer. Consequently, we have to look for an author in the Utrecht region and although it is not certain that the author is a woman, it is entirely probable. In which case, Aechte Eernstes is the best candidate.

Women's Authority

Status and Age

The sources offer various clues as to the basis upon which the authority of the women in the sample rested and it is clear that secular as well as religious elements contributed to it. Several of the women possessed considerable wealth and used it to the benefit of the religious communities that they fostered. The chronicle of St. Agatha in Delft, for example, is explicit about the importance of the material profit the community gained from Aleid Buser.[28] Her decision to enter the community is welcomed for its own sake, but also "because they had hitherto lived in poverty, and never before had a person joined the community whose admission had caused any progress worth mentioning."[29] Repeatedly, the chronicle calls her "honorable,"[30] using it as a foil for the humility that was the hallmark of her leadership. Machteld Cosijns had the habit of going around incognito in the villages of the region in order to beg on behalf of her congregation, concealing it from her husband and relatives.[31] High status in the world mattered, if only because it was something that could be sacrificed.

In contrast, marital status did not contribute to the position of the women under investigation, nor did age. Four women out of eight were virgins: Katrijn Jacobs, Katrijn Wouters, Aechte Willems, and Machteld Willems. When Machteld entered office, she was only twenty-six,[32] and Aechte, too, may have been very young when she started to lead the convent. Among the remaining four women, Aleid Cluten and Aleid Buser were widowed already at the start of their leadership, whereas Machteld Cosijns and Aechte Eernstes were still married. According to the Delft chronicle, Aleid was still a "young honorable woman" when she was first brought into contact with the sisters of St. Agatha, but she was then already a widow.[33] It is interesting to compare her life story with that of Machteld Cosijns. When Machteld started assembling a group of virgins together (in 1386), she was still "tied to her husband in marital bonds"; "she lavished alms on her virgins in their poverty insofar as she was allowed to do so as a married woman."[34] Probably she was only in her twenties, given the fact that she survived till 1439. The death of her husband gave her greater liberty to pursue her plans with the congregation but her widowhood did not entail a spiritual change. If such a conversion had ever occurred, this must have been long before the death of her husband.

Aleid Buser, however, did undergo such a metamorphosis. The chronicle relates in detail how first she was induced with some difficulty by her confessor to seek the company of the devout women of St. Agatha and only after long hesitation did she undergo radical conversion. This conversion itself was a rather theatrical event, with Aleid suddenly rushing into her house, stripping herself of her garment, grasping a crucifix, returning to the sisters' community in her underwear and there prostrating herself, claiming henceforth to wish nothing but to imitate the naked Christ.[35] The essential point here, however, is that this conversion is completely unconnected to her widowhood. The type of the widow who had reached the *aetas perfecta* (perfect age)[36] had no special appeal to the New Devout, nor did the "wise old mother" figure, as identified elsewhere by Mulder-Bakker.[37] If they had a preference for a specific type of sanctity, it was that of virginity.[38] Even the chronicle of St. Margaret's in Gouda, which has the married woman Machteld Cosijns as its protagonist, starts with an exalted praise of chastity (both *castitas* and *virginitas*).[39]

Management

All eight women were distinguished by a gift for management, thus exemplifying a quality that was considered indispensable for female leadership. The Rhenen ordinance, for example, prescribes that it is the woman who is "most wise and discriminate to reign and to provide things" who has to be elected as *maerte* (superior).[40]

Every movement pretending to durability is obliged to create institutions, if only to train younger generations in its values and to secure the administration of the goods that are accruing to it as a material underpinning of its religious life. The women in the sample appear to have made an important contribution of their own toward institutionalizing the New Devout. Katrijn Wouters assisted the lord of Warmond in founding a new convent.[41] With this lord himself providing for the material necessities, what else could Katrijn's contribution have been but to organize and discipline the new community? In Delft, it is true, the first rule adopted by the sisters of St. Agatha was proposed to them by Wermboud together with Martijn, their own confessor.[42] And in Utrecht and its surroundings, Wermboud van Boskoop was called by the inquisitor the "supreme legislator and governor of those congregations."[43] But when dissatisfaction with Wermboud's ordinances arose in the Rhenen community, triggering the intervention of the inquisitor, Wermboud entrusted Aleid Cluten with the task of defending them.[44] Earlier still, Katrijn Jacobs had imposed an ordinance on the religious house she was founding in Leiden, in which she reserved the direction of the community for herself together with one of the elder inmates. After her death, two senior members had to remain in charge of the community. Only in very difficult cases did they have to refer to an exterior board of supervision, consisting of the parish priest and two lay people who acted as executors of Katrijn's will.

The ordinances themselves exhibit much managerial common sense. In Katrijn Jacobs' community, for instance, the income of the women from rents and labor should be applied carefully for the common good, and those who bring in more will receive no preferential treatment. The two leading women will distribute the household duties among the remaining sisters and these have to obey. She who is ordered to cook has to do so without objection and the remaining sisters shall not complain about the result. But if the ill are in need of special dietary treatment, they will receive it.[45] Similar clauses are found in the Rhenen and Gouda ordinances and in the extensive regulation for St. Elisabeth's hospital in Leiden.[46]

A particular aspect of good management is eloquence, a quality that is attributed explicitly to Aechte Eernstes. In the process of founding

Jerusalem monastery, and in other instances, she showed a gift for negotiating with the city magistracy: "she was a wise and eloquent woman and beloved because of her honorable character, which enabled her to achieve a lot of things."[47]

Religious knowledge

In addition to management skills, religious qualities were also evidently conducive to leadership. Apart from asceticism—"true mortification"—which is praised both in Aleid Buser and in her daughter Aechte,[48] discernment in religious matters is required.[49] Discretion is required not only for practical aspects of community life: it is also applicable when furnishing spiritual guidance. In Rhenen and Gouda, together with the leadership team, the *maerte* is compelled to take in sisters who want to serve God or to dismiss those who deserve to be because of their disreputable behavior.[50] The two leading women in Katrijn Jacobs' congregation must admit an applicant on the basis of the "humility, virtue and honesty they trust to be in her."[51] If afterward the newly admitted gives cause for complaint, she should be issued with three successive warnings, following which the curate and the two lay supervisors should be consulted about expulsion.

None of the eight women exercised spiritual leadership more clearly than Aleid Cluten. The inquisitor depicts her repeated travels as *Martha principalis* [principal superior] to the convents in the Utrecht region as veritable visitation tours. On a given day, she used to take residence in a specific room in the convent and to interrogate the sisters one by one on the state of the house, on the functioning of the *maerte*, on harmony in the convent, on transgressions, and the proper observance of the customs. The inquisitor is shocked by this practice, the offense not only residing in the similarities with the routine of monastic orders, but also in the fact that Aleid exercised this task as a woman.[52]

Aleid Cluten is conspicuous for superior religious knowledge, something that she brought to bear within various settings. On visitation tours, as we saw, she subjected individual sisters to a concerted examination of conscience.[53] The chapter of guilt was presided over by her in an authoritative, not to say authoritarian, manner, with Aleid sitting and the sisters standing on either side of her.[54] Aleid also regulated the access of the sisters to the sacraments: they were not free to attend mass as they pleased. If they wanted to attend confession, Aleid instructed them on which facts to confess and which not to, and in doing so obliged them to undertake a kind of pre-confession. With specific priests she forbade the sisters all contact, on the grounds that there were many priests lacking in "savor of the

Scriptures" [saporem scripturarum].[55] Sometimes even—so the inquisitor insinuates—when Wermboud was too busy to hear confession himself, he referred confessants to Aleid, who acted as his deputy. She offered spiritual guidance not only to the sisters in her convent, but also to persons in the world still living in matrimony. These women disclosed to Aleid the secrets of their hearts as openly as though she were the priest hearing confession.[56]

The sources are not very revealing about the ways in which the women acquired their religious expertise but, in part, it was by studying and teaching. On her deathbed, Aleid Buser gave "edifying instruction, which she had well investigated."[57] The *Devout Letters*—if we are allowed to ascribe them to Aechte Eernstes—exemplify the type of religious learning received and transmitted by the women under scrutiny. In the first letter, the "daughters of Jerusalem"[58] receive instruction on how to cultivate their inner life so as to make them worthy of being true brides of Christ. The second constitutes a lesson on purity, of the body, of the heart, and of the spirit. The third letter consists basically of a series of prayers, to the suffering Christ, to the Virgin Mary, and to God the Creator.[59] The author did not have to compose the letters from scratch, however: the second letter contains extensive references to John of Ruusbroec's *Vanden XII beghinen*, a work lacking a final redaction and presently considered to be a late work by the famous Brabantine mystic.[60] In the first letter, too, borrowings from Henry Mande's *Boeckskyn van drien staten eens bekierden menschen* have been identified.[61] Mande was an inmate of Windesheim monastery but originally came from Holland. Early reception of his work in the western part of the diocese conforms to what else we know of the connections of this controversial visionary.[62] The free use Aechte Eernstes made of existing texts is not a sign of a lack of creativity, however; rather it exemplifies the way in which the devout were interconnected in an ongoing textual community that, in turn, produced a community of discourse.

Several of the women seem additionally to have had access to supernatural types of knowledge. For example, a paramystical experience received by Aechte Eernstes lay at the origins of the monastery of Jerusalem near Utrecht. Aechte received a vision of torches and burning lights approaching her and leading the way to the chapel of the Holy Sepulcher in the suburbs of Utrecht. Aechte interpreted the vision as a sign that people who were destined to lead an angelic life should be gathered together near the chapel. Thereupon she made every possible effort to acquire the chapel in order to turn it into a monastery.[63]

Supernatural experiences also befell Machteld Willems of the Gorinchem convent. Often, when she was in prayer, and especially during Holy Communion, she entered a trance and left her body.[64] During Christmas, her virginal breasts filled with milk as though she were ready to suckle the newborn Christ.[65] Aechte Willems of Delft benefited from the gift of being able to speak with the souls of the deceased.[66] Once she contacted the soul of a certain Aleid Wouter's daughter who had been condemned to remain in purgatory for fourteen days for disobedience against her superior. Aechte asked her whether the way of life they—the tertiaries in their Delft convent—lived pleased the Lord.[67] Aleid answered that Christ "would rather descend from heaven and have Himself crucified again than to permit such people to go to eternal damnation."[68] Aechte, however, realized the danger that was imminent if she took pride in her prophetic gift and humiliated herself instead.[69] The credibility of the report on Aechte's supernatural experience is enhanced by a detail added by the chronicle. On her deathbed, young sisters came to consult her for spiritual guidance, evidently relying on her special gift. But Aechte complained that it had forsaken her: formerly, she used to see the crucified Lord wherever she cast her eyes, but now her illness prevented her from seeing Him anymore.[70]

Setting

The authority of the women was further enhanced by the setting in which they operated. Between themselves, they entertained a veritable women's network. Aechte Eernstes had contacts with devout people all over the country. The authority of Aleid Cluten extended far beyond her own convent. She disciplined several other congregations in Utrecht beyond her own and intervened in convents in far-off Zwolle and in Rhenen. Together with Katrijn Wouters she appeared at the deathbed of Aechte Willems in Delft and supervised the election of a successor. Probably, she was also in contact with Machteld Cosijns. The ceremony with which the Gouda congregation adopted the Third Rule of St. Francis took place in St. Caecile's convent in Utrecht, Aleid's residence (1399).[71] Of course, this was also Wermboud's residence, which raises the problem of whether it is Aleid's own network we see at work here, or the female spin-off of Wermboud's many contacts.[72]

In fact, a recurrent phenomenon is the pairing of the female leader with a male counterpart, as I suggested earlier: the *ministra* and the confessor.[73] Naturally, a women's convent needed a priest to administer the sacraments, but the way the sources present the companionship between the priest and the *ministra* goes beyond this. A case in point is the cooperation between Aleid Cluten and Wermboud van Boskoop. Jointly, they exercise supra-local authority over a range of convents, Wermboud delegating part of his tasks to Aleid, including sacramental ones, if we are to believe the inquisitor.[74] Another instance of this dual setting can be found in Gouda. Here, Machteld Cosijns and the rector Dirk van der Aer are jointly responsible for the adoption by the sisters of St. Margaret of the status of regular canonesses.[75] The Gouda chronicle candidly reports that after Machteld Cosijns died, dissension arose between the rector and rectrix, which plunged the convent into a deep crisis.[76] This suggests that the harmony between the male and the female leader of the community is more than a hagiographical *topos*. Did these men and women in charge conform to a specific model in order to give shape to their cooperation? The example of St. Jerome and his spiritual friendships with pious ladies comes to mind here.[77] In any case, the effect of this dual setting can only have been to enhance the spiritual authority enjoyed by the women.

The women included in the sample have been selected on the basis of their association with one or more congregations of women. Was their sphere of action restricted to these congregations? In fact, the relationship between these communities and the outside world is rather complex. On the one hand, a clear boundary separated the congregations from the secular world. This was true even before full enclosure was introduced. Entering a community amounted to a radical conversion, as is exemplified by the case of Aleid Buser.[78] Within the convents, monastic values such as poverty, chastity, obedience, and humility prevailed. Evidently, these could have no direct validity in the outside world.

Nevertheless, the newly founded women's congregations remained part of the general society. They were dependent on their urban environment both for recruitment and for material support. At least in the early phase of their existence they lived according to secular law and were subject to the authority of the city magistracies. The striking point is the generous attitude with which these authorities approached the congregations. In this respect, the privileges granted by the city governments of Rhenen and Gouda to the congregations within their city walls reflect a general pattern. A more restrictive approach was adopted only after several decades, when the disadvantages of having to cope with an ever increasing number of immune convents became apparent.[79] In the early period, the urban environment welcomed the sister houses, whose prayer and intercession they appreciated, as is made clear by the wording of the Gouda privilege of 1396.[80] Although the secular environment did not adopt monastic values for application in its own sphere, it recognized them, if only because the holiness associated with the convents reinforced their intercessive power, which could be used for the benefit of society as a whole.

It is particularly evident at this juncture that the women in this sample enjoyed agency. They represented their newly founded convents, those highly valued places of holiness, and were therefore accepted as negotiating partners by secular authorities. But this very same setting allowed them, in specific circumstances, to extend their influences outside the direct sphere of their communities. This is why the founders of St. Elisabeth's hospital in Leiden turned to Katrijn Wouters for advice. A still more striking example is the pastoral care extended by Aleid Cluten to people outside her convent. To the dismay of the inquisitor, respectable lay persons, among them married ones, confessed to her openly as though she were a priest.[81]

Epilogue

The issue of female authority within the early Modern Devotion has not been very conspicuous within traditional research. This was due to the scarcity of sources originating directly from the women involved and to the bias in favor of their male counterparts, which seems to characterize the sources we do have. A new, critical examination, however, highlights the leading role women were allowed to play in the emerging movement. It relies on biographical texts and sources of a personal nature, such as letters. Apart from that and even more importantly, legal documents such as ordinances, founding charters, and reports by an inquisitor, if asked the right questions, yield interesting evidence.

A whole range of factors appears to have contributed to the authority these women enjoyed, including their social background and their personal capacities in several fields, both profane and religious. Their authority expressed itself in various roles, both formal—the position of *mater* in a convent—and informal, as founders, managers, and spiritual instructors. Their scope for agency was enhanced by the settings in which they operated, as leaders of their convents, as members of a women's network, and often in conjunction with priests, representatives of the ecclesiastical hierarchy, as male companions. Despite occasional tensions, the eight women of authority neither challenged this male bulwark, nor did they constitute an alternative to it. Instead, they supplemented it by their personal competence, doubling the learned knowledge embodied in the Church officials by means of their own experience, which combined practical skills and a discretion in religious matters acquired in a variety of ways. Consequently, they were better able to transfer the values of the newly chosen religious life to the next generation than the priests could ever have done alone. The fact that they were able to perform their roles in the ways that they did is a tribute to the wisdom both of the priests and of the women themselves.

Notes

1. On the Modern Devotion: John Van Engen, *Devotio Moderna: Basic Writings* (New York: Paulist Press, 1988); Wybren Scheepsma, *Medieval Religious Women in the Low Countries: "The Modern Devotion," the Canonesses of Windesheim and their Writings*, trans. David F. Johnson (Woodbridge: Boydel Press, 2004). On the tertiaries: Hildo van Engen, *De derde orde van Sint-Franciscus in het middeleeuwse bisdom Utrecht: Een bijdrage tot de institutionele geschiedenis van de Moderne Devotie*, Middeleeuwse studies en bronnen 95 (Hilversum: Verloren, 2006) [with English summary]. A survey by the present author will appear in *The Cambridge History of Religion*.
2. F.W.J. Koorn, "Hollandse nuchterheid? De houding van de Moderne Devotie tegenover vrouwenmystiek- en ascese," *Ons Geestelijk Erf* 66 (1992): 97–114; Koorn, "Het kapittel van Utrecht," in *Windesheim 1395–1995: Kloosters, teksten, invloeden. Voordrachten gehouden tijdens het internationale congres "600 jaar Kapittel van Windesheim" 27 mei 1995 te Zwolle*, ed. Anton J. Hendrikman, Middeleeuwse studies 12 (Nijmegen: Centrum voor Middeleeuwse Studies, 1996), pp. 48–66.
3. I refrain from giving the Dutch names an English flavor; Katrijn of course corresponds to Catherine. Most of the women involved are named after their closest male relative, either their father or their husband. My policy is to mention the complete name the first time it occurs and then to continue with an abbreviated form: "Katrijn Wouter's daughter" or "Katrijn Wouters".
4. Leiden, Regionaal Archief Leiden, Gasthuizen inv. 1052 and 1182, fols 18v–20v (deed of foundation and notice); fol. 7 (ordinance). Christina Ligtenberg, *De armezorg te Leiden tot het einde van de 16e eeuw* (The Hague: Nijhoff, 1908), pp. 106–109, with an edition of the sources on pp. 318–326. See also Madelon van Luijk, *Bruiden van Christus: De tweede religieuze vrouwenbeweging in Leiden en Zwolle, 1380–1580* (Zutphen: Walburg Pers, 2004), p. 215.
5. Leiden, Regionaal Archief Leiden, Kloosters inv. 1125 (foundation letter) and 1166 (donation of a house).
6. Chronicle of St. Agatha, edited by G. Verhoeven, "De kronieken van de Delftse tertiarissenconventen," *Ons Geestelijk Erf* 74:1–2 (2000): 133 (ll. 376–404, quotations at l. 377: "vaderen ende moederen" and ll. 389–390: "Welc woirt wi ontfinghen ghelijc oft ons van den hemel ghecomen waer") [105–152]. See also Van Luijk, *Bruiden van Christus*, p. 37.
7. Leiden, Regionaal Archief Leiden, Kloosters inv. 515.
8. Aleid Buser in Verhoeven, "Kronieken," 127–131 (ll. 145–293); Aechte Willems in Verhoeven, "Kronieken," 128 (ll. 157–160) and 131–133 (ll. 294–375).
9. Gouda, Streekarchief Midden Holland, Kloosters inv. 95, fols 1v–5v.
10. Weert, Minderbroeders (Museum voor Religieuze kunst "Jacob van Horne"), MS 6. Edition in excerpts: [J.W.L. Smit], "Het klooster der H. Agnes te Gorcum," *De Katholiek* 34 (1858): 95–126, for Machteld Willems, see pp. 114–115. For additional information on this manuscript I am grateful to Dr. Sabrina Corbellini.

11. For the quotation, see the following note.
12. Sources: (i) legal documents, including a privilege by bishop Frederick of Blanckenheim in favor of Aleid's convent of St. Caecile (1394) in: A. Matthaeus, *Fundationes et fata ecclesiarum* (Leiden: Lugduni Batavorum, 1704), pp. 303–304; (ii) fragments of the chronicle of St. Caecile's convent: Utrecht, Het Utrechts Archief, MS. Buchelius nr. 1840, fol. 131; (iii) a notice in the chronicle of St. Nicholas' convent in Utrecht in: P.J. Vermeulen, "Kronijk van het S. Nicolaasklooster te Utrecht," *Tijdschrift voor oudheden, statistiek etc. der geschiedenis van Utrecht* 4 (1852): 73–100, quotation at 77: "Soe hebben wi ons volkomeliken overgegeven onder her Warmbout ende onder die moeder van sint Cecilien, horen raet in allen te volgen"; (iv) a notice in the chronicle of St. Agatha's convent in Delft, see Verhoeven, "Kronieken," especially 133 (ll. 376–403); (v) a notice in the Diepenveen sister book, MS DV (Deventer, Stads- en Atheneumbibliotheek Suppl. 198 / 101 E 26), fols 62v-63r; (vi) two documents written by the inquisitor Eylard Schoneveld and included in P. Fredericq, *Corpus documentorum inquisitionis haereticae pravitatis Neerlandicae. Verzameling van stukken betreffende de pauselijke en bisschoppelijke inquisitie in de Nederlanden*, 5 vols (Gent: Vuylsteke and The Haque: Nijhoff, 1889–1906), 2:153–56 (nr. 106) and 2:181–185 (nr. 114). Literature: Koorn, "Kapittel van Utrecht," pp. 134–35.
13. (i) John Busch, *"Chronicon Windeshemense" und "Liber de reformatione monasteriorum,"* ed. Karl Grube, Geschichtsquellen der Provinz Sachsen und angrenzender Gebiete 19 (1886; repr. Farnborough: Gregg, 1968), pp. 363–364, quotation on p. 363; (ii) The Diepenveen sisterbook, MS DV, fols 272r; 360r–v; MS D (Zwolle, Historisch Centrum Overijssel, Coll. Van Rhemen inv. 1), fols 72d; 158c-159a; for an edition of this manuscript, see D.A. Brinkerink, *Vanden doechden der vuriger ende stichtiger susteren van Diepenveen ("handschrift D")* (Groningen: Wolters, 1904), pp. 141–42 and 301–302; (iii) The "Devote epistelen," edited by D.A. Brinkerink, "Devote epistelen (in Hs. No. 133 F 22 der Koninklijke Bibliotheek te 's-Gravenhage)," *Nederlandsch Archief voor Kerkgeschiedenis* 4 (1907): 312–38 and 388–409.
14. Busch, *Chronicon Windeshemense*, p. 363: "omnium religiosorum...pia mater et procuratrix."
15. MS DV, fol. 72d; Brinkerink, *Vanden doechden*, p. 142.
16. Busch, *Chronicon Windeshemense* (see note 13 earlier); see also Bertram Lesser, *Johannes Busch: Chronist der Devotio moderna: Werkstruktur, Überlieferung, Rezeption* (Frankfurt am Main: Lang, 2005).
17. Scheepsma, *Medieval Religious Women*, pp. 136–58; Annette M. Bollmann, *Frauenleben und Frauenliteratur in der Devotio moderna: Volkssprachige Schwesternbücher in literarhistorischer Perspektive* (Diss. Groningen, 2004), pp. 457–592.
18. Verhoeven, "Kronieken," 105–152; [Smit], "Het klooster der H. Agnes" (see note 10 earlier), pp. 95–126; M. Carasso-Kok, *Repertorium van verhalende historische bronnen uit de Middeleeuwen: heiligenlevens, annalen, kronieken*

en andere in Nederland geschreven verhalende bronnen, Bibliografische reek van het Nederlands Historisch Genootschap (The Hague: Nijhoff, 1981), pp. 157–158 (nr. 131) and 177–78 (nr. 150).
19. Leiden, Regionaal Archief Leiden, Kloosters inv. 1166.
20. Gouda, Streekarchief Midden Holland, Kloosters inv. 95, fol. 2v.
21. Ibid., fol. 21v (February 19, 1423).
22. Brinkerink, "Devote epistelen," (see note 13 earlier) pp. 312–38 and 388–409. Literature: J. van Aelst, "'Geordineert nae dye getijden'. Suster Bertkens passieboekje," *Ons Geestelijk Erf* 69 (1995): 147 [133–56]; Scheepsma, *Medieval Religious Women,* pp. 119–125; more extensive treatment in the original Dutch version: Wybren Scheepsma, *Deemoed en devotie: De koorvrouwen van Windesheim en hun geschriften* (Amsterdam: Prometheus, 1997), pp. 108–113; 227–228, and 236. For a description of The Hague, Koninklijke Bibliotheek MS 133 F22, which contains all three epistles, see Karl Stooker and Theo Verbeij, *Collecties op Orde: Middelnederlandse handschriften uit kloosters en semireligieuze gemeenschappen in de Nederlanden,* 2 vols (Louvain: Peeters, 1997), 2:409–410 (nr. 1224).
23. Busch, *Chronicon Windeshemense,* pp. 363–364; The Diepenveen sisterbook, MS DV, fols 60r–61v; MS. "D," fols 132d–133c; Brinkerink, *Van den doechden,* pp. 254–255. Cf. Scheepsma, *Medieval Religious Women,* 119–120.
24. Brinkerink, "Devote epistelen," 324 (rubric of the first letter).
25. Edition: W.J. Kühler, *Johannes Brinckerinck en zijn klooster te Diepenveen,* second edn. (Leiden: Van Leeuwen, 1914), pp. 362–380. For an English translation, see Van Engen, *Devotio Moderna* (see note 1 earlier), pp. 176–186. Cf. Scheepsma, *Medieval Religious Women,* pp. 113–119; Bollmann, *Frauenleben und Frauenliteratur,* pp. 164–172.
26. Brinkerink, "Devote epistelen," 326: "Ghi sult onderdanich wesen... uwen oversten ende alle den ghenen daer ghi bi sit."
27. On these sources, see later.
28. Katrijn Jacobs, Machteld Cosijns, and Aechte Eernstes put houses in their possession at the disposition of the devout.
29. Verhoeven, "Kronieken," 128 (ll. 185–89): "want si langhe jaren tesamen in groter armoeden gheweest hadden, ende hem noch nye persoen toe en quaem daer si merckelic onderstant eens voirtgaenden levens hope of hadden te vercrighen."
30. Verhoeven, "Kronieken," 127 (l. 146): "eersamich"; 128 (l. 185): "eersamen" (l. 189): "eersamer"; 129 (l. 197): "eersamer"; 130 (l. 251, 268, and 280): "eersamighe."
31. Gouda, Streekarchief Midden Holland, Kloosters inv. 95, fol. 1v.
32. [Smit], "Klooster der H. Agnes," 115.
33. Verhoeven, "Kronieken," 127 (l. 146): "eersamich jonc vrouwenpersoen."
34. Gouda, Streekarchief Midden Holland, Kloosters inv. 95, fol. 1v: "vinculo adhuc maritali copulate" and "beneficia et largas elemosinas utpote pauperculis quantum sub potestate viri constitute licuit, ministravit."
35. Verhoeven, "Kronieken," 128 (ll. 165–176).

36. Anneke B. Mulder-Bakker, "The Metamorphosis of Woman: Transmission of Knowledge and the Problem of Gender," *Gender and History* 12 (2000): 656 [642–664].
37. Anneke B. Mulder-Bakker, "Introduction," in *Sanctity and Motherhood: Essays on Holy Mothers in the Middle Ages*, ed. Anneke B. Mulder-Bakker (New York and London: Garland, 1995), p. 23 [3–30].
38. Mathilde van Dijk, *Een rij van spiegels: De heilige Barbara van Nicomedia als voorbeeld voor vrouwelijke religieuzen* (Hilversum: Verloren, 2000), pp. 140–145.
39. Gouda, Streekarchief Midden Holland, Kloosters inv. 95, fols 1r–v.
40. Utrecht, Het Utrechts Archief, St. Agnietenklooster Rhenen inv. 31, fol. 132v: "die wieste ende bescheidenste die dingen te regieren." The same clause: Gouda, Streekarchief Midden Holland, Kloosters inv. 95, fol. 2r.
41. Leiden, Regionaal Archief Leiden, Kloosters inv. 1125 and 1166.
42. Verhoeven, "Kronieken," 129 (ll. 218–224).
43. Fredericq, *Corpus documentorum inquisitionis* (see note 12 earlier), 2:183 (nr. 114): "istarum congregationum legislator est atque gubernator supremus."
44. Fredericq, *Corpus documentorum inquisitionis*, 2:154 (nr. 106).
45. Leiden, Regionaal Archief Leiden, Kloosters inv. 515.
46. Utrecht, Het Utrechts Archief, St. Agnietenklooster Rhenen inv. 31, fol. 132v; cf. Gouda, Streekarchief Midden Holland, Kloosters inv. 95, fol. 2r. Leiden, Regionaal Archief Leiden, Gasthuizen inv. 1182, fol. 7 with Ligtenberg, *Armezorg*, pp. 321–326.
47. MS. "D," fol. 158c; Brinkerink, *Van den doechden*, p. 301: "Want sij was een wijse walsprekende vrouwe ende seer gemynt om hore eerbaerheit willen also dat sij wal wat vercrijgen conde."
48. Verhoeven, "Kronieken," 128 (l. 191): "eens warachtigen stervenden levens" and 131 (l. 319): "een grondich stervende leven."
49. Utrecht, Het Utrechts Archief, St. Agnietenklooster Rhenen inv. 31, fol. 132v: "van geesteliken onderscheiden meest ondersocht."
50. Utrecht, Het Utrechts Archief, St. Agnietenklooster Rhenen inv. 31, fol. 132v; Gouda, Streekarchief Midden Holland, Kloosters inv. 95, fol. 2r.
51. Leiden, Regionaal Archief Leiden, Kloosters inv. 515 (unfol.): "overmids oetmoedicheit doechde ende reckelicheit die sier in ghetrouden."
52. Fredericq, *Corpus documentorum inquisitionis*, 2:183 (nr. 114).
53. Ibid.
54. Fredericq, *Corpus documentorum inquisitionis*, 2:153 (nr. 106) and 2:182 (nr. 114).
55. Fredericq, *Corpus documentorum inquisitionis*, 2:153–54 (nr. 106) and 2:182–83 (nr. 114), quotation at 2:183.
56. Fredericq, *Corpus documentorum inquisitionis*, 2:155 (nr. 106).
57. Verhoeven, "Kronieken," 131 (l. 284): "veel stichtiger leren die si selve wel ondersocht hadde."

58. Cf. Cant. 3.10–11.
59. For this and the following, see the fine analysis in Scheepsma, *Medieval Religious Women*, pp. 121–122, which is unaffected by the problem of authorship.
60. For an edition, see John of Ruusbroec, *Opera omnia*, ed. M.M. Kors and G. de Baere, trans. H. Rolfson, CCCM 107A, 10 vols (Thielt: Lannoo, 1981–2006), 7A. Cf. Geert Warnar, *Ruusbroec: literatuur en mystiek in de veertiende eeuw* (Amsterdam: Athenaeum, Polak & Van Gennep, 2003), pp. 274–279.
61. Edition: W. Moll, *Johannes Brugman en het godsdienstig leven onzer vaderen in de vijftiende eeuw*, 2 vols (Amsterdam: Portielje, 1854), 1:263–92. Cf. Thomas F.C. Mertens, *Hendrik Mande (?–1431): tekshistorische en literairhistorische studies* (Diss. Nijmegen, 1986), pp. 57–58, and 93–97.
62. The *Boeckskyn* is found a.o. in The Hague, Koninklijke Bibliotheek, MS 73 G 25, which is very early [around 1400?; Stooker and Verbeij, *Collecties op orde*, 2:429 (nr. 1294)] and belonged to the tertiaries of Weesp. These, too, were within the sphere of influence of Wermboud van Boskoop.
63. Busch, *Chronicon Windeshemense*, pp. 363–364.
64. [Smit], "Klooster der H. Agnes," 115: "Seer grote begheerte had si te gaen totten heiligen sacrament soe dat sy dicwijl in die weke dair toe ghinc als hair die drift des heiligen gheestes dair toe dranc."
65. MS Weert, Minderbroeders Nr. 6 (see note 10 earlier), fol. 5; omitted by [Smit], "Klooster der H. Agnes," 95–126. Koen Goudriaan, "Het Leven van Liduina en de Moderne Devotie", *Jaarboek voor Middeleeuwse Geschiedenis* 6 (2003): 195 n162 [161–236].
66. Verhoeven, "Kronieken," 132 (ll. 324–25).
67. Ibid. (ll. 325–332).
68. Ibid. (ll. 332–334): "Het behaecht den Heer also dat hi liever neder daelde van den hemel ende liet hem anderwerf crucen, dan hi aldusdanich volc verloren liet."
69. Ibid. (ll. 334–337).
70. Ibid. (ll. 338–343).
71. Gouda, Streekarchief Midden Holland, Kloosters inv. 95, fol. 2v–3r.
72. Wermboud was at the center of an extensive and ramified network of male devout, as I will explain in a separate publication: *Wermboud van Boskoop, een groot prediker en hoofd van alle devote mensen* (forthcoming).
73. See Brian Patrick McGuire, "Visionary Women Who Did What They Wanted and Men Who Helped Them," in *The Prime of their Lives: Wise Old Women in Pre-industrial Europe*, ed. Anneke Mulder-Bakker and Renée Nip (Louvain: Peeters, 2004), pp. 103–122.
74. Vermeulen, "Kronijk van het S. Nicolaasklooster," 77; Fredericq, *Corpus documentorum inquisitionis*, 2:154 (nr. 106), and 2:183 (nr. 114). Other instances are the ruling of St. Elisabeth's hospital in Leiden, see Ligtenberg, *Armezorg*, p. 319; the first flowering of St. Agatha's convent in Delft, see Verhoeven,

"Kronieken," 130 (ll. 268–278); and the foundation of Jerusalem monastery near Utrecht, see Busch, *Chronicon Windeshemense,* p. 363.
75. Gouda, Streekarchief Midden Holland, Kloosters inv. 95, fol. 5.
76. Ibid., fol. 5v.
77. Van Dijk, *Een rij van spiegels,* p. 166.
78. Verhoeven, "Kronieken," 127–129 (ll. 145–200).
79. Van Luijk, *Bruiden van Christus,* pp. 217–252.
80. Gouda, Streekarchief Midden Holland, Kloosters inv. 95, fol. 2v.
81. Fredericq, *Corpus documentorum inquisitionis,* 2:155 (nr. 106).

CHAPTER 3

PARTNERS IN PROFESSION: INWARDNESS, EXPERIENCE, AND UNDERSTANDING IN HELOISE AND ABELARD

Ineke van 't Spijker

Heloise and Abelard demonstrate how the experiential quality of thinking itself and the reciprocal influence of thought and feeling can function within Latin learning.

A development of inwardness has long been recognized as one of the defining elements of the twelfth century. In this development Peter Abelard played a major role. Recently, the influence of Heloise in the development of Abelard's thought has received renewed attention.[1] Indeed, in addressing her as his "partner in the profession of their sacred project" [in professione sacri propositi consors] Abelard acknowledged her importance.[2] Heloise's insistence on "the inner" is clear in her letters. Thus in her third letter she asks Abelard to compose a rule for her community that does justice to the inner.[3] She writes "whoever are real Christians are so totally concerned about the inner man...that they not at all or hardly take care of the outer."[4]

This inwardness has already been highlighted in scholarship on the Letters. Discussing Heloise's request for a rule fit for women, Linda Georgianna writes: "For Heloise, the goals of the spiritual life are absolute and strictly interior."[5] Abelard responded to her request with a history of the origins of female communities, in Letter Seven, and with a Rule, in Letter Eight. Mary McLaughlin sees in it "in essence, an elaborate gloss on the declaration of Heloise that 'the true Christian is wholly concerned with the inner man.'"[6] Abelard wrote several other works for the community of nuns at the Paraclete at the request of Heloise: hymns, sermons, and answers to questions about difficulties of scriptural interpretation. In many of these writings the notion of interiority is prominent.

Although Heloise and Abelard are thus both associated with an "inward turn," it is less common to see their names in connection with the increasing emphasis on "experience," equally considered as characteristic of the twelfth century. On the contrary, their shared project, with its insistence on scholarly understanding, seems to be at the expense of this experience, of which Bernard of Clairvaux is the most famous example. In the following I shall argue that we may question an over-narrow concept of experience on which such an image is based. Heloise's and Abelard's notion of inwardness in no way eliminates experience: their very activity of thinking is comprehended by it. Emblematic of their interiority, as I will demonstrate, is the Virgin Mary, as she is represented in Abelard's Sermo One in the scene of the Annunciation: alone with her thoughts, concentrating on reading and prayer, beyond any conflict between reason and experience.

Abelard and Heloise share their interest in the *homo interior* with many of their contemporaries. However, theirs is not the inwardness that we find in the Victorines, where the *homo interior* is architecturally modeled after, for example, the Ark of Noah;[7] nor is the emphasis, as it was in the Chartres philosophers' view, on the inner man as reflecting his place within a comprehensive cosmology.[8] It is also unlike the affective interiority that we find in Bernard of Clairvaux and William of Saint-Thierry.[9] The latter authors especially are associated not only with inwardness, but also with an increasingly affective devotion—and with experience. Experience, thus, is primarily associated with feeling [affectus].[10] It is often contrasted with (discursive) thinking, which both Abelard and Heloise exercise in their works. A dichotomy between these two aspects—perhaps even uneasiness—resonates when Linda Georgianna concludes that "Heloise focuses on the interior life more as a theoretical than as an applied principle. In comparison with Abelard's...meditations...Heloise's argument for a new rule seems rather technical."[11] Abelard's meditations were part of his effort to divert Heloise away from love of him to love of Christ. He suggests that she always keep Christ's suffering before her mind's eye and identify with the women at the Cross and at the grave. However, as Georgianna observes, Heloise does not engage in a "popular meditative mode,"[12] which in many other twelfth-century authors is connected with exactly the affective, experiential aspects of devotion. Abelard shows great imaginative power in this evocation of the suffering Christ, as well as in other biblical scenes and stories in his sermons and hymns. Yet meditation on these stories, in a Cistercian mode, was not their goal, neither for Heloise, nor, I would suggest, for Abelard.

As implicit as it is problematic, in the aforementioned opposition is a supposed superiority of feeling and experience, often as a reaction against the perceived claims for the superiority of reason. In the twelfth century, William of Saint-Thierry and Bernard of Clairvaux famously argued against what they saw as the arrogance of reason in Abelard and others. However, their pretensions based on their *experientia* might well be more absolute than those of which they accused Abelard. The privileging of experience taken in this affective sense, moreover, overlooks the very experience of thinking, of perceptively scrutinizing, of which Heloise is no less capable than Abelard. Abelard and Heloise sometimes appeal to experience in a general sense, as when Abelard in the opening of the *Historia Calamitatum* announces that he will write about "the experiences of my calamities."[13] Much more fundamental, however, for their own lived experience is their passion to understand. Heloise's introductory letter to her *Problemata* (questions she has put to Abelard about the meaning of several scriptural passages, and his "solutions") clearly illustrates her desire for understanding.[14] The activity of thinking, trying to understand, is not exempt from the realm of human experience.[15] And it is worth noting that in the medieval period an awareness of the affective quality of thinking and the reciprocal influence of thought and feeling was often present.[16]

It is the affective experience associated with, for example, Bernard of Clairvaux that women often arrogated as they were denied access to the experience of thinking. Even so, there is a risk that one may overlook the actual intellectual achievements of women, clothed as they may have been in the religious format of the time.[17] In the case of Heloise there is no doubt about the powers of her intellect—nor should this leave her on the "wrong" side of an experiential dichotomy.

From this background and perspective, I now go on to explore what is meant, in the work of Abelard and Heloise, by inner—and, inevitably, by what is opposed to it, outer. As we shall see, the opposition is not a stable one, nor is the relation between the two, inner and outer, symmetrical. "Outer" may refer to the material care within or outside the monastery, or to the care for the body. Often it refers to external rules and outward behavior, as opposed to inner intention, betraying a discrepancy between outer and inner. However, there is not necessarily a tension: often enough the outer also reveals or signifies the inner. As I intend to demonstrate here, the relation may also be associated with "works" and "the letter" as opposed to "faith" and the letter's hidden meaning. Thus the use of a well-known hermeneutical principle—that which governs the relation between the Old and the New Testament—contributes to a multifaceted notion of interiority as the mode of experience.[18]

Intentio and Discrepancy between Inner and Outer

Abelard's and Heloise's notion of inwardness centers on their concept of *intentio*. The importance of this concept to many twelfth-century thinkers, but especially in Abelard's philosophy, has long been acknowledged. For M.-D. Chenu it was Abelard's ethics of intention that made him into "the first modern man."[19] Mary McLaughlin sees Abelard's Rule in Letter Eight as "the work of a man profoundly convinced of the priority of reason over custom, the primacy of intention and the moral indifference of human actions."[20] The prominence of intention is easily illustrated in Abelard's works in general as well as in the Letters by both Abelard and Heloise. As Heloise says in Letter Six: "What we should consider is not so much what is done, but the mind with which [quo animo] it is done, if we try to please Him who tests the heart and the reins (cf. Ier. 20.12, Prov. 24.12)."[21] Abelard reflects this in his Rule in Letter Eight: "It is much better for us to do what we do well, than to do the good thing. We should consider not so much what is done, as the mind in which it is done."[22]

I shall return to Abelard's position on intention, different from that of his contemporaries and of Heloise. Before doing so, however, it is important to realize how for both Abelard and Heloise *intentio*, which seems to imply a withdrawal into the inner, is not synonymous with private experience. Nor can it be used as a defense of a purely inner devotion, where the outer circumstances do not matter—all Heloise's protestations about the unimportance of the exterior notwithstanding. The notion of the inner does not refer to some personal inner space that is safe from, or impervious and indifferent to, the outer world. On the contrary, there is a striking emphasis on the necessity of congruency between outer behavior and inner attitude, a correspondence whose lack in her own life Heloise had expressed, in her second Letter to Abelard, as failure: "Men call me chaste; they do not know the hypocrite I am."[23]

If ever the idea of interiority implies the notion of exteriority and the potential for a discrepancy between outer and inner, it is in the notion of *intentio* as seen by Heloise and Abelard. Heloise presents precisely the discrepancy between her outer actions and her inner motivation as what torments her most, or at least as much as her loss of Abelard. Behind Heloise's anxiety and complaint lies the question: "what is the standard of integrity for one who lives a life she has not chosen...?"[24] Or has she? As John Marenbon observes, she is not "making a protest against the life of religion she chose in obedience to Abelard's commands."[25] If this sounds like an unresolved paradox, what Heloise experiences as a discrepancy can be seen to illustrate her commitment to the values of monasticism—in which, ever since the Desert Fathers, the awareness of the possibility of ambiguity had been present, necessitating continuous self-examination.[26] This also shows how Heloise's inner experience, informed by her thoughtful self-scrutiny, is intimately linked to her awareness of an outside world.

Actual or potential discrepancy is a recurring issue in the letters. Abelard suggests the possibility of such a discrepancy when he first compliments Heloise on her attitude toward human praise, and then (in accordance with her own suspicions) admonishes her about the difficulty of really remaining immune to it: "May it be in your mind as it is in your writing."[27]

Heloise reacts to this Letter by announcing precisely a further discrepancy: "I will hold my hand from writing words which I cannot restrain my tongue from speaking"—words that, she had said, are "the ever ready indications of the heart's emotions," nothing being less under our control than our heart. At the same time she echoes Abelard's wish for congruency between her written words and her heart, with her wistful conclusion: "Would that a grieving heart would be as ready to obey as a writer's hand!"[28]

The Inner through the Outer

Not always is the incongruity between outer and inner a negative one, however. Immediately following the complaint about her own hypocrisy Heloise adds that maybe there is some merit in not giving outward offence, whatever the intention.[29]

Nor is the opposition negative when in Letter Five Abelard quotes the Canticle text: "I am black but comely" (Cant. 1:4), illustrating a contrast between outer and inner. Indeed, in Abelard's reply the long passage on the black bride contains a subtle nuancing of Heloise's view of hypocrisy of which she has accused herself. The blackness and coarseness of Heloise's outer habit, allegorically signaled by the Ethiopian bride, indicate bodily affliction (as opposed to the whiteness of inner virtues) and humility. Because of this humility the Bridegroom takes her into his chamber, which then is the secluded place where she can offer her prayer undistracted and purely—wholly different from the hypocrites who pray at street corners. Abelard here reconfigures hypocrisy in terms of purposeful looking for human glory—which do not cover Heloise's case as presented by her.[30]

Equally, when Abelard responds to Heloise's request for a history of the order of nuns, at first sight at least he does not extricate the exterior from his concerns. He quotes the example of the women who played a role in the community of Jesus' followers, showing women's importance and the excellence of Heloise's profession. Among these were Martha and Mary: when Jesus came into their house after Lazarus' resurrection (in an interesting externalization of the binary of inner and outer) one restored the inner man with food, the other cherished the outer man in his weariness, with ointment.[31] Presenting the Old Testament women who kept watch at the door of the tabernacle, and the mirrors they gave to Moses, Abelard interprets these mirrors as "those external works from which either the foulness or the beauty of the soul is perceived just as the quality of a human face in a physical mirror."[32] Discussing the role of deaconesses in the early church he quotes the Letter to Timothy (1 Tim. 5:9–11), in which the recommendations for a deaconess encompass her good works.[33]

Thus, in an understated way Abelard seems to hint at a more complex notion of the "inner man." He implies its inevitable connection with something external. Perhaps the reason why he does so is that, as John Marenbon has shown, Abelard developed his own view of intention, different from traditional ideas found in theories about morality and sin, and different from Heloise's own ideas. Heloise followed the tradition with its emphasis on the importance of inner states of mind and the potential sinfulness of even mere thoughts if one inwardly delights in, and in that sense consents to, sinful thoughts. By contrast, Abelard held that, whereas actions can only be described as good or bad by virtue of the intentions behind them, intentions in their turn are only sinful in relation to an intended action—if one has inwardly consented to carry out the act, whether it is then actually performed or not[34]: "Abelard's morality is one of intended actions: people are neither excused, nor inculpated, by a state of mind alone... Heloise was in Abelard's terms a heroine, no matter how she felt or thought, because of how she chose to live."[35]

Exteriora refers to outer and ultimately indifferent devotions, as Heloise repeated again and again, but also, especially in Abelard's Rule, to the care for the material well-being of the community and that for the bodily well-being of the nuns.[36] Abelard reflects Heloise's persistent privileging of the inner over the outer. Yet, it is impossible to eliminate considerations of the external. Thus simply such a thing as place, in itself not bringing salvation, may offer either opportunities or obstacles for easier observance.[37]

Abelard nevertheless fully engages with Heloise's concerns in his Rule, responding to her distinction between those things that are indifferent and what really matters. Heloise had quoted Augustine for the distinction between virtue and its external manifestation. Continence is a virtue not of the body but of the soul[38]: the less one cares for outer things, the greater can one's *devotio* for God be.[39] Abelard agrees: "Many afflict themselves more outwardly but make less progress before God who is the inspector of the heart rather than of the work."[40]

The Hidden Inner and its Legibility

This last quotation hints at the secrecy and inscrutability implied by the importance of inner dispositions. This secrecy seems to suggest that the inner as such is withdrawn from any possibility of human "reading," being open only to God.[41] It is symbolized externally in, for example, the bedchamber of the black bride,[42] or, in Abelard's sermon on the Annunciation, in Mary being alone in her bedchamber.[43]

However, the inner does not completely resist interpretation. As Heloise herself had pointed out at the beginning of Letter Six, the mind's feelings flow out through words.[44] Besides, outer things not only either facilitate or hinder devotion, they also have value as a sign. As Abelard explains, the black color of the nuns' habit fits the penitence to which they dedicate themselves, and the lambs' wool is suitable for the brides of Christ.[45]

Moreover, the initial intention usually becomes clear, if sometimes only after the event. Discussing the choice of an abbess, Abelard warns that it may be difficult to discern whether somebody is brought to the abbacy because she desires authority and status, or service. The outcome, however, will show the true nature of her previous behavior.[46]

The inner becomes further legible, when, as we saw, for example, in Letter Seven, Abelard pointed to the works that mirrored the soul.[47] On the one hand, man is judged not according to his works, but according to his intention. On the other, intention cannot be disengaged from external action, as Abelard explains also in his *Commentary on Romans*: "not the hearers of the Law, but the doers of the Law will be justified" (Rom. 2:13). Those who show outwardly in their works the goodwill that they have in their mind are the ones who, according to Romans 2:15, have that law written "in the heart, to which their own conscience bears witness... Their conscience and their right intention, known to them and not to others, makes them confident about the rightness of their works."[48] Even conscience, just as intention known only to its owner, is thus not without its external manifestation, if only to oneself.[49] *Conscientia* as employed by Abelard is not the modern seat of subjectivity. It is more "a sort of intellectual honesty."[50] Elsewhere Abelard says: in all that we do against our conscience and against what we believe, we sin,[51] showing that experience as represented in conscience is not a private space, but is to be subject to probing and informed by belief—itself, for Abelard and Heloise, open to reasoned examination.

Conscientia and Fama; Sinceritas and Caritas

Inner *conscientia* is, moreover, coupled with outer *fama*. Abelard quotes Augustine saying that caring for one's conscience without paying attention to one's *fama* is cruelty.[52] Heloise appeals to the benefit of at least avoiding scandal if she is a good abbess even without the right intentions. In Abelard's sermons Mary and Jesus are shown to obey the Law—Jesus being circumcised, Mary going through the rite of purification—partly to avoid scandal.[53]

If in her own view Heloise fails because of the discrepancy between actions and intentions, from another perspective she is successful: in controlling her behavior, indeed to the extent that the outside world knows her as an exemplary abbess. From a modern perspective one would perhaps question her sincerity. However, the issue is more complicated than this[54]: although sharing in the secrecy of the inner, *sinceritas* [sincerity]—or purity that is often seen as its equivalent—is not simply the opposite of Heloise's hypocrisy. It is not the sincerity of her intention that is the problem—it is that she does not have the intention demanded for her role, distracted as it is by her sincere and pure love for Abelard and by the anxieties that Abelard's letters cause her. *Sincere* is often connected with the lack of (outer) distractions—and fits in a monastic desire for concentration: "A heart overcome with sorrow has no rest, and a mind occupied with anxieties cannot truly [sincere] devote itself to God."[55]

If the idea of the inner and of (right) intention is thus connected with sincerity, it is further substantiated when sincerity, or purity, is associated with love [caritas]. Heloise famously declares how she loved Abelard for his own sake, not for anything else.[56] In his turn, Abelard counters this by telling her that it is really Christ who is her true friend.[57] Heloise's thinking about love and its necessary gratuity—love for the sake of the beloved—influenced Abelard, who developed his own theory of *caritas* from here.[58] This theory can also be found in his sermons for the Paraclete. In Sermo Five he writes about how God sent the Holy Spirit, that is, "he infused us with a chaste love for him, by which we would sincerely love him for his sake, not seeking in him our own convenience but only his glory and honour."[59]

It is *caritas* also that finally distinguishes Christians from others. Heloise writes: "Nothing so much separates Jews from Christians as the distinction between outer and inner works, especially since only love distinguishes between the children of God and the children of the devil, which the Apostle calls the fulfilment of the law and the aim of instruction."[60] This alerts us to another important aspect of *caritas*. Whatever its quality of purity and sincerity, informing and resonating in Abelard's and Heloise's concept of *caritas*, the concept of *conscientia*, and that of the *homo interior*, is their scriptural hermeneutics and theology.

The Mirror of Scripture

The inner, as we have seen, is not left to its own inscrutability. Words betray the mind. Works mirror the soul. So too does Scripture. Before Scripture can have this function, however, it needs to be studied and interpreted:

> Holy Scripture, indeed, is a mirror of the mind, in which anyone who lives by reading it and advances by understanding learns the beauty of their conduct or apprehends its hideousness...However, he who looks at Scripture while he does not understand it holds, as a blind man, a mirror in front of his eyes in which he is not able to see what he is, nor does he seek in Scripture for the teaching for which it solely is made...[61]

Scripture also informs the right intention. At the end of his Rule Abelard said that "no soul is pure except the one who meditates and ruminates about the divine precepts as much as she can understand them, doing not only the right things, but doing them in a right way, that is with the right intention."[62]

Answering the requests of Heloise and her sisters, Abelard offers interpretations of Scripture in his sermons, his answers to the *Problemata*, as well as in his *Hexaemeron* and in his hymns.[63] Heloise's questions prompted Abelard to discuss issues on which he would later elaborate in, for example, his *Commentary on Romans*.[64] They show her as a theologian in her own right and the works Abelard wrote for the Paraclete may be seen as a common project, of "partners in profession" indeed.

In his Sermo Nine Abelard, in a traditional allegorical way, explains the palanquin that Salomo—figure of Christ—has made for himself (Canticle 3:9) as signifying the Cross. Its posts were made of silver: they are the words of the Apostles, about which the Psalmist said: The words of the Lord are chaste, silver probed by fire (Ps. 11:7). "The words of apostolic preaching are said to be of silver, because they have the clarity of understanding, not the obscurity of a veil, as the Law and the Prophets, that use mystical more than plain [aperta] words."[65] In their obscurity the very words of the Old Testament are taken to refer to the greater clarity of the New Testament. The letter, of the prophet and the law, is a veil not immediately open to understanding as the words of the Gospel are. The secrecy of the inner, which at times can only be read through an interpretative effort, is paralleled in this hidden meaning of Scripture, equally demanding an act of understanding.

Law and Gospel

In his other works, the hidden nature of Scripture has a positive value. In his *Theologies* Abelard shows how a hidden truth is beautifully enfolded within Scripture. If a grimmer meaning sometimes surfaces—salvation history necessitating the Jews' blindness—his view primarily enables him to show how the words of pagan philosophers were consistent with Christian truth.[66] When in the Letters and Sermons, as well as in his *Commentary on Romans*, Abelard, and Heloise, discuss the distinction between law and prophets on the one side and gospel and apostles on the other, they offer no such positive rationale—and the greater clarity of the words of the apostles is now favorably contrasted with the mystical words of the Old Testament. The deeper meaning of the Law and the Prophets, hidden beneath the veil of their mystical words (which in Abelard's interpretation point to their own very hiddenness) lay waiting to be unveiled as the *figura* of the Truth, unveiled at the historical moment of the Incarnation. Jewish blindness to anything but the letter, instead of being virtually a cliché made in passing reference to salvation history, becomes the defining and contrasting background for Heloise's and Abelard's analysis of the inner.

The identification of Jewish interpretation as literal, as ignoring the deeper spiritual meaning, and of the Jewish religion as concerned with works rather than with faith is, of course, as old as Paul's Letters. It ignores the tradition of the Jews, who had their own spiritual interpretation. For Heloise and Abelard the Jew with whose works they contrast Christian faith is still predominantly what has been called a "theological Jew."[67] When Heloise asks Abelard to write a Rule that is fit for women she refers to New Testament texts, among others Paul's Letter to Romans and Peter. "Many are the witnesses by worldly as well as ecclesiastical teachers," she says, "that teach us that we should not care too much about the things that are done outwardly, and are called indifferent, otherwise the works of the law, and the insupportable yoke of its bondage, as Peter calls it, would be preferable to the freedom of the Gospel."[68]

The juxtaposing of Old Testament Law and New Testament Gospel; letter and spirit; fear and love; outer and inner is a recurring concern in several sermons. In Sermo Five, for the feast of Purification, Abelard discusses the relation between the two Testaments, and the limits of a literal understanding of the Law—when fear, not love, is the motivation—after its fulfillment. Abelard in his comments on Galatians 4:3–6: "While we were minors, we served under the elements of the world. But when the fullness of time had come, God sent his Son, born of a woman, born under the law, in order to redeem those who were under the law, so that we might receive adoption as children," writes:

> The understanding of the law, as of the letter that kills, is overshadowed by mystical words, not open to that [the Jewish] uncultivated people. The Jews thus have the words of the law as letters, because they have not understood their spiritual and mystical meanings, in which the usefulness of understanding mainly consists... They serve under those elements, who through fear of punishment... are forced into obedience, like servants, not through love, as sons.[69]

This passage reveals the connection between the "mystical meaning" and a regime of love, disclosed only by a process of understanding, which at the same time constitutes this regime.

Conclusion

Their biblical interpretation enabled Abelard and Heloise to establish and underpin their specific understanding of Christian identity as residing in the inner, where *caritas* and *libertas* take the place of *timor* and *servitudo*.[70] If *caritas* and *sinceritas*, *intentio* and *conscientia*, make up this inner, they nonetheless at the same time comprise the inner's outer facets, so to speak.

In his sermons Abelard fully mastered the traditional exegetical register with its figural interpretation of biblical stories. Yet, he does not often call for the usual tropological–meditational identification with the *personae* of these stories or with aspects of them. Even the evocation of Christ's suffering in Letter Five, with which Abelard tries to convince Heloise to love Christ rather than himself, is not, I would suggest, in the usual meditational mode. In Abelard's *crescendo* urging, to have Christ in view [prae oculis habe] and to keep him in mind [mente gere] as her true spouse, to look closely [intuere] at him on his way to the crucifixion, to be [esto] one of the crowd and the women who bewailed him, there is an immediacy that, totally within Abelard's literary mastery, is yet different from the orchestration of the readers' thoughts and feelings, which is the goal of much exegetical and meditational literature. Abelard is not interested in arousing his readers in the same way as, for example, Bernard of Clairvaux, or William of Saint-Thierry, or even, slightly earlier, Anselm of Canterbury in their Meditations or Commentaries on the Canticle. These almost compel their readers into devotional compliance. Nor does he see the *homo interior* as an interior object, to be cultivated in order to ultimately transcend one's individuality. Such a perspective may be seen in the works of Hugh of Saint-Victor and Richard of Saint-Victor.[71]

The goal, for Abelard and for Heloise, is more modest, though not necessarily easier to attain. Perhaps it is more like that which, as Abelard explains in the prologue to his *Commentary on Romans*, is the rhetorical aim of Scripture: to either teach, by insinuating to us what should be done or avoided; or warn us, drawing our will away from evil or applying it to the good.[72] Thus, the reader remains or is constituted as the subject of the story, enabled to doing as well as willing the good. She, as it were, creates in Scripture the mirror that "reflects her behavior." Such a reading does not subsume individual experience under a universal goal—be it that of the role of perfect abbess, or even of a restored *imago dei*. It transposes it into a key that accommodates both.

Perhaps the complexity and nuance implied in this reading are nowhere more compelling than in the way in which, in Abelard's view, the Virgin Mary embodies a multifaceted inwardness. At the end of his Rule Abelard showed how Mary "kept all these words in her heart"- implying just the sort of studious scrutiny that he recommended to the nuns and that should inform their *intentio*.[73] In Sermo One he returns to the Virgin. The biblical story as Abelard presents it to Heloise and the Paraclete is one of dramatic and psychological complexity,[74] transcending any potential dichotomy between thinking and feeling, rational understanding, and experience. Mary is shown as a connection between Old and New Testament and all that that implies. She married in obedience to the Old Law.[75] She chose Joseph, "whom she held dear because of his love of chastity and close familial ties, and whom she trusted she could draw into agreeing with her."[76] Alone with her thoughts, rather than in the company of other women, she was "never less alone than when she was alone."[77] She emphatically exemplifies and outwardly manifests inner concentration: her eyes fixed on her reading, or to the ground, in prayer, she totally desired that to which her mind was directed.[78] She is truly [sincere] free for God. Yet obeying the Law, she thus also embodies, if not the reconciliation, the combination of what pertains to *fama* and *conscientia*. Mary reflects for Heloise and her sisters how both external performance and inner conviction can be part of their experience.

Notes

1. See Peter Dronke, "Heloise," in his *Women Writers of the Middle Ages: A Critical Study of Texts from Perpetua (d. 203) to Marguerite Porete (d. 1310)*, (Cambridge, UK: Cambridge University Press, 1984), pp. 111–112 [107–139]; M.T. Clanchy, *Abelard: A Medieval Life* (Oxford: Blackwell, 1997),

pp. 169–172, 277–282, and 286; John Marenbon, *The Philosophy of Peter Abelard* (Cambridge, UK: Cambridge University Press, 1997), pp. 72–79 and 298–303. For more general considerations on Heloise's influence, see also Constant J. Mews, *Abelard and Heloise* (Oxford: Oxford University Press, 2005); and the articles in *Listening to Heloise: The Voice of a Twelfth-Century Woman*, ed. Bonnie Wheeler, The New Middle Ages (New York: St Martin's Press, 2000). I would like to thank John Marenbon for reading this article and making some helpful suggestions.

2. In his introductory Letter to the sermons, which he wrote for the Paraclete, in *PL* 179: 379–380. On Abelard's and Heloise's shared concern for the Paraclete, see Fiona J. Griffiths, "'Men's Duty to Provide for Women's Needs': Abelard, Heloise, and their negotiation of the *cura monialium*," *Journal of Medieval History* 30 (2004): 1–24.

3. I quote the Letters as follows: *Historia Calamitatum* [*HC*] in J. Monfrin, ed., *Pierre Abélard: Historia Calamitatum*, 4th edn (Paris: Vrin, 1979); *Epistolae* [*Ep*] 2–9 in J.T. Muckle, "The Personal Letters between Abelard and Heloise," *Mediaeval Studies* 15 (1953): 47–94 (in Muckle's numbering these are Letters 2–4); *Epistolae* 6–7 (= Muckle 5–6) in J.T. Muckle, "The Letter of Heloise on Religious Life and Abelard's First Reply," *Mediaeval Studies* 17 (1955): 240–281; *Epistola* 8 in T.P. McLaughlin, "Abelard's Rule for Religious Women," *Mediaeval Studies* 18 (1956): 241–292; *Epistolae* 9–14 in Edmé Renno Smits, ed., *Peter Abelard: Letters IX–XIV. An Edition with an Introduction* (diss. Groningen, 1983). Translations are generally my own, although I have consulted Betty Radice's translation of the Letters, see Peter Abelard and Heloise, *The Letters of Abelard and Heloise*, trans. and introd. Betty Radice (Harmondsworth: Penguin Books, 1974); see also the edition revised by M.T. Clanchy, ed., *The Letters of Abelard and Heloise*, trans. Betty Radice (Harmondsworth: Penguin Books, 2003). When I use this translation, it will be cited in the notes. For a clear summary and evaluation of the debate on the Correspondence, see John Marenbon, "Authenticity Revisited," in *Listening to Heloise*, pp. 19–33. I have not used the anonymous Letters that Constant Mews has also attributed to Abelard and Heloise. See Constant J. Mews, *The Lost Love Letters of Heloise and Abelard: Perceptions of Dialogue in Twelfth-Century France. With Translations by Neville Chiavaroli and Constant J. Mews* (New York: St. Martin's Press, 1999). The arguments against an attribution are weighty. See, e.g., Peter Dronke's review of *Listening to Heloise* in *International Journal of the Classical Tradition* 8 (2001): 134–139; Peter Von Moos, "Die 'Epistolae duorum amantium' und die säkulare Religion der Liebe. Methodenkritische Vorüberlegungen zu einem einmaligen Werk mittellateinischer Briefliteratur," *Studi Medievali* serie terza 44 (2003): 1–115; Jan M. Ziolkowski, "Lost and Not Yet Found: Heloise, Abelard, and the 'Epistolae duorum amantium,'" *Journal of Medieval Latin* 14 (2004): 171–202; Peter Dronke and Giovanni Orlandi, "New Works by Abelard and Heloise?" *Filologia mediolatina* 12 (2005): 123–177; Giles Constable, "The Authorship

of the 'Epistolae duorum amantium,'" in *Voices in Dialogue: Reading Women in the Middle Ages*, ed. Linda Olson and Kathryn Kerby-Fulton (Notre Dame: University of Notre Dame Press, 2005), pp. 167–178. Replies by C. Stephen Jaeger, "'Epistolae duorum amantium' and the Ascription to Heloise and Abelard," in *Voices in Dialogue*, pp. 125–166; and C. Stephen Jaeger, "A Reply to Giles Constable," in *Voices in Dialogue*, pp. 179–186.
4. *Ep* 6, ed. Muckle, p. 250.
5. Linda Georgianna, "'In Any Corner of Heaven': Heloise's Critique of Monastic Life," in *Listening to Heloise*, p. 201 [187–216].
6. Mary Martin McLaughlin, "Peter Abelard and the Dignity of Women: Twelfth-Century 'Feminism' in Theory and Practice," in *Pierre Abélard, Pierre le Vénérable: Les courants philosophiques, littéraires et artistiques au milieu du XIIe siècle*, ed. René Louis, Jean Jolivet and Jean Châtillon, Colloques internationaux du Centre national de la recherche scientifique 546, abbaye de Cluny 1972 (Paris: Editions du Centre National de la Recherche Scientifique, 1975), p. 329 [287–333].
7. See my *Fictions of the Inner Life: Religious Literature and Formation of the Self in the Eleventh and Twelfth Centuries* (Turnhout: Brepols, 2004).
8. See, e.g., Winthrop Wetherbee, *Platonism and Poetry in the Twelfth Century: The Literary Influence of the School of Chartres* (Princeton, NJ: Princeton University Press, 1972).
9. On Bernard of Clairvaux, see, e.g., M.B. Pranger, *Bernard of Clairvaux and the Shape of Monastic Thought: Broken Dreams* (Leiden: Brill, 1994). On William of Saint-Thierry, see my *Fictions of the Inner Life*, chapter four, pp. 129–184, and the literature mentioned there.
10. For an analysis of the meaning of *affectus*, see Damien Bocquet, *L'Ordre de l'affect au Moyen Age: Autour de l'anthropologie affective d'Aelred de Rievaulx* (Caen: Publications du CRAHM, 2005).
11. Georgianna, "'In Any Corner of Heaven,'" p. 202.
12. Ibid., p. 204; Abelard, *Ep* 5, ed. Muckle, p. 91. See later where I argue that Abelard does not engage in the meditative mode either.
13. *HC*, ed. Monfrin, p. 63.4. On this aspect of Abelard's life, see also Clanchy, *Abelard*, chapter six, "*Experimentum*—'Experience,'" pp. 121–129.
14. See her Introductory Letter, *PL* 179: 677–678. Within the context of Abelard's writings for the Paraclete one has only to read the last pages of *Ep* 8, ed. McLaughlin, pp. 285–291, and *Ep* 9, ed. Smits, pp. 219–237.
15. On the problematic nature of the notion of experience and its (modern) history, see Martin Jay, *Songs of Experience: Modern American and European Variations on a Universal Theme* (Berkeley: University of California Press, 2005). On the "experience of thinking," e.g., the works of Hannah Arendt, see especially *The Life of the Mind* (New York, London: Harcourt Brace Jovanovich, 1978).
16. On this aspect in, e.g., Hugh of Saint-Victor, see my "'Ad commovendos affectus': Exegesis and the affects in Hugh of Saint-Victor," in *Bibel und Exegese in der Abtei St. Victor zu Paris. Form und Funktion eines Grundtextes*

im europäischen Kontext, ed. Rainer Berndt (Berlin, 2008), pp. 194–215. On medieval views of emotions, see Simo Knuuttila, *Emotions in Ancient and Medieval Philosophy* (Oxford: Clarendon Press, 2004).
17. See Patricia Ranft, *Women in Western Intellectual Culture, 600–1500* (New York: Palgrave Macmillan, 2002), p. 35. At the moment of finishing this article, Fiona J. Griffiths, *The Garden of Delights: Reform and Renaissance for Women in the Twelfth Century* (Philadelphia: University of Pennsylvania Press, 2006) was not yet published. Griffiths' book contains a revaluation of the role of twelfth-century monastic women in the intellectual life of the period as being much more important than hitherto assumed.
18. I use the Letters, the Sermons, and *Problemata*, occasionally connecting the discussion there and in the Letters with Abelard's other writings. On the Sermons, see Paola De Santis, *I sermoni di Abelardo per le monache del Paracleto* (Louvain: Louvain University Press, 2002). I quote the *Problemata* and the Sermons from the edition in *PL* 178, unless the sermons (*Sermo 2, 4, 14, 32, 26, 34*) have been edited by De Santis, *I sermoni*. On Abelard's Sermons, see also Mews, *Abelard and Heloise*, pp. 165–168.
19. M.-D. Chenu, *L'éveil de la conscience dans la civilisation médiévale* (Montréal: Institut d'Études Médiévales and Paris: Librairie J. Vrin, 1969), pp. 17–21.
20. McLaughlin, "Peter Abelard and the Dignity of Women," (see note 6 earlier) p. 319. Marenbon, *Philosophy of Peter Abelard*, pp. 91–92, and chapter eleven, pp. 251–264, discusses Abelard's distinctive view of *intentio*, see later.
21. *Ep* 6, ed. Muckle, p. 251.
22. *Ep* 8, ed. McLaughlin, p. 265. See David Luscombe, "The Bible in the Work of Peter Abelard and of his 'School,' " in *Neue Richtungen in der hoch- und spätmittelalterlichen Bibelexegese*, ed. Robert E. Lerner and Elisabeth Müller-Luckner (Munich: Oldebourg Verlag, 1996), pp. 79–93. For further references to this quotation, see pp. 82–83, n27.
23. *Ep* 4, ed. Muckle, p. 81. Abelard and Heloise, *The Letters* (see note 3 earlier), p. 133; and Clanchy, *The Letters*, p. 69.
24. Peter Dronke, "Heloise's *Problemata* and *Letters*: Some Questions of Form and Content," in *Petrus Abaelardus (1079–1142): Person, Wirk und Wirkung*, ed. Jean Jolivet, D.E. Luscombe, and L.M. de Rijk, *Trierer theologische Studien 38* (Trier: Paulinus Verlag, 1980), p. 58 [53–73]. Cf. Georgianna, "'In Any Corner of Heaven,'" p. 205, about Heloise's "search for her own authenticity"; Catherine Brown, "'Muliebriter': Doing Gender in the Letters of Heloise," in *Gender and Text in the Later Middle Ages*, ed. Jane Chance (Gainesville: University Press of Florida, 1996), p. 42 [25–51], draws attention to the way in which Heloise's "rhetorical and ideological control of her discourse in fact *constructs* such a sense of personal authenticity."
25. Marenbon, *Philosophy of Peter Abelard*, p. 311.
26. For this view, see Chrysogonus Waddell, *The Paraclete Statutes: Institutiones Nostrae. Troyes, Bibliothèque Municipale Ms. 802, ff. 89r–90v. Introduction, Edition, Commentary*. Cistercian Liturgy Series 20 (Gethsemani Abbey, Kentucky, 1987), especially pp. 48–50.

27. *Ep* 5, ed. Muckle, p. 87.
28. *Ep* 6, ed. Muckle, p. 241. Abelard and Heloise, *The Letters*, p. 159; and Clanchy, *The Letters*, p. 93.
29. *Ep* 4, ed. Muckle, p. 81.
30. *Ep* 5, ed. Muckle, pp. 83–85. See also Brown, "'Muliebriter,'" p. 37: Abelard accuses "the 'hypocrite' Heloise of insincere insincerity."
31. *Ep* 7, ed. Muckle, p. 254.
32. Ibid., p. 262.
33. Ibid., pp. 263 and 265. See also *Ep* 8, ed. McLaughlin, p. 252.
34. Marenbon, *Philosophy of Peter Abelard*, especially pp. 251–64.
35. Ibid., p. 92.
36. See, e.g., *Ep* 8, ed. McLaughlin, pp. 258 and 260.
37. Ibid., p. 246.
38. *Ep* 6, ed. Muckle, p. 250.
39. Ibid., p. 251.
40. *Ep* 8, ed. McLaughlin, p. 275.
41. *Ep* 6, ed. Muckle, p. 251.
42. *Ep* 5, ed. Muckle, p. 85.
43. *Sermo* 1, *PL* 178: 382D; see also *Sermo* 26, *PL* 178: 540A. Cf. *Sermo* 14, *PL* 178: 491D–492A, about the secluded space required for prayer.
44. *Ep* 6, ed. Muckle, p. 241.
45. *Ep* 8, ed. McLaughlin, p. 281.
46. Ibid., p. 256. In *Sermo* 33 there is a discussion on the requirements for a superior with the same warning, *PL* 178: 599B–D.
47. See earlier, notes 32–33.
48. Peter Abelard, *Commentaria in epistolam Pauli ad Romanos* I, ed. Eligius M. Buytaert, CCCM 11 (Turnhout: Brepols, 1969), p. 85, ll. 307–309.
49. Ibid., ll. 299–300.
50. Marenbon, *Philosophy of Peter Abelard*, pp. 273–276.
51. *Ep* 8, ed. McLaughlin, p. 268.
52. *HC*, ed. Monfrin, *Pierre Abélard*, p. 102, ll. 1393–1394.
53. In *Sermo* 3, *PL* 178: 405; *Sermo* 5, *PL* 178: 419CD.
54. On the historical aspect of sincerity, see William M. Reddy, *The Navigation of Feeling: A Framework for the History of Emotions* (Cambridge, UK: Cambridge University Press, 2001), pp. 108–110. For the view of the ideal of sincerity as emerging in the sixteenth century, see John Jeffries Martin, *Myths of Renaissance Individualism* (New York: Palgrave Macmillan, 2004), especially chapter six, pp. 103–122.
55. *Ep* 4, ed. Muckle, p. 78: "Confectus moerore animus quietus non est, nec Deo sincere potest vacare mens perturbationibus occupata." Cf. *Ep* 6, ed. Muckle, p. 253: "ut sincerius Deo vacare possimus," and *Ep* 8, ed. McLaughlin, p. 247: "ut videlicet Deo possent sincerius vacare."
56. *Ep* 2, ed. Muckle, p. 70–71. Clanchy, *Abelard*, pp. 163–164, humorously takes Heloise's "piece of bravado" with a grain of salt.
57. *Ep* 5, ed. Muckle, p. 92.

58. Marenbon, *Philosophy of Peter Abelard*, p. 300; Mews, *Lost Love Letters*, pp. 136–138. For example, in Peter Abelard, *Commentaria in epistolam, add. III* (see note 48 earlier), pp. 201–204.
59. See *Sermo* 5, *PL* 178: 423C.
60. *Ep* 6, ed. Muckle, p. 248. For the same idea, see Abelard, *Commentaria in epistolam*, 195, ll. 285–286; *Sermo* 17, *PL* 178: 502C.
61. *Ep* 8, ed. McLaughlin, p. 285. Heloise quotes this in her introductory Letter to the *Problemata*, *PL* 178: 678B.
62. *Ep* 8, ed. McLaughlin, p. 292.
63. On Abelard's and Heloise's biblical studies, see Eileen Kearney, "'Scientia and Sapientia': Reading Sacred Scripture at the Paraclete," in *From Cloister to Classroom: Monastic and Scholastic Approaches to Truth*, ed. E. Rozanne Elder (Kalamazoo, Mich: Cistercian Publications, 1986), pp. 111–129; Eileen Kearney, "Heloise: Inquiry and the 'Sacra Pagina,'" in *Ambiguous Realities: Women in the Middle Ages and Renaissance*, ed. Carole Levin and Jeanie Watson (Detroit: Wayne State University Press, 1987), pp. 66–81. Abelard often claims to apply just the historical or literal sense. He announces as much in his Introductory Letter to the Sermons, *PL* 178: 379–380. See also *Sermo* 11, *PL* 178: 453C. Often, however, he uses an allegorical reading. Kearney has also drawn attention to the character of Abelard's "historical" exegesis in his *Hexaemeron*; see Eileen Kearney, "Peter Abelard as Biblical Commentator: A Study of the Expositio in Hexaemeron," in *Petrus Abaelardus*, pp. 199–210.
64. See Mews, *Abelard and Heloise*, chapter eight, pp. 145–173, especially p. 167. On Heloise's and Abelard's cooperation, see also Griffiths, "'Men's Duty to Provide for Women's Needs'" (see note 2 earlier). On the later influence of their thoughts about the mutuality of men and women within the religious life, see Fiona J. Griffiths, "'Brides' and 'Dominae': Abelard's 'Cura Monialium' at the Augustinian Monastery of Marbach," *Viator* 34 (2003): 57–88.
65. *Sermo* 9, *PL* 178: 445D. For an analogous treatment of words of the Old Testament as a veil containing the reference to New Testament clarity, see *Sermo* 21, *PL* 178: 521CD.
66. See, e.g., Peter Abelard, *Theologia Christiana; Theologia scholarium, recensiones breviores; accedunt Capitula haeresum Petri Abaelardi*, ed. Eligius M. Buytaert, CCCM 12 (Turnhout: Brepols, 1969), p. 122. For the necessity of blindness to a deeper meaning, see Abelard, *Theologia Christiana* 1.105, p. 116.
67. Gilbert Dahan, *Les Intellectuels Chrétiens et les Juifs au Moyen Age* (Paris: Cerf, 1990), p. 585.
68. *Ep* 6, ed. Muckle, pp. 251–252. Abelard equally refers to the opposition; see, e.g., *Ep* 8, ed. McLaughlin, pp. 265–266. On the issue of the different Laws, see Marenbon, *Philosophy of Peter Abelard*, pp. 267–272.
69. *Sermo* 5, *PL* 178: 418AB.
70. On this connection as explored in Abelard's *Collationes* and in the Sermons, see also Mews, *Abelard and Heloise*, pp. 177–179.

71. These authors can be seen to follow a tradition as described by Pierre Hadot, "Reflections on the Notion of the 'Cultivation of the Self,'" in *Michel Foucault Philosopher*, trans. Timothy J. Armstrong (New York: Harvester Wheatsheaf, 1992), pp. 225–232.
72. Abelard, *Commentaria in epistolam*, p. 41. Regarding the correction by Peppermüller, (*monere* rather than Buytaert's reading of *movere*): Rolf Peppermüller, "Zur kritischen Ausgabe des Römerbrief-Kommentars Abaelards," *Scriptorium* 26 (1972): 85–86 [82–96].
73. *Ep* 8, ed. McLaughlin, p. 292.
74. Marenbon, *Philosophy of Peter Abelard*, p. 318.
75. *Sermo* 1, *PL* 178: 382C. On this Sermon, see also Marenbon, *Philosophy of Peter Abelard*, pp. 317–318.
76. *Sermo* 1, *PL* 178: 382C.
77. *Sermo* 1, *PL* 178: 382D–383A. Abelard quotes Ambrose who uses a widely known Ciceronian dictum. Cf. Cicero, in *De officiis* III.1; see also *De Republica* I.17.
78. *Sermo* 1, *PL* 178: 384AB: "fixis quippe oculis in lectione, vel terrae affixis in oratione, quo animus intendebat tota inhiabat."

CHAPTER 4

COMMUNITIES OF DISCOURSE: RELIGIOUS AUTHORITY AND THE ROLE OF HOLY WOMEN IN THE LATER MIDDLE AGES

Carolyn Muessig

This essay considers the teachings of Angela of Foligno, Clare of Montefalco, and Margaret of Faenza, and how these pedagogical endeavors were both negatively and positively received by their male contemporaries.

The teaching of theology is not often associated with women in the medieval period. Perhaps this is because the term "theology" is frequently coupled with scholasticism, a pedagogical method that excluded female students from the university classrooms of religious learning. Scholastics attempted to clarify the mysteries of Christian theology with faith, Scripture, and Aristotelian logic. According to some scholastics, the level of rationality required for the theological venture meant that women were barred from this investigation because their intellectual capabilities were inferior to men's. Nevertheless, theology—or *sacra doctrina* the term more commonly used in the Middle Ages—had a variety of meanings.[1] In monastic schools of thought, theology focused on the moral development of the individual as the person progressed toward the understanding of oneself and God.[2] In the thirteenth and fourteenth centuries, these monastic ideals permeated the boundary walls of religious houses and made their way generally into the hearts and minds of individuals. Communities of like-minded folk spoke in local idioms to discuss the way to perfection. This religious communication, termed "vernacular theology," was more accessible than scholastic and monastic discourses as it was not necessarily practiced within the walls of an exclusive institution, nor was it inevitably relayed in Latin.³ It could occur anywhere: in towns, cities, and the countryside. It facilitated a "community of discourse" wherein men and women, clerics and lay people, shared their religious aspirations.⁴

This essay will focus on these diverse forms of theology (i.e., monastic, scholastic, and vernacular) when considering the role of women in religious formation in the thirteenth and fourteenth centuries. The examples will mainly come from Italy, but illustrations from different geographical areas could be used as well. The sources for this analysis are from four different genres: theological treatises, *vitae*, a commentary on a prophecy, and a canonization process; these date from the later thirteenth and early fourteenth centuries.

Scholastics were warned to keep three things from their lodgings: "rain, smoke and evil women."⁵ Thomas Aquinas underscores this desire for gender segregation in his *Summa theologiae* when he asks: "Does the charism of wisdom in speech and knowledge pertain to women?" His reply was typical of the scholastic outlook: "But to teach and persuade publicly in Church is not the task of subjects but of prelates. Men, when commissioned, can far better do this work, because their subjection is not from nature and sex as with women, but from something supervening by accident."⁶

Henry of Ghent, a secular master and teacher of theology in Paris from 1275 to 1291, represented a view similar to Thomas Aquinas's regarding women's involvement in the teaching of theological matters. In his *Summa quaestionum ordinarum* (*articulus* 11, *quaestio* 2), he asks if a woman could be a *doctrix* of theology. He quotes 1 Timothy 2:12, "I suffer not a woman to teach," which was one of the main texts used to undermine the idea of women as preachers and teachers of doctrine in the Middle Ages.⁷ He argues that a person can teach by office if they have a constancy of teaching; effectiveness of the execution of teaching; authority to teach; and vigorous speech.⁸ He concludes that a woman is deficient in these four respects and so she cannot teach. In extraordinary cases Henry does concede that a woman can preach publicly. In these rare instances the grace of preaching may descend upon a woman, but Henry stresses that this is only in unusual circumstances when men are not upholding their responsibility to teach.⁹ In this scenario women's preaching indicates a negative or unnatural state of affairs because they can only preach when men fail.

Henry presents theology as a science of salvation that is exclusively the right of men to learn and to teach. Women are required to know just enough of this science to save themselves. Men, however, need to study this science in depth for they are to lead others to salvation.¹⁰ Henry notes the foolishness of some men who try to teach women theology: "Therefore how very stupidly do men act who instruct women about this science beyond what is fitting and expedient for women to know; and especially men who both explain to women and translate for them into the vernacular sacred books for reading."[11]

More often than not, Thomas and Henry's negative view of female learning has been portrayed as normative for the Middle Ages. But Henry's objection against men who taught women vernacular theology indicates that not all male educators shared his disdain to educate women in a more thorough manner. However, those who taught women, and women who taught, are often overlooked to a degree that has led some to argue that by the late Middle Ages women had become insufficiently educated.[12] For example, Prudence Allen in her magisterial *The Concept of Woman: The Aristotelian Revolution 750 BC–AD 1250* posits that with the rise of Aristotle at the University of Paris, Aristotelian logic took over as the main school of thought in all areas of learning.[13] This, she maintains, was particularly disastrous for women as Aristotelian learning had a far-reaching impact on the history of sexual identity in that it promoted a theory of sex polarity that claims "that there are philosophically significant differences between the sexes and that one sex is superior to the other."[14] Armed with this theory, those educated in Aristotelian thought promoted the belief that women as the inferior sex had little value or worth in comparison to men, especially in the domain of philosophy and theology.

It is true that women were barred from theological training at the University of Paris. However, women's involvement in theological learning and teaching did not become obsolete, and was not universally deemed inferior in the thirteenth and fourteenth centuries. While Aristotle did indeed change the face of learning, not every student agreed with this change and some rebelled. The "Aristotelian Revolution" did not eradicate the influence of women in religious education.[15]

The monastic tradition promoted an ideal of education that maintained a leveling of theological training because a woman's soul, like any man's soul in the monastic enterprise, needed to be reformed in the image of Christ;[16] in this endeavor, the experience of the Book of Life was emphasized.[17] The procedure for a soulful reformation was relatively accessible to all. Any monk, friar, and priest who believed that the soul was redeemable through moral reformation could not completely forget the obligation to allow women an inclusive place and, in some cases, an active position in religious training. In the thirteenth and fourteenth centuries we find several women at the forefront of what constitutes part of a larger pedagogical alternative rooted in these concepts of monastic dialogue and spiritual counsel. While some scholastic theologians, like

Thomas Aquinas and Henry of Ghent, wrote their treatises and narrowly defined their profession into a specialized science that implied women were not normally accepted as religious teachers, other monks, friars, and theologians did not cut their ties with women; these men continued a discourse of community with women.

Coupled with the tendency of some theologians to support the place of women in religious dialogue and education was a larger debate concerning what was "true" theology. For example, not all theological contemporaries of the Aristotelian movement were supportive participants. A powerful challenge to the Aristotelian model was put forth by Ubertino of Casale (1259–c.1328).[18] Ubertino was a Franciscan who endeavored passionately to preserve the first bloom of Franciscanism against the encroaching frost of the Order's institutionalization. His sentiments toward Spiritual Franciscanism are contained in his *Arbor Vitae Crucifixe Jesu*, which was composed in 1305. The *Arbor* is notable for many reasons. From it we glean significant autobiographical information regarding Ubertino and learn about his spiritual friends and influences. In addition to Francis of Assisi, Hugh of Digne, John of Parma, Bonaventure, and Peter John Olivi, Ubertino indicates the women who influenced his religious life.[19] He discusses Cecilia of Florence,[20] Clare of Assisi (c.1193–1253),[21] Margaret of Città di Castello (d. 1320),[22] and Angela of Foligno (c.1248–1309).[23] In the prologue of the *Arbor*, Ubertino states that after nine years in Paris resulting in a spiritual lethargy, he visited Angela, a Franciscan tertiary, in her native Foligno; this visit transformed his life:

> And by his secret graces, Jesus revealed to her the defects of my heart so that I was not able to doubt that it was he who spoke in her. And all my own gifts, lost through my evilness, she restored beyond measure so that from then on I was no longer that person I had been. And in the vigilant brightness of her inflamed virtue she changed the whole shape of my mind and in such a way she beat back the infirmities and feebleness from my body and soul and transformed my prior distractions into more excellent things so that no one of sound mind who had known me before had a doubt that the spirit of Christ was born in me again.[24]

The main source we have for Angela of Foligno is the *Memorial*, a biographical and theological report/treatise that she dictated to a Franciscan friar, Brother A.[25] Little is known about Brother A., not even his name. His mediating role in the production of the *Memorial* has led to the questioning of how much this work accurately reflects Angela's voice.[26] Some see the text as mainly that of Angela's with little or no influence from Brother A.[27] Some have argued that Angela's theological persona and teachings were actually a literary creation of Brother A.[28] Others have proposed that while the ideas and language of the scribe most likely shaped the tenor of her views, by and large what we have are Angela's thoughts.[29] And others have posited that the *Memorial* is the product of a collaboration between a questioning and respectful scribe and a sometimes unsure but devout religious woman.[30]

To posit Angela as an ahistorical, literary creation is to succumb to the medieval scholastic rhetoric that denied women a role in theological dialogue. Furthermore, the textual evidence of the *Memorial* bears out rather convincingly the idea of authorial collaboration as the book is embroided with editorial difficulties indicating the struggle Brother A. and Angela experienced in the understanding and subsequent recording of her words.[31] In many ways the *Memorial* encapsulates the nature of the community of discourse as a mutual endeavor to comprehend one's soul and God through conversation with others. It presents a woman who experiences the divine directly. For example, during Lent Angela intently meditated on a scriptural passage contained in her missal. Resisting the temptation to open the missal and read the written words she was led into a vision by a divine guide. The vision enabled her to understand the scriptural passage—and divine goodness—with perfection. Her newly established insight and confidence is striking:

> Recalling this experience still gives me great pleasure. From then on, I was filled with such certitude, such light, and such ardent love of God that I went on to affirm, with the utmost certainty, that nothing of these delights of God is being preached. Preachers cannot preach it; they do not understand what they preach. He who was leading me into this vision told me so.[32]

Through avoidance of reading the written word and through meditation on the word of God, her wisdom waxes: she questions the authority of preachers and apparently trained theologians. This view dovetails perfectly with Ubertino's who argues in the *Arbor*:

> Because the foundations of our faith come from invisible things just as the Apostle says [in II Corinthians 4:18], "while we look at the things which are not seen," and the origins of secular philosophy have their origin based on the experience of our blindness, it is a manifest fallacy to want to argue with pagan rules formed from such blindness against the excellent states of Jesus both in himself and in his members.[33]

In taking a direct shot at scholastic theologians he writes:

> I am stunned at the deductive arguments which some masters—who are called theologians—gather to prove (at one moment) the perfection of

Christ's mind and (at another moment) to diminish Christ's excellence. And I do not want to name the arguments because of the abhorrence and repulsion [I have for them].[34]

So too, Angela takes a sharp aim at the intellectual theologian. The Lord tells Angela: "A harsh judgment awaits those who look at your lives but do not act accordingly." And then she reflects: "My soul understood that this harsh judgment concerned the lettered more than lay people because the former despise these works of God though they know about them through Scriptures."[35] The similar viewpoints of Ubertino and Angela provide powerful examples of how individuals upheld knowledge gained through the dialogue of love of God rather than through scholastic method and disputation[36]; these educational ideologies clearly emphasized *experientia* over a pedagogy based on the written word.[37]

When one starts to scratch the surface of late medieval theology, alternative views emerge that challenge scholasticism and indicate that antagonism against the Parisian theological model was rife. Another individual who indicates an alternative view to Parisian learning and Aristotelian authority is Gentile of Foligno. Gentile was a fourteenth-century Augustinian friar and friend of the Spiritual Franciscan, Angelo Clareno.[38] Gentile studied at Paris in the early fourteenth century and he may have been associated with Angela of Foligno.[39] When he was in Paris, he copied a prophecy that was circulating regarding the arrival of the Antichrist and the punishment of wayward Christians.[40] Some thirty years later coming across his old notes from his Paris days, he rediscovered the prophecy and set about to decipher its meaning. Gentile comments on a sentence in the prophecy that reads: "The wasting nest of Aristotle will be emptied, because the horrible gabbling of the chicks will cover up the truth, by deriding its ministers."[41] In his commentary on this particular sentence, Gentile's anti-scholastic stance is obvious:

> *The nest of Aristotle* can be interpreted as Paris, where the study of Aristotle specially thrives...these [in the nest of Aristotle] with the greatest effort diligently study this philosophy against the commands of the holy Fathers and the founders of their orders...the disciples of *Aristotle* are said to *gabble*, because the science of *Aristotle* makes people loquacious and *gabbling*. And such *gabbling* is horrible for pious minds, because it knows faithlessness rather than Catholic *truth*.
>
> For if the mind at the beginning of its education, before it is rooted in Catholic faith, is occupied with the study of philosophy, it is imbued with the opinions and errors of philosophers and gradually *the truth* of faith is stolen away from it, and so the fat of the sacred devotion dries up.[42]

The tone of this commentary indicates that there were clearly expressed opposing views of theology. Hence, if Thomas Aquinas and Henry of Ghent are not read as normative indicators of what constitutes theology but as two of many voices vying for theological authority, the examples of women in positions of religious influence begin to appear less as exceptions and more as alternatives.

If we turn to Clare of Montefalco (1268–1308) we find more evidence of theological alternatives. Clare came from a devout family;[43] her older sister Giovanna entered a *reclusorium* and Clare followed at the tender age of six, while their younger brother Francis entered the Franciscan order. Clare's father, Damiano (d.c. 1282) oversaw the maintenance of his daughters' *reclusorium*.[44] Giovanna attracted a following of devout women, which resulted in both sisters moving to a larger building. In 1290, the bishop of Spoleto, Gerard, formalized this group of religious women by placing them under the Augustinian rule and establishing them as nuns with Giovanna as abbess.[45] The following year, Giovanna died and Clare became abbess of the community. For the next seventeen years she was popular both within her convent and with the lay community who visited her for spiritual advice. Upon her death the nuns of her convent claimed that the symbols of the passion of Christ were embedded in Clare's heart. This claim led to an investigation of her sanctity; ultimately, however, she was not formally canonized.

Her process of canonization was held between 1318 and 1319 and contained the accounts of 486 witnesses.[46] The fact that a woman who never strayed far from Montefalco had nearly five hundred witnesses for her process indicates an immediate impact on the people of her town and beyond. Ubertino of Casale was a witness in this process of canonization. His testimony has been lost but the process does preserve why he was included as a witness—Clare's miraculous sudden cure of his hernia that he had endured for seventeen years.[47] Notwithstanding far-reaching miraculous cures, Clare's influence was most felt both within her monastic community and the lay community of Montefalco. Among the most extensive testimonies are by three sisters of her convent: Marina, Thomassa, and Francescha.[48] Her monasticism was greatly rooted in the late medieval focus on the passion of Christ. Thomassa explained: "Clare frequently spoke to the sisters with tears, compassion and great devotion. She discussed the passion of Christ, leading them to the consideration and meditation of Christ's death."[49]

But Clare, like Angela (although not as accessible due to enclosure), did meet and did counsel individuals from all walks of life. She established herself as a person who was equally sought out by theologians and heretics for advice. In her process of canonization we find that: "truly and profoundly she used to respond to weighty and difficult theological questions when she was asked and sometimes great lectors experienced in theology used to come questioning her, and this holy Clare would satisfy them and respond well and sufficiently."[50] The process attests to frequent visitors who spoke to her at the iron grate in the convent. Lord Bartolo of Spoleto, a lawyer, often went to see Clare because of her excellent counseling abilities:

> he said that he heard her talking often about God, but never did he see her or her sister ever in their lives because whenever he spoke to them at the iron grate it was locked and affixed with a cloth on the interior side. And he heard her speaking about God and spiritual matters both deep and profound, which he had no doubt anyone would be able to say such things unless they were imbued with divine grace. And he said that he saw and heard many lecturers and masters of theology and in his judgment none of them spoke about divine matters as well as she did.[51]

Her brother Francis explains why so many came to hear Clare: "her expression was of such eloquence and virtue that the hearts of each person changed effectively either from evil into good and from sin into God's grace if they were in sin, or from good into better if they were in a state of virtue."[52] His explanation of Clare's spiritual abilities is striking in its similarity to Angela of Foligno's effect on Ubertino of Casale—through the holy woman's words the individual was transformed to a purer self. Therefore, it is no surprise that Ubertino of Casale held Clare in high esteem.[53] Women also visited Clare for precious advice; a woman named Angeluccia would come to Clare's monastery in order to speak with the holy woman and have counsel about hidden and spiritual affairs.[54]

The process of canonization indicates that Clare's level of training was such that she met with problematic theologians who were accused of heresy. This is witnessed with her encounter with Bentivenga of Gubbio, a Spiritual Franciscan and alleged heretic. In her brother's testimony we witness a debate between Clare and Bentivenga. Clare is so appalled by Bentivenga's heretical replies that she reports him to the ecclesiastical authorities.[55] As a result of Clare's unofficial inquisition, Bentivenga is ultimately imprisoned for life.[56]

The theological discussions that are witnessed in the process of Clare's canonization give us insight to the extent that holy women shaped and influenced the people in their communities. Women may have been barred from teaching at universities but this did not preclude them from touching the hearts and minds of eminent lay people such as Bartolo of Spoleto and theologians such as Ubertino of Casale, or condemning heretics such as Bentivenga.

We see these trends with another example from early-fourteenth-century Italy. Margaret of Faenza (d. 1330) was abbess of the Florentine convent of St John the Evangelist. This Vallombrosan nun and disciple of Humility of Faenza (d. 1310), although eclipsed in history by the fame of her teacher, was well known by her contemporaries because of her outstanding ability to provide spiritual counsel.[57] Her *vitae* indicate that she brought solace to men and women, counts and barons, prelates, monks, and nuns who sought her spiritual advice.[58] Margaret had two hagiographers: one was a Franciscan friar, Peter the Florentine;[59] the other was John the rector of St Anthony of Faenza.[60] In addition to Margaret's excruciatingly painful sensations of Christ's passion in her side and feet, the *vitae* emphasize how she distributed elegant spiritual advice.[61]

The practicalities of how a nun could learn such eloquence is indicated in John's account. At the start of Margaret's monastic career, Humility of Faenza provided her with a *magistra* who taught her how to read Latin. But Margaret dismissed the *magistra* believing that God would open up the meaning of scripture to her.[62] John, perhaps acting as a more advanced pedagogical replacement for the dismissed *magistra*, gives an account of the first time he read to her: "When I, John, read to her for the first time, I asked her if she wanted me to read in the vernacular. She responded: 'Not at all! I understand Latin very well.'"[63]

With Peter's account we learn about Margaret as spiritual counselor. He was asked by her nuns to record Margaret's life. He accepted the task because he knew Margaret since he was a boy and she confided many arcane things to him that she hid from her sisters.[64] He describes how many hearing of her saintly reputation were drawn to her: "those attracted by the sweetness of her words thought themselves unworthy to be in her presence, and to divulge to her their secret plans, but Christ had conferred such grace on her that those who heard her returned consoled in their own particular affairs."[65] He describes a vision in which Margaret feeling doubtful of her advisory position was reassured by Christ who told her: "Do not doubt that I am always with you and would never leave you: I want you not to withdraw but to apply your consolation to everyone; I place the words in your mouth and through your words I penetrate the hearts of the listeners, so that they may know without any doubt that I am in you."[66]

Unlike the strict enclosure that Clare observed, Margaret was free to move outside her monastic community. John first explains that Margaret desired to stay in the cloister to pray lest divine grace be lost due to human conversation and daily concerns.[67] This sentiment is found in the papal bull *De periculoso* promulgated by Boniface VIII in 1298 which demanded strict perpetual enclosure for all nuns. Keeping in mind the spiritual succor that the lay and clerical community received from holy women, strict observance did not have a realistic chance to be implemented successfully.[68] This is attested by Margaret's vision, which follows her attempt at observing strict enclosure: "Then she was taken before the Lord in spirit and he said to her: 'I do not want you to be enclosed; but I want you to go outside and spend time with people and speak my words to these same people: I send you my grace and power in this [endeavor].'"[69]

Peter too, perhaps eager to push forward this point of overt and noncloistered discourse presents a graphic vision that Margaret had early in her religious career. Having been transported to a visionary state she looks at Christ crucified. She sees his wounds rushing forth with blood as if they had been recently inflicted. Christ, touched by her sorrow for his suffering, speaks and asks if there is anything he can grant her. At first she responded that she wanted nothing but his grace. She then thought a bit longer and said:

> "You know Lord, I am a simple woman and have to keep company and speak to both wise and foolish people. Therefore, I ask that my tongue be governed according to your pleasure in silence and in conversation." Then Christ touched his tongue to hers and from that moment she received such efficiency and virtue that verily God was [always] recognized on her tongue.[70]

As delightful as this image of a divine French kiss of eloquence is, we must not get distracted by it. Margaret's role, like those of the other women mentioned in this chapter, points to a widespread acceptance of religious counsel by women, which was not exceptional but frequent. The roles of Angela of Foligno, Clare of Montefalco, and Margaret of Faenza, and the support they found among like-minded men and women, indicate alternative modes of theological conversation. Such evidence demonstrates that, in spite of the likes of Thomas Aquinas and Henry of Ghent, women continued to thrive as influential players in a community of religious discourse in the later Middle Ages.[71]

Notes

1. Thomas Aquinas (1224–1274), *Summa theologiae* 1 (*questio* 6, *responsio* 1), ed. Thomas Gilby, 61 vols (London: Blackfriars, 1964–1975), 1: 22–23: "Holy teaching (sacra doctrina) assumes its principles from no human

science, but from divine science, by which as by supreme wisdom all our knowledge is governed."
2. The *locus classicus* of the debate between scholastic and monastic notions of theology is the debate between Bernard of Clairvaux and Peter Abelard. See Thomas Renna, "Bernard vs. Abelard: An Ecclesiastical Conflict," in *Simplicity and Ordinariness*, ed. John R. Sommerfeldt, Studies in Medieval Cistercian History 4 (Kalamazoo, MI: Cistercian Publications, 1980), pp. 94–138.
3. See Bernard McGinn, *The Flowering of Mysticism, Men and Women in the New Monasticism 1200–1350*, vol. 3 of *The Presence of God: A History of Western Christian Mysticism* (New York: Crossroad and Herder, 1998), p. 19. See also Margaret E. Klotz, *Clare of Montefalco (1268–1308): The Life of the Soul is the Love of God* (diss. University of Toronto, 2001), pp. 70–71, 80–89, where she discusses vernacular theology.
4. The phrase comes from Bernard McGinn's introduction to a collection of papers on Eckhart and the beguines. "These papers are not really interested in what Meister Eckhart may have *learned* from the Beguine authors, but rather seek to grasp what Eckhart *shared* with them, that is, the community of discourse and joint concerns in which his thought and theirs developed and enriched each other." See Bernard McGinn, *Meister Eckhart and the Beguine Mystics: Hadewijch of Brabant, Mechtild of Magdeburg, and Marguerite Porete* (New York: Continuum, 1997), p. 4. I am grateful to Anneke Mulder-Bakker for drawing my attention to McGinn's idea of "community of discourse." See also Mulder-Bakker's introduction to this present volume.
5. Astrik L. Gabriel, *Student Life in Ave Maria College, Mediaeval Paris. History and Chartulary of the College* (Notre Dame: University of Notre Dame Press, 1955), pp. 101–102. Gabriel cites this from the *Facetus* and explains: "The *Facetus*, one of the most popular books of behavior, of which Ave Maria College possessed both the Latin and the French versions, advised students to keep three things out of the house: rain, smoke, and evil women: 'Trois choses sont qui le preudon, Enchassent hors de sa maison: Pluye, fumee et male femme, Ces choses sont males, par m'ame.'" The *Facetus* quote comes from J. Morawski, *Le Facet en françoys, Édition critique des cinq traductions des Facetus latins*, Société Scientifique de Poznan, Travaux de la Commission Philologique 2.1 (Poznan: Gebethner i Wolff, 1923), p. 29.
6. Thomas Aquinas, *Summa theologiae* 45:133 (*quaestio* 177, *articulus* 2), ed. Roland Potter, 61 vols (London: Blackfriars, 1964–1975), p. 44.
7. Darleen Pryds, "Proclaiming Sanctity through Proscribed Acts: The Case of Rose of Viterbo," in *Women Preachers and Prophets through Two Millennia of Christianity*, ed. Beverly Mayne Kienzle and Pamela J. Walker (Berkeley: University of California Press, 1998), p. 159 [159–172].
8. *Svmmae quaestionum ordinariarum theologi recepto preconio solennis Henrici a Gardauo, cum duplici repertorio*...(Paris: Badius, 1520), fol. 78. See A.J. Minnis, "The 'Accessus' Extended: Henry of Ghent on the

Transmission and Reception of Theology," in *Ad litteram: Authoritative Texts and Their Medieval Readers*, ed. Mark D. Jordan and Kent Emery, Jr. (Notre Dame: University of Notre Dame Press, 1992), pp. 311–312 [275–326].
9. *Summae quaestionum ordinariarum theologi*, fol. 78. See Minnis, "The 'Accessus' Extended," p. 313 and 315.
10. Minnis, "The 'Accessus' Extended," pp. 314–315.
11. *Svmmae quaestionum ordinariarum theologi*, fol. 83. For further discussion on Henry's *Summae* and women's learning, see Alcuin Blamires, "The Limits of Bible Study for Medieval Women," in *Women, The Book and The Godly: Selected Proceedings of the St Hilda's Conference*, ed. Lesley Smith and Jane H.M. Taylor (Cambridge: D.S. Brewer, 1995), pp. 1–12.
12. Penelope D. Johnson, e.g., has argued: "But keeping a high educational level became difficult for nuns, who as women were not able to take advantage of the university educations available to men. From the twelfth century on, as universities grew and proliferated, orders sent their brightest male monastics to become educated in university towns; this option was not open to any women, even in nunneries. By the tail end of the Middle Ages, in the fourteenth and fifteenth centuries, the under education of women had become the norm." See Johnson, *Equal in Monastic Profession: Religious Women in Medieval France* (Chicago: The University of Chicago Press, 1991), p. 147; Jacques Verger's *Men of Learning in Europe at the End of the Middle Ages*, trans. Lisa Neal and Steven Rendall (Notre Dame: University of Notre Dame Press, 2000), p. 40, argues that education for boys began in the home with the mother teaching the boy how to read. But Verger argues that this was quite unusual for women were rarely literate. For alternative discussions on the subject of women and learning, see the articles in *Seeing and Knowing: Women and Learning in Medieval Europe 1200–1550*, ed. Anneke B. Mulder-Bakker, Medieval Women: Texts and Contexts 11 (Turnhout: Brepols, 2004).
13. Prudence Allen, *The Concept of Woman: The Aristotelian Revolution 750 BC–AD 1250*, 2nd edn. (Grand Rapids and Cambridge, UK: Eerdmans Publishing Company, 1997).
14. Ibid., p. 77.
15. Ibid., p. 413: "The Aristotelian Revolution had conquered the minds of intellectuals in Europe." Allen argues that this was influential outside of the University: "Finally, Aristotle's thought reached beyond the academic world into the homes of ordinary citizens... These clerics simplified concepts and arguments in order to 'preach in the streets.' In this way, Aristotelian sex polarity was transmitted in an organized way outside of the universities."
16. For example, the Cistercian abbot, Adam of Perseigne (d. 1221) wrote to Agnes, a spiritual friend and Cistercian abbess: "It is necessary that the soul be transfigured and lays aside the appearance of the pilgrim of earthly lust, so that she is capable of seeing the hidden splendour of her

transfigured Bridegroom. [Transfigurari enim necesse est ipsam animam, et peregrinam terrenae cupiditatis deponere formam, ut idonea sit transfigurantis sponsi secretam cernere claritatem]." In "Epistola 22, ad Agnetem Virginem," *PL* 211: 663a–663b. For a discussion of the nature and significance of Adam and Agnes's exchanges, see Brian Patrick McGuire, "The Cistercians and Friendship: An Opening to Women," in *Hidden Springs: Cistercian Monastic Women. Book One*, ed. John A. Nichols and Lillian Thomas Shank, Medieval Religious Women 3 (Kalamazoo, Mich: Cistercian Publications, 1995), pp. 176–177 [171–200].
17. See Bernard McGinn, "The Changing Shape of Late Medieval Mysticism," *Church History* 65:2 (1996): 197 [197–219].
18. Recent works on Ubertino of Casale include: Charles Davis, *Ubertino da Casale and His Conception of "Altissima Paupertas"* (Spoleto: Centro Italiano di Studi sull'Alto Medioevo, 1984); Marino Damiata, *Pietà e storia nell'Arbor vitae di Ubertino da Casale,* Bibliotheca di Studi Francescani 19 (Florence: Studi Francescani, 1988); Gian Luca Potestà, "Ubertin de Casale," in *Dictionnaire de Spiritualité*, 17 vols (Paris: Beauchesne, 1932–1995), 16:3–15; Marino Damiata, *Aspettando l'Apocalisse in fervore e furore con Ubertino da Casale* (Rome: Tiellemedia, 2000); David Burr, *The Spiritual Franciscans: From Protest to Persecution in the Century after Saint Francis* (University Park: Pennsylvania State University Press, 2001). See also Ubertino of Casale's entry at the website "Franciscan Authors, 13th–18th Century: A Catalogue in Progress," created and maintained by Bert Roest and Maarten van den Heijden: http://users.bart.nl/~roestb/franciscan/index.htm.
19. For discussion of how these men influenced Ubertino, see Damiata, *Pietà e storia*, pp. 26–42.
20. Ibid., p. 46.
21. Ibid., pp. 45–46.
22. Ibid., pp. 46–48.
23. Ibid., pp. 50–55.
24. Ubertino of Casale, *Arbor Vitae Crucifixe Jesu*, ed. Charles T. Davis, Monumenta politica et philosophica rariora ex optimis editionibus phototypice expressa 1.4 (1485; Turin: Bottega d'Erasmo, 1961), p. 5.
25. Angela of Foligno, *Il libro della beata Angela da Foligno*, ed. Ludger Thier and Abele Calufetti, Spicilegium Bonaventurianum 25 (Grottaferrata: Editiones Collegii S. Bonaventurae ad Claras Aquas, 1985). The works attributed to Angela are the *Memorial* and the *Instructions,* which are entitled the *Book* (*Il libro*). Henceforth, the *Memorial* will be referred to as *Il libro*. The *Instructions*, which is made up of a variety of writings (visions, letters, and theological writings), are directed to her following of men and women who shared her religious views. The exact authorship of the *Instructions* is widely debated.
26. For an excellent overview and analysis of the relationship between Brother A and Angela of Foligno, see Catherine M. Mooney, "The Authorial Role of Brother A. in the Composition of Angela of

Foligno's 'Revelations,'" in *Creative Women in Medieval and Early Modern Italy: A Religious and Artistic Renaissance*, ed. E. Ann Matter and John Coakley (Philadelphia: University of Pennsylvania Press, 1994), pp. 34–63. Some refer to Angela's scribe as Brother Arnaldo, but there is no evidence supporting this view (see Mooney, "The Authorial Role of Brother A.," p. 36).

27. See Mooney, "The Authorial Role of Brother A.," p. 36. See also Antonio Blasucci, "L'itinerario mistico della B. Angela da Foligno," in *Vita e spiritualità della Beata Angela da Foligno*, ed. Clément Schmitt (Perugia: Serafica Provincia di San Francesco, 1987), p. 207 [199–227].
28. See Jacques Dalarun, "Angèle de Foligno a-t-elle existé?," in *Alla Signorina. Mélanges offerts à Noëlle de La Blanchardière*, Collection de l'Ecole française de Rome 204 (Rome, Ecole française de Rome, 1995), pp. 59–97. This text is also available online: http://www.sismelfirenze.it/mistica/ita/studiArticoli/angelaDalarun1.htm. I am grateful to Bert Roest for informing me about this article.
29. Paul Lachance stresses that Brother A. is a "co-protagonist": "Even if it is Angela's book, he is in many ways the artisan of its composition, and, as such, a co-protagonist of her communications from God." See Paul Lachance, "Introduction," in Angela of Foligno, *Angela of Foligno: Complete Works*, trans. Paul Lachance, The Classics of Western Spirituality (New York: Paulist Press, 1993), p. 51.
30. Mooney, "The Authorial Role of Brother A," pp. 34–63; Diane Watt, *Medieval Women's Writing: Works by and for Women in England, 1100–1500* (Cambridge: Polity, 2007), pp. 1–18.
31. Brother A. did not understand how the Holy Spirit could communicate to her: Angela of Foligno, *Il libro*, p. 190; for an English translation, see *The Book of Blessed Angela (Memorial)*, in Angela of Foligno, *Complete Works*, trans. Lachance, pp. 144–145. Brother A. discusses how he had great difficulty trying to write down everything in the exact way Angela had intended: Angela of Foligno, *Il libro*, pp. 398–400; trans. Lachance, pp. 217–218. See also *Memoriale*, pp. 172–174; trans. Lachance, pp. 137–138. See also Mooney, "The Authorial Role of Brother A.," pp. 53–54.
32. Angela of Foligno, *Il Libro*, p. 150, ll. 243–247; trans. Lachance, pp. 130–131.
33. Ubertino of Casale, *Arbor Vitae Crucifixe Jesu* (see note 24 earlier), p. 38, column b; see also Damiata, *Pietà e storia*, p. 148, n69.
34. Ubertino of Casale, *Arbor Vitae Crucifixe Jesu*, p. 38, column b; see also Damiata, *Pietà e storia*, 148, n69.
35. Angela of Foligno, *Il Libro*, p. 202 (ll. 32–37); trans. Lachance, p. 148.
36. For a discussion of Angela da Foligno's possible involvement with the Spiritual Franciscans, see Burr, *The Spiritual Franciscans*, pp. 334–344.
37. See Mulder-Bakker's introduction to this volume.
38. Matthias Kaup and Robert E. Lerner, "Gentile of Foligno Interprets the Prophecy 'Woe to the World.' With an Edition and English Translation,"

Traditio: Studies in Ancient and Medieval History, Thought and Religion 56 (2001): 151 [149–211].
39. Ibid., 158, n29.
40. Ibid., 160. The prophecy "Woe to the World" was appended to the treatise *De cymbalis ecclesie* written by Arnald of Villanova. *De cymbalis* argued that the Antichrist would come sometime before the end of 1376. The prophecy, Arnald claimed, was revealed to a "nearly illiterate man." Kaup and Lerner convincingly speculate that this prophecy was most likely Arnald's creation.
41. The text of Gentile of Foligno's commentary on the "Woe to the World" in ibid., 205 (for the Latin original, see p. 204).
42. Gentile of Foligno's commentary on the "Woe to the World" in ibid., 205; emphasis in the original.
43. For an overview of Clare of Montefalco's life and influence, see *S. Chiara da Montefalco e il suo tempo: Atti del quarto Convegno di studi storici ecclesiastici organizzato dall'Archidiocesi di Spoleto, Spoleto 28–30 dicembre 1981*, ed. Claudio Leonardi and Enrico Menestò, Quaderni del Centro per il collegamento degli studi medievali e umanistici nell'Università di Perugia 13 (Florence/Perugia: La nuova Italia/Regione dell'Umbria, 1985). For the most extensive work in English on Clare of Montefalco, see Klotz, *Clare of Montefalco* (see note 3 earlier).
44. Klotz, *Clare of Montefalco*, p. 9.
45. For an analysis of how semi-religious groups of women came to be institutionalized into monastic communities in late medieval Spoleto, see Mario Sensi, "La monacazione delle recluse nella valle spoletina," in *S. Chiara da Montefalco*, pp. 71–94.
46. For a critical edition of her process of canonization, see Enrico Menestò, Claudio Leonardi, and Silvestro Nessi, eds., *Il processo di canonizzazione di Chiara da Montefalco*, Quaderni del Centro per il collegamento degli studi medievali e umanistici nell'Università di Perugia 14 (Florence: La nuova Italia, 1984). [Henceforth: Menestò, *Il processo*.] Not all of the testimonies are extant.
47. Menestò, *Il processo*, p. 32, ll. 17–18. See also Damiata, *Pietà e storia*, p. 49, n175; Silvestro Nessi, "Appendice storic-documentaria," in Menestò, *Il processo*, p. 625.
48. Respectively, these are witnesses 38, 39, and 67 in the process of canonization. See Menestò, *Il processo*, pp. 329–348.
49. Testis 39, art. 46 in ibid., p. 193, ll. 16–18. See also Klotz, *Clare of Montefalco*, p. 174.
50. Menestò, *Il processo*, p. 20, ll. 2–6. See Damiata, *Pietà e storia*, p. 48, n171.
51. Menestò, *Il processo*, p. 363, ll. 17–24.
52. Ibid., p. 278, ll. 3–6.
53. Ubertino most likely met Clare after he composed his *Arbor Vitae Crucifixe Jesu*. For a summary of Ubertino of Casale's relationship with Clare of

Montefalco, see Nessi, "Appendice storico-documentaria," in Menestò, *Il processo*, p. 625. See also Koltz, *Clare of Montefalco*, p. 68.
54. Menestò, *Il processo*, p. 461, l. 31 and p. 462, ll.1–2. Others commented on Clare's sage abilities. Her confessor Thomas of Gubbio compared her to Solomon regarding her knowledge of Sacred Scripture: "Salomon non respondit melius." Menestò, *Il processo*, p. 68, l. 34.
55. Testis 45 in Menestò, *Il processo*, pp. 287–291. See also Klotz, *Clare of Montefalco*, p. 163.
56. Romana Guarnieri, *Il movimento del Libero Spirito*, Archivio italiano per la storia della pietà 4 (Rome: Edizioni di Storia e Letteratura, 1965), 410: "1307, estate, Arezzo. Bentivenga e sei altri frati minori son condannati al carcere a vita, da scontarsi a Firenze." See also p. 406 and 409.
57. For a discussion of how the hagiographical account of Margaret differs from Humility, see Adele Simonetti, "Introduzione," in *I sermoni di Umiltà da Faenza*, ed. Adele Simonetti (Spoleto: Centro Italiano di Studi Sull'Alto Medioeveo, 1995), pp. xxv–xxviii.
58. Peter the Florentine, *Vita B. Margaritae Faventinae*, in: *AASS*, Aug. V (Antwerp, 1746), pp. 847–851 (850E).
59. Peter the Florentine may be the same Tuscan friar known as Petrus Acciajuoli. Petrus Acciajuoli was a member of the Santa Croce friary as well as a master of theology. He wrote philosophical works, but none of them is extant. See Roest and van den Heijden, "Franciscan Authors, 13th–18th Century," on the Internet: http://users.bart.nl/~roestb/franciscan/franautp.htm#PetrusAcciajuoli. For further information on Peter the Florentine, see Jo Hyacinth Sbaralea, *Supplementum et Castigatio ad Scriptores Trium Ordinum S. Francisci*, 3 vols (Sala Bolognese: Forni, 1921), 1: 339. See also August Potthast, ed., *Repertorium fontium historiae Medii Aevi*, 11 vols (Rome: Instituto storico italiano per il Medio Evo, 2002), 9:145–146.
60. John the rector of St. Anthony of Faenza, *Revelationes et miracula*, in *AASS*, Aug. V (Antwerp, 1749), pp. 851–854. John may have been a nephew of Margaret. See J. Stiltingo, "Commentarius praevius," *AASS*, Aug. V, pp. 845E [845–847].
61. Regarding her sensation of the wounds of Christ, see especially Peter the Florentine, *Vita B. Margaritae*, 849A.
62. John the rector of St. Anthony of Faenza, *Revelationes et miracula*, 851F.
63. Ibid.
64. Peter the Florentine, *Vita B. Margaritae*, 847C.
65. Ibid., 850E.
66. Ibid.
67. John the rector of St. Anthony of Faenza, *Revelationes et miracula*, 852D.
68. For the history of this bull, see Elizabeth Makowski, *Canon Law and Cloistered Women: Periculoso and Its Commentators, 1298–1545* (Washington, D.C.: Catholic University of America Press, 1997). One of the functions of *Periculoso* perhaps was to silence women who were in unison with enemies of the pope. For example, Angela of Foligno and

Clare of Montefalco were supported by Bishop James Colonna, opponent of Pope Boniface VIII. For James Colonna's relationship with these women, see Burr, *The Spiritual Franciscans*, pp. 316–317, 338–339.
69. John the rector of St. Anthony of Faenza, *Revelationes et miracula*, 852D/E.
70. Peter the Florentine, *Vita B. Margaritae*, 849C.
71. I would like to thank George Ferzoco for reading and commenting on this essay.

CHAPTER 5

TWO WOMEN OF EXPERIENCE, TWO MEN OF LETTERS, AND THE BOOK OF LIFE

Anneke B. Mulder-Bakker

The new genre of the "book of life" results from the cooperation of (prophetic) women whose experiential knowledge is embodied as *experientia* and articulated as *prophetia* with learned men.

What happens when so-called women of experience come into contact with men of letters? Or rather, what happens when religious discussions undertaken by women of experience are registered by men of letters and recorded by them in writing? Who is to be considered as the author or authors? What is the nature of their texts and how do they represent the women in question? In this essay, I wish to explore these issues by referring to two examples.

The first is Juliana of Cornillon from Liège (1192–1258), a religious woman (but not a nun) whose history was recorded in French by Eve, anchoress of Saint-Martin, and subsequently reworked into an official Latin *vita* by a learned hagiographer. Both texts were produced within a few years of Juliana's death. The French text has been lost, but can be partially reconstructed; the Latin *vita*, which is the one I will consider here, is available in a sumptuous codex from Cornillon itself dated c. 1280.[1] The second case is that of Agnes Blannbekin, also a religious woman but one living in Vienna a half century after Juliana (before 1244–1315). Her visions were written down by her confessor, a Franciscan from Vienna, and the text is available in an early edition based on a fourteenth-century manuscript entitled *Vita et Revelationes* [Life and revelations].[2]

Both women lived long enough to accumulate a great deal of experience; moreover, they were lettered and well versed in church doctrine.

We should therefore consider them to be female theologians or "common theologians," as I have called them elsewhere.³ Their biographers were proficient in Latin and were therefore men of letters. What, then, does a study of their texts reveal about the nature of these writings? I will argue that a "book of life" is created, a composition that is not a saint's Life, as frequently supposed, but a "book" that has become "life."⁴ I view it as a new genre emerging in the late Middle Ages and gaining the status of a book of wisdom or *vademecum*. Two anecdotes will introduce my argument.

Juliana of Cornillon

Juliana, the prioress of a lepers' convent near Liège and in her later years a free roaming beguine and anchoress, was the originator of the Feast of Corpus Christi—a main festival in the Roman Catholic Church to this day. She composed a Latin office for the feast, *Animarum Cibus* or "Food for souls."

Juliana had a studious nature from her early youth. She would take advantage of every opportunity, however brief, to study or to meditate; "semper meditativa erat" [she was always deep in contemplation] writes her biographer. As a child, she had her own cell into which she could retreat; as an adult, she lived apart from her fellow sisters and passed her final years as an anchoress in an anchorhold. Growing up as a rich orphan in Cornillon, Juliana was given every opportunity to blossom intellectually. She could read and write at an early age, and mastered Latin too. She could recite the Psalms from heart, as well as the basic texts of the Christian faith. She studied the Bible in both French and Latin, along with a number of the writings of Augustine and Bernard of Clairvaux. She knew an entire series of the latter's sermons by rote, especially the sermons on the Song of Songs. "In studying, she forgot her sex and her age," says her biographer, making what is for us an intriguing remark.⁵ At a young age, she was brought into contact with scholars outside the convent. There is some question about whether she even went to one of the Latin schools in the city to which girls were regularly admitted. She was strongly drawn to her disciple, Eve. There was an intimate bond between the two, so that Juliana was able to reveal herself to Eve more than to any other. The two women understood each other impeccably. When Eve allowed herself to be enclosed in Liège as an anchoress of Saint-Martin, Juliana regularly visited her and lived with her in the anchorhold, sometimes even for lengthy periods. As a result, Eve was in a favorable position to write the history of

Juliana, which she did in what we can call the *Vie de Julienne*, the text used by the learned hagiographer.

Both women regularly met in the anchorhold to say divine office, at which time Juliana was sometimes rapt. As the Latin hagiographer tells us, Eve eagerly relates that, during one such rapture, Juliana "fixed her eyes on heaven...and fell into an ecstatic vision of the Trinity." She then "witnessed" how, in the incarnation, Christ "descended wholly to earth yet nevertheless remained wholly in heaven. She saw how Christ shows himself whole, unbroken, and perfect in the bread...and remained unbroken and perfect in himself."[6] For Juliana, this was a true "revelation"; at last she understood that the ostensible religious problem of how Christ, as the Son of God, can simultaneously rule with his Father in heaven and be present with us on earth in the communal bread and wine was simply not a difficulty at all. In this visionary way, Juliana received thorough insight into "all the articles pertaining to the Catholic faith..., she had no need to consult masters or books about them."[7] This anecdote together with its commentary leads us to the heart of the issue concerning visionary experience and it relationship to literacy and book learning.

Agnes Blannbekin

Agnes Blannbekin was an independent religious woman living in Vienna during the last decades of the thirteenth and first decade of the fourteenth centuries. She lived alone near a Franciscan convent and had her own *oratorium* [oratory], just as Juliana did. She had contact with other religious women, who like her were called beguines. Perhaps, she even lived together with them in one house. A good friend of hers was summoned to court by the duchess in order to instruct the courtiers. Religious women were evidently held in high esteem.[8] Agnes lived under the guidance of a Franciscan confessor; they began to work together on the book of visions when Agnes was about forty years old.[9]

Our knowledge about Agnes's education and activities is much poorer than the information we have about Juliana, as we lack the intimate details recounted by a close friend. Interpreting the remarks of the confessor, we know that she could read, was even sufficiently literate to read the Divine Office in Latin and must have had sound theological schooling. She refers to Augustine, Gregory, Bernard of Clairvaux, and the German popular preacher Berthold of Regensburg. She also mentions Bernard's sermons on the Song of Songs. She meditated on important theological questions. Older scholars, such as Kurt Ruh, automatically assumed that this sort of information must have been added by the editor, adhering to the common belief that women in the Middle Ages were deprived of schooling. However, such assumptions are without basis—as I shall argue to the contrary.[10]

Agnes made daily visits to churches in the city, went to communion at least once a week, and often had visions in church. We read that she was lifted up into the spirit, saw the heaven open so hidden secrets could be revealed to her, and a voice within her spoke to her. Her visions usually followed the church calendar. For instance, she once saw at Christmas how "the child was born by the Virgin and how it lay naked in the mother's lap, suckling her breasts and wrapped in the mother's headscarf." We recognize the generally familiar manner of representation, but then the editor continues, "And she saw him lying on straw in the manger. The ox and the donkey stood not above, but next to the manger"[11]: a revealing detail. Here, Agnes betrays the fact that she probably derived her vision from the art of her time, for example, the representations of Mary and child on the type of ivory diptychs common during this period. The artists of these representations, working on the narrow space of the ivory plate, always located the ox and the donkey "above" the manger, as her editor suggests. But Agnes, in her lifelike vision, saw them standing directly beside the crib. In a later year, she had a nativity vision at Christmas that displays some similarity to the Christmas vision of Sister Bertken, an anchoress in the Netherlands, who evidently was inspired by the representation of the apocalyptic woman.[12] Agnes tells how "bright and shining Mary gave birth" without midwives but surrounded by singing angels: "And God intended that the boy would be placed onto the earth after parturition like other boys."[13]

These anecdotes alert us to three points requiring further research. First, they reveal something about the visual culture in which people lived and thought in the Middle Ages: the religious culture that furnished images on which to model personal religious experiences.[14] People looked through the eyes of faith, as a result of which they were granted a glimpse into the history of salvation. They modeled their experiences on images from their own culture and saw these images coming to life before their inner eyes. Second, they allow us to understand the public function of this visual and visionary material. The reception of visions was no unique occurrence, no subjective affair that the visionary kept to her or himself, but created experiential wisdom that had to be passed on. It was, in this sense, comparable to written knowledge or book learning, but it was at the same time much more. It served to give the religious community a deeper insight into scripture and granted people new modes of language and thought in order to express their relation with God. In this sense, Juliana and Agnes had messages for their fellow believers. Third, it shows how Eve and the Latin editor attempted to incorporate experiential religious knowledge in the form of a book. Their texts have performative functions for communities of faith that are integral parts of their meaning. Therefore, these texts should also be analyzed in the context of their discourse communities.

The Religious Culture

Characteristic of the religious culture in which both women grew up was that people lived out their faith by going to church, primarily in their own parish. At the time when Juliana and Agnes lived, these churches were being rebuilt with the assistance of townspeople, whose combined powers were helping to erect these awe-inspiring new sanctuaries. At church, these people experienced their love of God both individually and collectively. While Juliana went to Saint-Martin, Agnes frequented the churches in Vienna: neither woman received her visions at home or in her private cell. Indeed, the faithful often remained at church even outside worship, staying there for hours not just to pray but to remain in the company of God and his Saints whom they encountered through images and relics. There they communed with God in the consecrated Host or via the True Countenance of Christ.

In the course of the ecclesiastic year, the faithful recreated the entire history of salvation; they lived through all the important events in the life of Christ, as well as that of his Mother. For Juliana, her *annus affectionis*, her celebration of the church year perceived through the "eyes of a lover," began with the Annunciation. She then experienced how Mary accepted her preordination to bear the Christ child and also came to accept her own role: "do with me what you will (as well)."[15] At Christmas, she recreated the birth of the child; in Holy Week, she joined in Christ's suffering. Emotionally, her year ended with the feast of the Ascension. She then ran outside and "saw" her Lord rise to heaven in human form. When the feast was over, "a great sadness overcame her, as if she was left behind and orphaned."[16] Of course, she knew that the Holy Spirit would descend at Pentecost, but she was evidently uncertain about this event. She longed for a rite that would (re-)present God's presence among the faithful until the end of time. This formed the affective background to the celebration of the Sacrament and provided the basis on which she developed her Eucharistic theology.

Agnes also underwent a similar reliving of the liturgical year. Her ecclesiastic year began with Advent.[17] At Christmas, she felt great joy, reliving the birth of Christ in the manner described earlier. The joy transformed into a deep suffering during Holy Week and into a subsequent melancholy: "From the time of Easter to Pentecost sadness had filled her heart...however much the Church may celebrate the joy of resurrection,"[18]—the new celebration of the Sacrament of Juliana, with her revived faith in God's presence, had clearly not spread yet to Vienna and to Agnes.

From this we can perceive that the imagery in the church, the mental images, the metaphors, the liturgical festivals, the bread and wine opened the eyes of the viewers' faith and allowed them to experience deeply the things to which they referred. The visible images were not symbols in the contemporary sense of referring to things that are absent; they actually *were* their own meaning. The consecrated host or the True Countenance of Christ *was* Christ; it was the earthly incarnation of His salvation. The faithful were literally holding God in their hands.

Such a worldview has enormous consequences.[19] For example, in believing that God is "at hand," ordinary believers had immediate and personal relationships with the divine. This made them more or less independent in matters of faith—well suited to townspeople who were also assuming the political and socioeconomic initiative for themselves. Moreover, since the faithful were looking through to what lies hidden behind the surface of appearances, they were immersed, as it were, in the history of salvation and were present when salvation occurred before their eyes. In this respect, they were eye witnesses, participants. Like Simeon, they were able to say: "My eyes have seen thy salvation" (Luke 2:30). As a result, they were themselves raised to the level on which the history of salvation unravels. They experienced salvation in their bodies. Women of holy experience especially embodied salvation in this way; salvation radiated from them to their fellow believers. Raised to the biblical level, they were themselves actors in sacred history and instructed their fellow believers using these same images, figurative language, and visions.

The Charism of Prophecy

In the prologue to his *Vitae et Revelationes*, the Viennese Franciscan editor places Agnes in the tradition of Old Testament prophets: "It pleases You [the Lord] to reveal secrets to Your little and humble ones. As You have done in the days of old for the forefathers in the Books of the Prophets, You disclose the unknown and hidden content of Your wisdom in order to edify and console believers." Agnes was such a humble one and the editor saw it as his task to communicate her wisdom to fellow believers "for the edification of faith, the nurturing of devotion, and the stimulation of love for God which I have learned or will learn from the holy and trustworthy persons to whom You, Lord, have revealed Yourself." Agnes was therefore regarded as a prophetess, a devout with a message for the community, rather than as a self-enclosed mystic undergoing private experiences or a fasting ascetic closed off from the external world living at a gateway to heaven; indeed, her teaching is recorded by the editor in a guidebook for others.[20]

It is precisely in this way that the Latin hagiographer characterizes Juliana as a prophetess elaborating on what Eve has provided him with. He also adds a learned or even scholastic explanation. Prophetesses, he contends, are religious women who express their views on important religious questions. "It may be worthwhile to inform readers about the spirit of prophecy, however briefly, to increase true knowledge of it," he writes. "As St. Gregory clearly proves in his exposition of the prophet Ezekiel, in the first homily, prophecy includes past, present, and future tenses." Etymologically speaking, *pro-phetia* means "to speak forth" and "prophecy is rightly so called not because it predicts the future, but rather because it reveals the hidden." Prophets could therefore be concerned with the future (the sense in which the concept is understood today), the present (which we would label "telepathy" or, in certain contexts, "mind reading"), or even the past[21]: for example, Agnes saw how the Christ child was born thirteen hundred years earlier, and Juliana spoke to the apostles Peter and Paul. While this might strike us as remarkable, if we consider how people in the Middle Ages hungered after details about the life of the baby Jesus and his mother—her joy at the baby and her sorrow at the cruel death of her son, all bits of information that the Bible does not mention—we can then understand how this sort of detail may have been revealed to prophetesses. Their prophecies were taken by their fellow believers as revealed truth of the same order as that provided by Bible stories. And that also holds true for theological questions, answers to which were also revealed to them.

Both Juliana and Agnes were placed within the tradition of women who discovered an opportunity in prophetic agency to expand into the public domain. Hildegard of Bingen and her protégée Elisabeth of Schönau were earlier examples of such women, both of whom lived in the twelfth century.[22] In the religious writings composed by these women, they claimed to have the authoritative voices of prophets, something that was radical and new. For example, in a vision an angel took Elisabeth by the hand and led her into a tent where she saw an enormous pile of books. "Do you see these books? They are still all to be written before the end of time comes," spoke the angel. After which he took one book from the pile and said, "This is the book *Liber Viarum Dei* [The Book on the ways of God], and it must be written by you." In this way, Elisabeth saw her religious insights in the form of prophecies granted by God.[23] Moreover, the prophetesses, and the male theologians who worked with them, fully believed that they received insights not revealed to ordinary men and women. Elisabeth worked together with her brother, Egbert of Schönau, a theologian who had studied in Paris. It was there that he encountered theological problems for which no one had a solution, even the most learned of masters. Egbert therefore asked his sister if certain questions could not be presented to the angel whenever he visited her again. Sometimes, Elisabeth complied, other times not, but when she did, it was often with a satisfying result.

Looking back from our perspective, we can view the prophetic gifts of these educated and pastorally inspired women as a form of response to developments in the Church after the Gregorian Reform. When the priesthood began to claim the study of theology and the Bible for itself and to forbid the laity, especially women, from engaging in such study—not to mention meddling in preaching and pastoral care—they could not with all their learning prevent the fact that "God's Spirit entered where it would." If God or Mary or an angel sent inspirations to pious women who everyone regarded as important and orthodox, they were interpreted as prophecies, revelations of God's secrets that must be communicated to fellow worshippers, an imperative that ultimately allowed these women a voice.

However, Juliana's hagiographer went even further than this, for the era of Juliana and Eve saw a reaction from the Church to these developments, specifically from the masters at the University of Paris. A growing excitement about the question of prophecy began to infect the masters of this epicenter of Latin Christianity during the years 1220–1260. In particular, those theologians who had an eye on the religious needs of their time were keen to get involved. One of these, Hugh of Saint-Cher, produced an entirely new interpretation of the concept of prophecy in his tractate *De Prophetia* written in 1235–1236.[24] As I have argued elsewhere, those are precisely the years during which he came into contact with Juliana and Eve in Liège. It is therefore tempting to link one with the other, especially since Hugh offered an unexpected form of recognition in his reinterpretation of the role of such women as Juliana. Hugh's definition enabled these women to find some support within scholastic theology for their self-appointed roles as intercessors. And, similarly, it prompted the hagiographer's account of Juliana's life in the *Vita*.

What, then, was new about Hugh's scholastic views and why were they so eminently important for Juliana and other prophetesses? To begin with, Hugh differed from older theologians in stating that prophecy was a charism, a gift from God that was not intended for the recipient alone but meant to be passed on to the fellow faithful. As a charism, prophecy belonged to the series of gifts for servants of the Church, similar to the ones given to priests, teachers, and overseers as presented in Romans 12:6–8. Since it also included the task of making God's will known to others, a prophet, even a prophetess, had a well-defined duty in the church community, a line of argument that was clearly attractive to women craving a public role.

Hugh subsequently distinguishes three stages in each prophecy. First, a person receives a visionary image, often a symbolic representation such as the incomplete round moon seen by Juliana. Such an image was not immediately understandable, however; it was more like a coded message. The recipient therefore had to receive further explanation from God concerning the meaning of the symbol and to translate the code into intelligible language, which constituted the second stage. For instance, Christ told Juliana that the incomplete moon was a symbol for the universal Church that missed the important Feast of Corpus Christi and he charged her with the task of elaborating a theology and a liturgy for this celebration. She proceeded to spend more than twenty years on this work. Only after completing it was the recipient empowered to address the external world and communicate the message to fellow worshippers—the third stage of the process identified by Hugh.

A similar division into stages is discernible in Agnes's visions. "Experiencing raptures and enfolded in unspeakable light," we read at the beginning of the *Vita et Revelationes*, "she saw a man, handsome before the sons of man...and in that man and the divine light, she saw the elements, and creatures and the things made thereof...All of this was in that man, that is, Christ."[25] It is with this vision that the book opens and the editor requires twenty-three chapters to explain it. The vision appears as condensed holy doctrine presented in images and mental pictures, thus comprising the first of Hugh's stages.

In the second stage, Agnes proceeds to receive small explanatory visions of a different nature on a daily basis[26]: the editor writes, "The Lord honored her by granting her a new type of visitation...She felt and heard within her chest a serene voice, mild and sweet,"[27] continuing, "she realized also that it was the celestial voice" that gave bits and pieces of explanation. When Agnes wonders if this is God's voice, she hears, "You poor little one, what are you doubting... It is Me who speaks, who in the past spoke through the mouth of prophets."[28] From that time on, Agnes had daily conversations with the Lord. By means of such internal dialogue between her and this voice within her she sought the meaning of the various elements of the opening vision, interpretations of the liturgical feasts, and an understanding of church doctrine, and so on.[29] She systematically worked through all the issues involved until she came to a solution. Frequently, we read that she began to think about something and the voice within her answered.[30]

The visions are often exceedingly "homely" and drawn from ordinary daily life: Christ is presented as the good housewife, for example, or as the pharmacist making medicine. And they occurred in the church, that same church building in which worshippers experienced their faith. More specifically, they occurred during worship, often after Agnes had taken communion and literally had the Lord "in her body." The inner dialogues therefore had the character of a Christian *exemplum*: what the story relates reoccurs on the spot. They are moments of incarnated, experiential salvation.[31] On a few occasions, the editor becomes involved in the discussion himself: "I asked her whether the Blessed Souls move from one place to another. She answered, 'No.'"[32] For Agnes, this second stage lasted many years, probably for the rest of her life, and was interspersed with new visions and the transference of her acquired wisdom to her confessor and fellow believers.

The third stage reveals itself in what the confessor recorded of such experiences in the *Vita et Revelationes,* which proves to be a sort of *vademecum* for the spiritual life, anchored in images and visions. Noteworthy is the emphasis on the physical, experiential nature of the acquired wisdom that I focus on in more detail in the following section entitled "Book of Life." The editor reveals that this is something other than the fruit of Bible study and theology. Nevertheless, reading between the lines of the editor's allusion to book reading, it is likely that the knowledge was based on such study—or at least in part: "She said that the questions that she asked came to her easily and without any difficulty and effort of thought, as if she had read them in a book."[33] While Agnes herself may have given oral lessons, the editor continued her teaching in written form; but in any event, as Ulrike Wiethaus has observed, the book reveals that "[m]ystically gifted women could exercise spiritual authority and independence in their respective local communities."[34]

Returning, then, to Hugh of Saint-Cher and the meaning of his *De Prophetia,* it is clear that his new definition of prophecy enabled him to create what, in contemporary terms, would be a "win-win situation" for both the female prophets and the troubled clergy. The great advantage for prophetic women was that not just their prophecy but they themselves were taken seriously; they could be called upon to account for the interpretations that they gave. Not merely divine megaphones but independent-thinking Christians, these women acquired, through prophecy, a recognized medium to issue opinions on religious—even theological—questions. The gain for the theologians was that they did not have to accept without question the visions as God's dictation but could guide the interpretation and, if they did not like it, even forbid it. In turn, the women could intercede as "theologians" in the religious discourse and could make their own suggestions, at least insofar as the clergy accepted them as inspired prophetesses (and there was, as we know, a need to grant such acceptance).[35] In the later Middle Ages, however, theologians would pose stringent conditions for women to meet if they wanted to be recognized as such. Jean Gerson, also a Parisian master, was one who made such demands, and he even had his doubts in the case of Bridget of Sweden. In the time of Juliana and Agnes, however, their position was still much more admissible.

It is clear that a form of intellectual debate must have taken place between the learned men in Paris and the learned women in Liège: a debate not just about the women's opinions themselves but about how they should reveal them to others and how they might persuade the Church to take their views seriously. Such collaboration between the clergy and women was more prolific and productive than until recently we thought possible. It did not, however, take place in the organized Church itself, as women could not don clerical office and had no institutional power. Nor did it happen much at the level of cathedral schools or universities, as women did not have any access to them. But it happened in the church insofar as the church constituted a community of worshippers, the church as a community of discourse. "Prophetic" women and "inspired" men were able to find each other in the living community. And we see this happening elsewhere, too: in Magdeburg, for example, where Mechthild of Magdeburg, the recluse Lame Margaret, and inspired Dominicans worked together; or in Italy, where devout women also collaborated with Dominicans, the ambulant mendicants providing easily interconnecting links.[36] We find it also in the Upper Rhine, where the manuscripts of Agnes's visions were copied, in Bavaria, Austria, and, in particular, Vienna. The texts written there were—and are—the silent witnesses of such interactions and they had their function in the living community.[37]

Book of Life

Finally, we arrive at an answer for the initial research questions posed in this essay: what happens when learned men record in books the lessons and/or stories of similar types of women?[38] What type of books do they write and how do they represent the women themselves? In providing answers to these questions, I will draw upon the conceptual apparatus developed by Mary Douglas who distinguishes a general conceptual world shared by people in a given society (these she identifies as the "thought world") and its several specific conceptual models (which she names "thought styles"), recognized by (groups of) individuals within that society.[39] In my study, the (oral) world of medieval Christianity with its experiential culture can be regarded as such a general thought world. Scholars and laypeople, men and women, all share the key elements of this world, as do the religious women in question. However, inside the larger thought world, there are various systems or models of thought employed by various people to phrase their faith, to air their views, to formulate their doctrine, the thought styles. Learned men were a part of the general thought world, insofar as they were ordinary believers as well as theologians. They had learned in their youth to believe in the visionary language of images but were then educated in the Latin schools and the universities, where they learned to study the Book of Scripture on the basis of commentaries by the Church Fathers. They were trained in logic and in a rational manner of thinking; they employed the scholastic method in putting their insights to paper, as did Hugh of Saint-Cher in his *De Prophetia*. They developed a specific thought style. In modern scholarship we have a tendency to view this learned style as *the* medieval thought style and to forget how limited it actually was. It was just *one* style among many.[40]

The same theological insights, however, could also be expressed in another thought style represented first in visions and inner dialogues and second in writing—in the form of a book of life. I argue that this is precisely what the religious women undertook and what the men of letters attempted to record in their Latin writings about them. Together, the men and women tried to provide a written record of the effects and stylistic elements of this visual and experience-based thought style. The resulting texts were not rational and discursive in design like scholastic tractates, but rather dialogic and imaginative. They were not ordered logically and chronologically, but were cyclical, following the ecclesiastic year. They were not rationally structured on the basis of a scholastic *sententia*, but were mnemotechnically attached to an image or the points elaborating a mnemonic device. They combined life experience and writing. The goal, however, was the same as that of the scholarly tractates or sermons: to communicate the same faith—although each, of course, emphasized its own generic points. Even learned *scholastici* had at times to recognize the greater persuasiveness of the book of life, something, perhaps, demonstrated most clearly by the learned church prelate James of Vitry (d. 1239). After leaving the barren world of the Paris academia to sit at the feet of the experiential Mary of Oignies, James saw in Mary the embodiment of the book of life. To this effect, he writes, "Then you belched forth many and wondrous readings from a wondrous and unheard of fullness, and...you read to us from the book of life, suddenly changing from a disciple into a master."[41] His *vita* of Mary is not a saint's Life in the traditional sense but a series of readings enabling readers and listeners to reexperience the *religion vécue* of Mary. It is for this reason that I began to label these sorts of texts as books of life.[42]

In this way, both Eve and the Latin hagiographer of Juliana's Life, along with the Viennese editor of Agnes's visions, follow in the footsteps of James of Vitry. Eve's *Vie de Julienne*, the Latin *Vita Julianae* and the *Vita et Revelationes* of Agnes Blannbekin are not saint's Lives in the traditional sense, even if they are usually placed within this category.[43] They are not written as evidence for a canonization process—neither Juliana nor Agnes were considered for canonization in the Middle Ages. They do not contain a series of miracles revealing what the saint has done with the help of God in heaven. The narratives are collections of short stories with a didactic purpose; they provide the "life principles" of these women in a way that includes the *experientia* of their exemplary lives. They instigate imitation and allow listeners/readers to share in their lived salvation. Ultimately, they have a salvational purpose.

As *exempla*, the short stories adhere closely to the definition posited by Aaron Gurevic[44] who claims that medieval *exempla* are chronotopes, salvational stories that "happen" at the very moment they are being told. They not only tell a salutary tale, they grant salvation on the spot, as it were. They are therefore comparable to the women of holy experience themselves who felt salvation in their own bodies and radiated it to their fellow faithful. In this way, *exempla* are the written *experientia* of living saints. It can be no accident that James of Vitry, who remains among the inventors of the medieval genre of the *exemplum*, transformed his *Life of Mary of Oignies* into a long string of *exempla*. His book is much less a saint's Life intended to promote canonization than a didactic textbook replete with examples, a manner of teaching by graphical illustration or preaching by means of *exempla*. In writing it, he initiated a new tradition.

In this regard, Eve consciously or unconsciously imitated him. Viewing the chapters in the Latin *Vita* attributed to her in their entirety, it becomes clear that they elucidate Juliana's theological insights in a consistent and systematic way. As I have written elsewhere, Eve strings together seemingly innocuous episodes and lifelike dialogues, she appears to give verbatim renderings of entire conversations between Juliana and herself. In her text each anecdote becomes in itself an *exemplum* intended to instruct the reader or listener, and the succession of *exempla* forms a treatise of common theology in *exemplum* form.[45] As a woman Eve was not entitled to use the discursive or abstract theological thought style, nor was she, I suspect, willing to do so. She chose the *exemplum* form within the framework of a book of life for its persuasive and salutary function.

The Latin hagiographer continued in a similar direction. Although he was given the task of converting Eve's book into a fully fledged saint's Life, he describes her deeds in a way that he hopes will bring her back to life. He locates her in the circle of holy men and women, *sancti*, who are still alive and whose examples of virtuous living can be imitated by the faithful, both men and women. He tries to revive her *religion vécue*,[46] his text also being an *exemplum*, a salvational story that "happens" at the very moment it is being told. It is common theology incarnate.

This new genre comes to fruition in the *Vita et Revelationes* of Agnes. What makes this book special is its portrayal of the intimate collaboration of a man and a woman and the fusion of two thought styles into a unified book of life. The composition is further noteworthy for the fact that it is constructed on the relationship between a female persona and a male scribe. Evidently, this gave the book greater authority and persuasiveness in the world outside academia, which is to say in the greater community of discourse. We must therefore ask ourselves who the actual author is. Assuming the nineteenth-century concept of the author, most contemporary scholars attribute authorship to the Latin editor.[47] McGinn, however, in his history of mysticism refers to "new forms of cooperation between women and men, in terms of both a shared dedication to the pursuit of the *vita apostolica* [the apostolic way of life] and a joint concern for attaining the 'loving knowledge of God.'" This opens the prospect of a more satisfactory allocation of authorship for the texts: "what we hear comes to us in the form of a dialogue in which the contributions of male and female voices are both present in varied ways, often in a mutually enriching fashion."[48] In other words, they are the products of joint authorship.

This, then, is ultimately the answer to my initial research question: the cooperation of prophetic women whose experiential knowledge is embodied as *experientia* and articulated as *prophetia* results in a new genre of text written down by learned men—and, in due time, a growing number of learned women. Neither the experiential woman nor the learned man can be regarded as the single author; the *Liber Vitae* [Book of Life] is the work of both.

Notes

1. On Eve and Juliana, see Anneke B. Mulder-Bakker, *Lives of the Anchoresses: The Rise of the Urban Recluse in Medieval Europe* (Philadelphia: University of Pennsylvania Press, 2005), chapters 4 and 5 pp. 78–147.

    The *Vita Julianae* has been edited with French translation by Jean-Pierre Delville, ed., *Fête-Dieu (1246–1996) II: Vie de Sainte Julienne de Cornillon* (Louvain-La-Neuve and Turnhout: Brepols, 1999). [Henceforth referred to as *Vita Julianae* with book and chapter number.] For an English translation, see *The Life of Juliana of Mont-Cornillon*, trans. Barbara Newman (Toronto: Peregrina Publications, 1988). [Henceforth referred to as trans. Newman, with page number.]

2. Anneliese Stoklaska, "Weibliche Religiosität im mittelalterlichen Wien unter bes. Berücksichtigung der Agnes Blannbekin," in *Religiöse Frauenbewegung und mystische Frömmigkeit im Mittelalter*, ed. Peter Dinzelbacher and Dieter Bauer (Cologne: Böhlau, 1988), pp. 165–84; Kurt Ruh, *Geschichte der abendländischen Mystik*, 4 vols (Munich: Beck, 1990–99), 2:132–136. The vision book has been published as *Ven. Agnetis Blannbekin, Quae sub Rudolpho Habspurgico et Alberto I Austriacis Impp. Wiennae floruit Vita et Revelationes*, ed. Bernardus Pez (Vienna: Petrus Conrad Monath, 1731) (copy in the Royal Library of The Hague); new edition in Peter Dinzelbacher and Renate Vogeler, eds. and trans., *Leben und Offenbarungen der Wiener Begine Agnes Blannbekin (d. 1315)*, Göppinger Arbeiten zur Germanistik 419 (Göppingen: Kümmerle Verlag, 1994). [Henceforth referred to as Dinzelbacher and Vogeler, *Leben und Offenbarungen*, with chapter number.] English translation by Ulrike Wiethaus, *Agnes Blannbekin, Viennese Beguine, Life and Revelations* (Woodbridge: Brewer, 2002). [Henceforth referred to as trans. Wiethaus, with page number.]

3. Mulder-Bakker, *Lives of the Anchoresses*, pp. 100–101, 176–177.

4. See the paragraph "Book of Life" later; for the term see note 54 of the introduction to this volume.

5. *Vita Julianae*, Prologue, trans. Newman, p. 26.

6. *Vita Julianae* 1.16, trans. Newman, pp. 53–54.

7. *Vita Julianae* 1.20, trans. Newman, p. 54. See also my "Introduction" to *Seeing and Knowing: Women and Learning in Medieval Europe 1200–1550*, ed. Anneke B. Mulder-Bakker (Turnhout: Brepols, 2004), pp. 1–21.

8. Dinzelbacher and Vogeler, *Leben und Offenbarungen*, chap. 142–143. As a property owner she would have belonged to the wealthier class of citizens and enjoyed corresponding rights. This duchess (queen in the German Empire) must have been Elisabeth, the wife of Albrecht I, also known as the Franciscan king because of his sympathies for mendicants.

9. Dinzelbacher and Vogeler, *Leben und Offenbarungen*, chap. 39: "Hoc cruciatu famis voluntariae propter deum bene per decem annos vitam actitabat, incipiens, cum septem foret annorum. Carnes per triginta annos vix ad unum comedit pastum." [Beginning at age seven, she spent a good ten

years of her life with such martyrdom of voluntary hunger for God's sake. For thirty years, she hardly ate any meat at meals.] She was therefore older than 37 (7 + 30 including 10) or 47 (7 + 10 + 30) when the confessor wrote this.
10. See also my argument in the paragraph on "School education" in the introduction to this volume.
11. Dinzelbacher and Vogeler, *Leben und Offenbarungen*, chap. 54.
12. *Mi quam een schoon geluit in mijn oren. Het werk van Suster Bertken*, ed. José van Aelst, e.a. (Hilversum: Verloren, 2007), pp. 96–103.
13. Dinzelbacher and Vogeler, *Leben und Offenbarungen*, chapter 193.
14. Cate Gunn, "'A recluse atte Norwyche': Images of Medieval Norwich and Julian's Revelations," and Alexandra Barratt, "'No such sitting': Julian Tropes the Trinity," in *A Companion to Julian of Norwich*, ed. Liz Herbert McAvoy (Cambridge: D.S. Brewer, 2008), pp. 32–41 and pp. 42–52, respectively.
15. *Vita Julianae* 1.16, trans. Newman, p. 47.
16. *Vita Julianae* 1.19, trans. Newman, p. 52. See Mulder-Bakker, *Lives of the Anchoresses*, pp. 78–117.
17. Dinzelbacher and Vogeler, *Leben und Offenbarungen*, chapter 25: St. Nicholas's day, then chapter 33: Christmas period, and so on.
18. Dinzelbacher and Vogeler, *Leben und Offenbarungen*, chapters 81–82.
19. Cf. Craig Harbison, "Visions and Meditations in early Flemish Painting," *Simiolus* 15 (1985): 87–117; the studies of the art historian Jeffrey Hamburger collected in *The Visual and the Visionary: Art and Female Spirituality in Late Medieval Germany* (New York: Zone Books, 1998); Barbara Newman, "What Did It Mean to Say: 'I Saw'? The Clash between Theory and Practice in Medieval Visionary Culture," *Speculum* 80 (2005): 1–44, and the studies on "experience" quoted in the introduction to this volume.
20. Dinzelbacher and Vogeler, *Leben und Offenbarungen*, Prologue.
21. *Vita Julianae* 1.21, trans. Newman, pp. 55–56.
22. The Chronicle *Annales Palidenses* published in the MGH SS 16:90 noted for the year 1158: "two women...were filled with the spirit of prophecy." Cf. Paul Alphandéry, "Prophètes et ministère prophétique dans le Moyen Âge latin," *Revue d'histoire et de philosophie religieuses* 12 (1932): 334–359; André Vauchez, *Saints, prophètes et visionaries: Le Pouvoir surnaturel au Moyen Age* (Paris: Albin Michel, 1999); Rosalynn Voaden, *God's Words, Women's Voices: The Discernment of Spirits in the Writing of Late-Medieval Women Visionaires* (York: York Medieval Press/Boydel & Brewer, 1999).
23. Anne L. Clark, *Elisabeth of Schönau: A Twelfth-Century Visionary* (Philadelphia: University of Pennsylvania Press, 1992), p. 18 and 54.
24. Hugh of Saint-Cher, *De Prophetia*, in *Théorie de la prophétie et philosophie de la connaissance aux environs de 1230: La contribution d'Hugues de Saint-Cher (Ms. Douai 434, Question 481)*, ed. Jean-Pierre Torrel

(Louvain: Spicilegium Sacrum Lovanense, 1977); Mulder-Bakker, *Lives of the Anchoresses*, pp. 93–101.
25. Dinzelbacher and Vogeler, *Leben und Offenbarungen*, chapters 1–23, quotation in chapter 1.
26. Dinzelbacher and Vogeler, *Leben und Offenbarungen*, chapter 187, trans. Wiethaus, p. 127, where the editor explains: "The visual sense of the soul is contemplation, through which she sees God and uncertain and hidden matters are shown her [first stage]. The soul's sense of hearing [of the voice within] is intelligence, through which the soul receives Divine revelations within and understands them without an interpreter [second stage]." He also identifies this as an "auditory experience." Prior to all this, there is a preliminary stage in which Agnes had visions but could not remember them, not to mention interpret them. This was before she collaborated with the confessor, or rather before she had reached the age of discretion. On this age of discretion, see Anneke B. Mulder-Bakker and Renée Nip, eds., *The Prime of their Lives: Wise, Old Women in Pre-Industrial Society* (Louvain: Peeters, 2004).
27. Dinzelbacher and Vogeler, *Leben und Offenbarungen*, chapter 30.
28. Ibid., chapter 34.
29. A good example occurs in ibid., chapter 108. Cf. Bernard McGinn, *The Flowering of Mysticism: Men and Women in the New Mysticism (1200–1350)* (New York: Crossroad, 1998), p. 30: "specifically with regard to visions, I suggest that it is helpful to think of them primarily as 'visualizations,' in the sense of powerful imaginative creations based on intense meditation on the imagery of the Bible and the liturgy, as well as artistic representations of Christ, the angels and Saints, heaven and hell, and so on."
30. For a good example, see Dinzelbacher and Vogeler, *Leben und Offenbarungen*, chapter 115.
31. Aaron J. Gurjewitsch [Gurevic], *Himmlisches und Irdisches Leben: Bildwelten des schriftlosen Menschen im 13. Jahrhundert: Die Exempel*, trans. Erhard Glier (Amsterdam and Dresden: Verlag der Kunst, 1997), pp. 55–128.
32. Dinzelbacher and Vogeler, *Leben und Offenbarungen*, chapter 23.
33. Ibid., chapter 135, trans. Wiethaus, p. 134. Bernard McGinn, "The Language of Inner Experience in Christian Mysticism," *Spiritus* 1 (2001): 164 [156–171] notes: "since women could not be scriptural commentators *ex officio* the way that monks and friars could, they use the *liber scripturae* in a different way—by way of illustration and secondary confirmation, not as the essential context of their presentation of mystical consciousness."
34. In her commentary to the translation: Wiethaus, p. 164. As Mary Suydam remarks in "Beguine Textuality: Sacred Performances," in *Performance and Transformation: New Approaches to Late Medieval Spirituality*, ed. Mary Suydam and Joanna E. Ziegler (New York: St. Martin's Press, 1999), p. 176: "Every visionary taken up in the spirit had an involved audience that enabled, witnessed, and participated in shared religious performances."

35. Voaden, *God's Words*.
36. Mulder-Bakker, *Lives of the Anchoresses*, pp. 148–173; see also chapter four by Carolyn Muessig in this volume.
37. Five manuscripts have survived that contain the text of Blannbekin, parts of which carry translations. These texts are not direct copies of each other and it is necessary to construe several intervening links between them. There must, therefore, have been a significantly wide circulation.
38. Once again it is good to remind ourselves that, for the life stories of Juliana and Agnes, we have to rely on the revisions of their life stories as produced by learned men. In the case of Juliana we also have her own Office and references to Eve's notes; for Agnes, we only have the vision book *Vita et Revelationes*. There is thus a danger of circular reasoning when studying these texts.
39. Mary Douglas, *Thought Styles: Critical Essays on Good Taste* (London: Sage, 1996); Douglas, *How Institutions Think* (Syracuse, NY: Syracuse University Press, 1986).
40. See also Muessig's comments in chapter four in this volume.
41. James of Vitry, *The Life of Mary of Oignies* 2.48, trans. Margot H. King, in *Mary of Oignies: Mother of Salvation*, ed. Anneke B. Mulder-Bakker (Turnhout: Brepols, 2006), p. 84 [33–127].
42. In the late Middle Ages, the title "Buch des Lebens" [Book of Life] was more often used for a spiritual *vademecum*; see *Die deutsche Literatur des Mittelalters: Verfasserlexikon*, 5 vols, 2nd edn (Berlin: De Gruyter, 1978–2006), 1:1092–1093. [Henceforth: *Verfasserlexikon*.]
43. In his investigation into the new emphasis on visions and revelations in some saints' Lives Peter Dinzelbacher continued to refer to them as *vitae*. Dinzelbacher, "Die 'Vita et revelationes' der Wiener Begine Agnes Blannbekin (d. 1315) im Rahmen der Viten- und Offenbarungsliteratur ihrer Zeit," in *Frauenmystik im Mittelalter*, ed. Peter Dinzelbacher and Dieter R. Bauer (Stuttgart: Schwabenverlag, 1985), pp. 152–177.
44. Current definitions are found in Claude Brémond, Jacques Le Goff, and Jean-Claude Schmitt, *L'Exemplum* (Turnhout: Brepols, 1982), pp. 37–38: "un récit bref donné comme véridique et destiné à être inséré dans un discours (en général un sermon) pour convaincre un auditoire par un leçon salutaire"; and in Gurjewitsch, *Himmlisches und irdisches Leben*, p. 55: "Die Ewigkeit bricht...für einen Augenblick in den Zeitverlauf ein und wandelt ihn um oder vernichtet ihn. Die Raum-Zeit-Einheit im Exemplum besteht darin, dass in einem gewissen kurzen Moment...ein ungewöhnliches, wunderbares Ereignis geschieht."
45. Mulder-Bakker, *Lives of the Anchoresses*, pp. 139–140; cf. Amy Hollywood, *The Soul as Virgin Wife. Mechthild of Magdeburg, Marguerite Porete, and Meister Eckhart* (Notre Dame: University of Notre Dame Press, 1995), pp. 57–61.
46. *Vita Julianae*, Prologue 2: "et sic exempla eorum qui iam de hoc seculo sunt assumpti, velut in rem presentem per scriptorum memoriam revocari."

47. See the definitions in *Verfasserlexikon* (see note 42 earlier), 1: 1092–1093.
48. McGinn, *The Flowering of Mysticism*, p. 17. Amy Hollywood, in her review of Wiethaus' translation, has similarly remarked: "Although the text has been read as hagiographical, it can also be understood as a collaboratively-produced devotional text, closer in its hybrid genre to the works of Hadewijch, Mechthild, and Marguerite than to thirteenth-century beguine and Cistercian hagiographers," in *Spiritus* 4 (2004), p. 97 [91–97], n6.

CHAPTER 6

"[A]N AWNGEL AL CLOTHYD IN WHITE":
REREADING THE BOOK OF LIFE AS
THE BOOK OF MARGERY KEMPE

Liz Herbert McAvoy

Margery Kempe's spiritual authority, as articulated in her *Book*, is traced via her use of the experiential hermeneutic of the child figure in her writing.

In her critique of the delimiting effects upon women and their productivity imposed by the masculine language in which they have traditionally had to operate, Hélène Cixous imagines what would happen if women were to express themselves using a language of their own: "Then, all the stories would have to be told differently, the future would be incalculable, the historical forces would, will, change hands, bodies; another thinking, as yet not thinkable will transform the functioning of all society."[1] Cixous's utopian ideal for women and this female use of language, of course, remains just that—a utopian ideal that, paradoxically, although continuing to be striven for, will ultimately remain unobtainable.

But neither is Cixous's utopian vision radical, nor even new. The debate surrounding women's relationship to language has long been around in literary and intellectual circles. Indeed, at the same historical moment as Margery Kempe was about to embark upon marriage and motherhood in late-fourteenth-century Bishop's Lynn, the strident voice of another urban wife was being constructed to resound on this issue—in this instance penned by a male author, Geoffrey Chaucer.

In his "Wife of Bath's Prologue" Chaucer has his "new woman,"[2] The Wife of Bath, demand:

> Who peyntede the leon, tel me who?
> By God, if women hadde written stories,
> As clerkes han withinne hire oratories,
> They wolde han written of men moore wikkednesse
> Than al the mark of Adam may redresse.[3]

> [Who painted the lion, tell me who?
> By God, if women had written stories
> As clerics have done within their oratories,
> They would have written of more wickedness
> Than all the male sex may redress.]

Here, Chaucer's Wife of Bath touches on an issue that is of major concern to her living contemporary Margery Kempe, at least as recorded in the book of her own life, *The Book of Margery Kempe*.[4] This issue is the problem of how a woman is to operate within a male-dominated world, within male-sculpted ideological systems that deny women any form of linguistic self-expression on their own terms. Chaucer leaves the question floundering in ambivalence: does Alisoun effectively subvert male linguistic and ideological practices by means of performance and imitation, or does she remain ultimately trapped within hegemonic constraints that she is helpless to overturn? Critics remain divided on these questions but, like it or not, Alisoun of Bath confronts male authority as something to be challenged and debated, rather than accepted, and demonstrates clearly that the female perspective should be regarded as an alternative, rather than an "other" to accepted practices and viewpoints. It should provide an alternative way of taking life on.

Margery Kempe's similar clashes with male authority have been very well documented.[5] However, in this essay, I want to examine her particularly problematic relationship with what feminist theory terms "phallogocentric" language[6] and, in so doing, I will examine the extent to which her life—and her written account of it—can be read in terms of a struggle to find a personal linguistic idiom that can work on a variety of levels simultaneously. This idiom will be one that, while appearing to uphold the socioreligious order, will at the same time subvert it by offering a specifically female/feminine lexis for explication and interpretation of her highly singular experiences.

In the scribe's proem to Margery Kempe's book,[7] we are told that Margery resolutely resisted for over twenty years the instruction proffered by her anchorite confessor and other clerics to write down her remarkable mystical experiences. Indeed, as she tells her readers, "sche myth neuyr expressyn it with her word lych as sche felt it in hyr sowle" [she might never express it in words as she felt it in her soul].[8] In keeping with a familiar topos within mystical texts that illuminates the ultimate elusiveness of the mystical experience and its resistance to linguistic communication, Margery here points toward the failure of language and its traditional hermeneutics of the masculine to capture the enormity of her own mystical experiences, which she configures everywhere as intensely feminine.[9] For Margery, those experiences are deeply affective and cataphatic, received by and within a body that is in itself intensely gendered. Margery's early pronouncement of communicative failure, therefore, serves as the ultimate caveat within the *Book* and is also closely tied to the limitations imposed upon articulating the mystical experience and the body that receives it.

At this juncture Margery, via her scribe, also insists on pointing the reader toward the necessity of dispensing with normal, culturally conditioned reading practices and to regard what she has to express—in written language—as only ever provisional, as an approximation of what remains, for Margery, a private narrative of divine truth received by and felt within her own gendered body. This book, we are told, defies traditional written logic: it is not linear, it resists organization and Margery's experiences are collated "not in ordyr as it fellyn but as þe creatur cowd han mend of hem" [not in order as it happened but as the creature recollected them].[10] Ultimately, it will not conform to the masculine literary logic of chronological accuracy and structural linearity that Cixous and others have identified in more recent times as being both patriarchal and "the orchestrator of values."[11] And, in keeping with Cixous's later theories of female fluidity and multiplicity, Margery too will draw upon the type of cyclical and liquid repetitiveness that is not only symptomatic of the life cycle of the medieval wife and mother,[12] but—as Cixous has also argued—is a part of a woman's own Imaginary based on a rounded, fleshly body and multifaceted, "cosmic" libido.[13] As I will argue in this essay, Margery's disruption of traditional masculine logic and the accepted practices of literary production allow for the development of a language that is closer to Cixous's utopian ideal than is generally recognized. Moreover, such a language will enable the time-honored, androcentric "grand narratives" concerning divine love and human salvation to be told differently. As a result of Margery's efforts, then, the book of her own life will be reinscribed as the sacred Book of Life itself, articulated by a palimpsestic language based on the patterns laid down by her own body and its lived experience.

Such lived experience, however, dictates that, although Margery Kempe's conversion to the holy life takes place during her childbearing and childrearing years, it is not until the birth of her fourteenth and last child when she is forty years of age that she is able to extricate herself from the inexorable rhythms of domestic and familial duties in order to embark upon the life of holy woman. For much of her married life sex with her husband, the long-suffering John Kempe, had been abhorrent to her,[14] and yet she continued to bear child after child until eventually negotiating a vow of chastity with him.[15] By this time, almost two-thirds of Margery's life had been lived, one-third of it with an intense religious calling subjugated by the endlessly spiraling demands of earthly wifehood and motherhood. It is hardly surprising, then, that she resisted for two decades the call by her priestly supporters to write her experiences down. When she does come to write—well into old age by medieval standards[16]—we hear of how she spends protracted periods locked in her room alone with her amanuensis. This, of course, would have been unthinkable in her more youthful and sexually active days, not only because of the restrictions of time and space but also because it ran counter to the type of behavior expected of a young bourgeois housewife in fourteenth-century Bishop's Lynn.

So, Margery fails to write: first because of the inexplicability of her experiences; second because of the failure of human language to express them; and third because she is not yet old enough to get away with it and her youthful body still poses a threat to any potential audience.[17] More than this, though—and this will comprise the main argument of my essay—Margery fails to write because she has not yet experienced all she needs to experience of being a woman in the world in order to have a suitable and malleable enough language with which to write of the mystical. Hers is not an education steeped in Latin and Theology. She may or may not read English but the language she requires is not just simply a form of the local vernacular. Margery's education and the language that enables her to write are rooted deeply within the gendered body she inhabits, within the gendered socioreligious body into which she is born and within her response to the gendered language that constructs and polices both of these bodies.

All three of these, however, rarely cohere, except on the level of ideology and its resultant cultural narratives. There is no body that *is* these things but, as Simone de Beauvoir has famously asserted in the context of the operation of the female within patriarchal culture, ideology and narrative cohere to give that body meaning, rendering the body ultimately a "situation."[18] In the context of Margery Kempe I argue that it is within the conflict between Margery's own experiences of the body on the one hand and the fact of its "situatedness" on the other that a suitable language for her writing emerges through which her narrative is engendered. Her mystical experiences are, after all, embodied; but, although rendering her "al inflawmyd with þe fir of loue" [all inflamed with the fire of love],[19] they resist accurate representation because of the failure of what de Beauvoir, Cixous, and others regard as the masculine logic deeply embedded within language: "sche myth neuyr expressyn hem wyth hir bodily tunge liche as sche felt hem. Sche vndirstod hem bettyr in hir sowle þan sche cowed vttyr hem." [she might never express them with her bodily tongue in the way that she felt them. She understood them better in her soul than she could utter them.][20] The *impasse* necessitates the development of some kind of alternative articulation with a logic that can evade masculine linguistic strictures if Margery is to relay her singular experiences for the benefit of others. It is not until the life has been lived that the means for its articulation can be realized and the book of that life can be produced. So, it is at that very point when, free from years of compulsory sex, the cycles of childbirth, childrearing, and other marital concerns, a new space, both psychological and ideological, begins to manifest itself within which this more appropriate language may be produced. From that point onward, Margery's bodily experiences will be increasingly translated into compelling literary hermeneutics: conjugal sex transmutes into nuptial mysticism; misogynistic persecution becomes salvific suffering; and eventually, as we shall see, the experiences of Margery's body will become written into the sacred Book of Life itself.

Margery's Own Children and the Child

While I have dealt in depth with some of these issues elsewhere,[21] an issue that I have not examined previously in this context is how Margery's treatment of children in her narrative functions as part of this strategy to create a language by which her mystical chosen-ness by God may be understood and articulated. Indeed, on the subject of the importance of Margery's children to her book, I run counter to many commentators—both past and contemporary. The fate of Margery's children is one that has perplexed critics ever since the manuscript's discovery in 1934. Many scholars have been highly critical of the readiness with which Margery appears to abandon her fourteen children, including a newborn baby, in 1413 in order to embark upon the holy life and travel to Jerusalem on pilgrimage.[22] Others have been quick to identify this as symptomatic of some kind of psychological disturbance.[23] More speculatively, still more have either attempted to excuse this apparent abandonment by suggesting that Margery's children were farmed out to others in a type of "extra-mural fostering"[24] or even—according to one self-evidently erroneous assessment—must all have been dead.[25] Interestingly, even the most convincing of feminist readings have remained tellingly silent on the issue of Margery's children. In the next section, therefore, I aim to address the problem of Margery's children and their influence upon her mode of literary production. In so doing I will demonstrate that, far from being silent onlookers or absent victims within this text, they are very much to its fore, forming part of a sustained performance of the feminine and a carefully constructed literary hermeneutic that impact significantly upon the language of her writing. In other words, I will argue that Margery's children are reconfigured as a language with which to articulate those mystical insights received within the female body and to obtain a measure of authority for that body within the female-authored text itself.

Before turning my attention to two of the three references to specific children of her own, I want to focus on some of the many other children who populate this text in order to see how the figure of the child might be functioning in this context. There is, for instance, the small child named after Saint Bridget of Sweden (1303–1373) to whom Margery becomes godmother in Rome on her way back from pilgrimage to the Holy Land:

> Þan was þer a gret jentyl woman in Rome preyng thys creatur to be godmodyr of hir childe & namyd it aftyr Seynt Brigypt, for they haddyn knowlach of hir in hir lyue-tyme. & so sche dede.[26]
>
> [Then there was a great gentlewoman in Rome who begged this creature to be the godmother of her child and named it after Saint Bridget, for they had known of her in her lifetime. And so she did.]

Margery's frequent identification with her most consistent role model, Saint Bridget, is consolidated at this point by the close relationship she forges with both child and mother in the very place in Rome where Bridget met her saintly end. Moreover, this mother had known Bridget personally and there is the sense that she recognizes in Margery the reincarnated presence of the Swedish saint and seeks to unite holy woman and saint by means of the child, also called Bridget. Similarly, other children appear and disappear at regular intervals—some nursing at their mothers' breasts, or playing at their mothers' feet, but always inducing Margery to respond with tears of maternal love and compassion as she reads the nursing Virgin or *pietà* onto their vulnerable bodies:

> Þe powr woman clepyd hir into hir hows & dede hir sytten be hir lytyl fyer, ȝeuyng hir wyn to drynke in a cuppe of ston. & sche had a lytel manchylde sowkyng on hir brest, þe which sowkyd o while on þe moderys

brest; an oþer while it ran to þis creatur, þe modyr syttyng ful of sorwe & sadness. Þan þis creatur brast al into wepyng, as þei sche had seyn owr Lady & hir sone in tyme of hys Passyon... but euyr sat & wept plentyvowsly a long tyme.[27]

[The poor woman called her into her house and sat her down by her little fire, giving her wine to drink in a stone cup. And she had a little male child nursing at her breast who nursed a while at the mother's breast; another time it ran to this creature, the mother sitting full of sorrow and sadness. Then this creature burst out into weeping, as though she had seen our Lady and her son at the time of his Passion... but she continued to sit and weep plenteously for a long time.]

As on this occasion, the appearance of a child in Margery's narrative and the author's own response to it serves both to redefine and underscore the type of flexibility that Margery has come to recognize within her subjectivity as mother and its importance for her achievement of authority as a holy woman. Here, Margery can exploit all the societal expectations attached to the empathetic worldly mother and the unconditional love of the child, expectations that she has, no doubt, been subject to in her own lived life and that in apocryphal tales were fully inherent to the Mary–infant Christ relationship. While drawing upon such cultural paradigms for her dramatized maternal response to this child, Margery's performance, therefore, also allies her to the mother of Christ and establishes the child as verifier of her own special religious status.

Such a bodily performance allows for the production of a language that is initially extra-linguistic, that is to say beyond the bounds of spoken language, but that, nevertheless, succeeds in articulating Margery's "situatedness" as a woman, as a mother, as a holy woman, and spiritual mother and, in so doing, demonstrates the divine grace and insight to which she is privy. On the level of the text the figure of the child constitutes part of a central hermeneutic and validating strategy that is created out of the author's experiential knowledge of, and former immersion in, earthly maternal practices. Not only does this validate her past but it also approves her future as sought-out holy mother and privileged *sponsa Christi* [bride of Christ]. On the level of the body and the level of the text, therefore, Margery develops a language suitable for expressing the mystical, an experience that ultimately eludes all spoken language, especially the language of the masculine that Cixous terms "the law [which] organizes the thinkable."[28] In other words, the earthly child is adopted to help define and organize Margery's otherwise unthinkable situatedness as mystic by placing her back within the frame of earthly mother while concurrently allowing her to occupy the feminine site of vessel of the Word of God.

The few fleeting appearances of Margery's own children in her text[29] are all equally expedient and form part of the same hermeneutic structure as I have been identifying. Both Books One and Two, for example, open with accounts that focus on one or other of her children, casting her definitively in the role of mother for her readers. Indeed, Book One's disturbing account of the difficult birth of Margery's first child provides us with a primary example of how, even at this early stage in the text, what appears to be unproblematic autobiographical detail actually constitutes the basis of what will become an ongoing strategy toward self-validation:

> Whan þis creatur was xx ȝer of age or sumdele mor, sche was maryed to a worshepful burgeys and was with chylde within schort tyme, as kynde wolde. And aftyr þat sche had conceyued, sche was labowrd with gret accessys tyl þe child was born, & þan, what for labowr sche had in chyldyng & for sekenesse goyng beforn, sche dyspered of hyr lyfe, wenyng sche mygth not leuyn.[30]
>
> [When this creature was 20 years of age or a little more, she was married to a respectable burgess and became pregnant within a short time, as nature would have it. And after she had conceived, she was troubled by severe attacks of illness until the child was born. And then, what with the labor she had in giving birth and the preceding sickness, she despaired of her life, believing she might not live.]

This opening narrative firmly establishes a direct link between marriage, childbirth, suffering, and patriarchal proscription that will constitute a recurrent refrain in this text. Moreover, it is a refrain that is produced in part by the long, retrospective appraisal of a life lived by an aging woman who has newly come to writing. The onset of motherhood, after all, is where it all began and where, like the newly born child to whom she gave birth, both Margery's text and its language are engendered with great difficulty. In her account of this early episode, therefore, we are given not only a glimpse of a common legacy of medieval childbirth but also an insight into the situation of the frustrated writer and mystic that Margery will later become. As she sinks into dementia following the problematic birth, the physically manacled Margery is chained to her bed within the chamber and unable to leave the room.[31] Even after her recovery, perhaps even as a result of it, the *ideologically* manacled Margery is equally unable to leave her situation to follow her new religious calling, enchained there as she is by the gendered constraints of earthly motherhood, wifehood, and domesticity. Her hands remain well and truly tied. Meanwhile, the artistic task will be repeatedly evaded, attempted, aborted, abandoned, and—decades after its imaginative inception—completed, and its accomplishment will have been reliant in part upon Margery's transformation of a language of repression into a complex, female-focused expression of her own vision of the transcendent. In this episode, therefore, the body of the child operates as hypostatic signifier for the creative process that will, after much suffering and endeavor, eventually result in the production of "þis lityl boke" [this little book].[32] Such hermeneutic use of the figure of the child, whether divine or earthly, becomes fully consolidated within this text as part of a process for making intelligible to author, to amanuensis, and to audience what lies ultimately beyond language. In the words of Lee Edelman concerning the politico-ontological position of the Child within human culture:

> That Child remains the perpetual horizon of every acknowledged politics, the fantasmatic beneficiary of every political intervention... How could one take the *other* "side" when taking any side at all necessarily constrains one to take the side *of*, by virtue of taking a side *within*, a political order that returns to the Child as the image of the future it intends?[33]

For Edelman, the hegemony of the Child as "embodiment of the telos of the social order"[34] has become conflated with the "one" for whom the order is perpetually "preserved." Margery's sense of her own role in such a preservation (whether of the teleological future or of her own role within it) is clearly evidenced in her continual predilection for casting herself as nurturing mother in a wide variety of contexts; even in her visions, it is often a child who is brought center stage as a means of underscoring this role. In one mystical encounter, for example, Margery becomes actively involved as handmaid at the birth of the Virgin and proceeds to become responsible for the care and upbringing of the young Mary.[35] In the same way as she brought about a conflation between herself and Saint Bridget over the body of a small child, so Margery's care of the Virgin–child in this visionary episode allows for a mother–daughter synthesis in which Margery offers motherly advice to the young Virgin and which is entirely dependent upon Margery having supplanted the birth-mother, Saint Anne. Later, using the same stratagem and warming to her theme, Margery will also envision herself as midwife and handmaid to the parturient Virgin upon the birth of Christ in order to bring about a conflation between the Virgin Mother and herself:

> Sche beggyd owyr Lady fayr white clothys & kerchys for to swathyn in hir Sone whan he wer born, and, whan Ihesu was born, sche ordeyned bedding for owyr Lady to lyg in with hir blyssed Sone... Aftyrward sche swathyd hym with byttyr teerys of compassion, hauyng mend of þe scharp deth þat he schuld suffyr for þe lofe of sinful men.[36]

[She begged for our Lady fair white cloths and kerchiefs for her to swaddle her Son in when he was born and, when Jesus was born, she ordained bedding for our Lady to lie in with her blessed Son...Afterwards, she covered him with bitter tears of compassion, having mind of the sharp death that he should suffer for the love of sinful men.]

It would seem here that Margery is bringing to bear on her narrative a considerable amount of personal authority based on her situation as earthly mother; indeed, the hypostatic infant moves again to the forefront of the narrative in order to enhance the language of Margery's own authority. Mary as child, Mary as parturient mother, the infant Christ—all demand Margery's maternal services and, furthermore, depend upon them in order to fulfill their preordained destiny. Thus, their childish or childlike dependencies upon Margery become part of a powerful hermeneutic that validates Margery's production of self as maternally informed mystic who holds the key to salvation. In keeping with those "real" children in the text, then, these visionary children further reinforce the role of the child as delineating and defining Margery's holy credentials and her futurism. Now, however, far from constituting the manacles with which she was tied down, they announce the spiritual freedom and authority necessary for Margery to minister to the world and to articulate that ministry in the book of her life. Thus, in her old age Margery Kempe will become the female evangelist "at hom in hir chambre with hir writer" [at home in her chamber with her scribe][37] who, in a sense, reconfigures the sacred scriptures through the retrospective lens of her own bodily situation as earthly mother *and* mystic. In effect, she is inserting her own life and situated body into the sacred text and the sacred text itself becomes, in effect, the book of her own life.

One of the most arresting of incidents recounted in the *Book* that serves to bring the earthly and the visionary child together in the formation of a workable hermeneutic is that of Margery's encounter with a group of women while on the road to Rome on her way back from the Holy Land where she has been on pilgrimage.[38] Here, Margery encounters a woman carrying with her a casket that opens to reveal a doll-like effigy of the infant Christ whom the women remove in turns and care for, as if for the infant Christ himself. Such dolls tended to be popular in medieval nunneries on the Continent and, according to Caroline Walker Bynum, rendered the nuns simply "little girls playing at dolls."[39] However, there is nothing "simple" about what this doll represents for Margery—or, at least, what it comes to represent in the text—and there is certainly no sense of these "mothering" activities constituting any type of game. From her own account, the ministering to this doll by the woman and her companions is a deadly serious reenactment of the Virgin's ministering to Christ and—inevitably—it stirs up a deeply affective response from Margery.[40] On the simplest level it re-invokes in terms of memory and text her own visionary ministrations to the infant Christ that I have discussed earlier; on another it fully endorses the lived life of childbearing and child-caring that Margery has left behind her. Years later, however, the recounting of this episode to her amanuensis forms part of a literary strategy that invokes the figure of the child as the reification of what is patently a decidedly maternal ministry. On another level too, the child–doll can be read as an acerbic, nonverbal critique of a patriarchal world having no place within a female economy that, for Margery, has the maternal at its core. To this end, this becomes one of the handful of episodes from which men are entirely excluded in this text. The only male player here is the figure of the Christ–doll who, as both passive and inanimate and the focus of female ministrations, is marked by an inscription of the feminine. It is, however, just this feminized passivity that facilitates female access to the divine. In a sense, then, the doll reconfigures the child in this text as talismanic figure that guarantees access to and articulation of the author's female-focused mystical insights. It throws into firm relief the specifically human and maternal drama that lies at the heart of Christianity—identifying one of the few locations where the potential for action, and therefore articulation, remains with the woman.[41]

The Prodigal Son

The mother–child bond within this text, however, is not restricted to a configuration in terms of the infant. At one point Margery uses a fraught relationship with her own adult son to consolidate her position as holy woman and to further develop the hermeneutic of the child for her literary expression.[42] The episode in question comprises the opening section of Book Two and is billed as one of the episodes that Margery overlooked in her first account and that her second scribe thought worthy of inclusion. In this sense it takes up position as counterbalance to the opening of Book One, which documented the delivery of Margery's first child and her subsequent postpartum dementia, as we have seen. Now, at the beginning of Book Two we get a detailed insight into the problematic relationship Margery shares with a son in his early adulthood. It is possible that this son may also be the child of the Book's opening account and, even more pertinently, its first amanuensis.[43] If this were to be the case, then what we would have is the text's primary hermeneutic further hypostatizing into the child whose very hand puts pen to paper to write the book of his mother's life. Whether the case or not, the inclusion of Margery's quarrel with an adult son not only parallels the earlier childbirth narrative but also acts as a temporal pointer that illuminates the changed situation that Margery Kempe and her maternal body have become since the early days of her marriage. This time we are presented with a recalcitrant adult son who has abandoned his religious sensibilities in favor of an active and pleasurable social life that takes its toll on his health:

> [Þ]e same ȝong man passyd ouyr þe see..., & þan, what thorw euyl entisyng of oþer personys & foly of hys owyn gouernawnce, he fel into þe synne of letchery. Sone aftyr hys colowr chawngyd, hys face wex ful of whelys & bloberys as it had ben a lepyr.[44]
>
> [The same young man crossed over the sea..., and then, what through the evil enticing of other persons and folly of his own governance, he fell into the sin of lechery. Soon afterwards, his color changed, his face became full of wheels and pustules as if he had been a leper.]

Now, just as we saw in the earlier childbirth narrative, the relationship between mother and child becomes fragmented, leading to rupture and separation. This time, however, it is not a visitation from Christ that resolves things, nor does Margery demonstrate any self-recriminations; instead she unleashes what appears to be a recognizably maternal anger—a type of "hard love"—which is devised to bring her son back to the straight and narrow:

> "Now sithyn þu wil not leeuyn þe world at my cownsel, I charge þe at my blissyng kepe þi body klene at þe lest fro womanys feleschep tyl þu take a wife aftyr þe lawe of þe Chirche. And, ȝyf þu do not, I pray God chastise þe & ponysch þe þerfor."[45]
>
> ["Now since you will not abandon the world on my advice, I order you at my blessing to keep your body pure at least from woman's company until you take a wife according to the law of the Church. And, if you do not, I pray that God will chastise you and punish you as a result."]

This "maternal" voice, however, is also recognizably that of the preacher and Margery is able to slip into this role with ease and without censure because of its masquerading as maternal duty[46] rather than presupposing an usurpation of the male evangelical position—something explicitly forbidden by Saint Paul in 1Timothy 2:1–15 and for which she has been vilified on a number of other occasions.[47] While we are apparently witnessing an episode from a local and familial drama, Margery's written treatment of this filial conflict conjures up many elements of the biblical parable—specifically that of the Prodigal Son in Luke 15:11–32—into which sacred narrative she then again inserts herself. However, as on the previous occasion, she removes the sacred text from its patriarchal and androcentric context and injects it with a salvific economy that is entirely dependent upon the intervention—and absolution—of the female as primary mediatrix:

> He [Margery's son] preyid hys modyr of hir blissyng, & specialy he preyd hir to prey for hym þat owr Lord of hys hy mercy wolde forȝeuyn hym þat he had trespasyd.[48]
>
> [He prayed to his mother for her blessing, and he especially entreated her to pray for him so that our Lord in his mercy would forgive him that he had trespassed.]

In previous treatments of this episode I have tended to read it purely in terms of Margery's attempts to cast herself in the role of spiritual mother.[49] However, returning to it afresh, I am struck by its resonances, albeit much more prosaically articulated, with aspects of Julian of Norwich's Long Text version of her *Revelations*.[50] Margery had visited Julian some years prior to this episode, just before she embarked upon her visit to the Holy Land,[51] and just at the very moment when she was about to shed the restrictions of home and family to embark upon a new life and vocation. Julian's advice to her had been to follow the directive of God at all times and not to fear the words of the world, that is to say, public opinion,[52] and there is evidence throughout Margery's text of the influence upon her of Julian's advice, both at the level of language and of doctrine.[53] At the time of their meeting, Julian may well have been completing, or have completed, the revised version of her own text that contains several significant extended additions to the initial Short Text, one of which constitutes a similarly parabolic story and its protracted exegesis.[54] In this story there features a powerful lord who, while appearing initially in the guise of Old Testament patriarch, reveals himself to be both paternal *and* maternal in his concern for his lowly—and childlike—servant. In seeking to do his lord's work, the servant has carelessly fallen into a mire—an allegorical version, of course, of the mire of immorality into which Margery's own son also falls. As a result, in Julian's text the relationship between lord and servant takes on the dynamics of mother and child as the text attempts to negotiate a resolution to the fall:

> The servant standyth by, aforn his lord reverently, redy to don his lords will. The lord lookyth upon his servant ful lovely and sweetly, and meekly he sendyth hym to a certain place to don his will...Anon he fallith in a slade and takith ful grete sore...but he ne may risen ne helpyn himself be no manner wey...Than seith this curtes lord in his menyng: "Lo, lo, my

lovid servant. What harme and disese he hath takeyn in my service for my love, ya, and for his good will! Is it not skyl that I award hym his afray and his drede, his hurt and his maime and al his wo?...and ell me thynkyth I dede hym no grace."⁵⁵

[The servant stands nearby, reverently before his lord, ready to do his lord's will. The lord looks upon his servant sweetly and with much love, and sends him meekly to a certain place to do his bidding...Soon he falls into a mire and is greatly hurt...but he is unable to get up or help himself in any way at all...Then this courteous lord says in his grief: "Ah, behold my beloved servant. What harm and discomfort he has suffered in my service for my love, yes and because of his good will! Is it not appropriate that I reward him for his fear and dread, his hurt and injury and all his anguish?...Otherwise, I think I have done him no grace."]

This entire episode bears considerable resemblance to Margery's own structural treatment of the parabolic form: an initial unity is followed by abrupt severance, by separation, by suffering and anxiety, by contrition, by forgiveness, by return to unity. In both texts, too, these concepts are again removed from the masculine frame of reference and repositioned within an economy of the feminine and maternal—albeit in different ways. Whereas Margery is at pains to cast herself as mother, mediatrix, evangelist and inject those roles into the body of the text as language of a hierarchized feminine, Julian prefers to superimpose a femininity upon her masculine lord in order to create a synthetic balance that leads inexorably into the second major addition within her Long Text: the fully blown narrative of the Motherhood of God for which she is most renowned.⁵⁶ As in Margery's narrative too, the maternal love envisaged by Julian is both compassionate and hard-edged:

And whan it [the child] is waxen or more age, she [the mother] suffrid that it be bristinid in brekyng downe of vices to makyn the child to receivyn vertues and graces. This werkyng, with al that be fair and good, our lord doith it in hem be whom it is done.⁵⁷

[And when it is grown or is older, she suffers it to be beaten to break down vices in order to make the child receive virtues and graces. This working, with everything that is fair and good, our lord does it in them by whom it is done.]

In Julian's text, God becomes the mother of all humanity offering mercy and chastisement where appropriate for the greater good of her children—and, by implication, the human soul. Within Margery's text, it is Margery herself who takes on this role, both in her treatment of her own son, her reactions to the children of others, and to other religious miscreants whom she encounters on her travels. In *The Book of Margery Kempe* it is Margery herself who is invested with the motherhood of God; it is Margery who writes herself as distributor of its benefits on earth; it is Margery who thus casts herself in the same frame as God himself. By deploying an aberrant, yet redeemed, adult–child figure at the center of the narrative in these episodes, and by focusing on the concomitant and determined maternal responses of the figure of authority, both Julian and Margery demonstrate how the intervention of the feminine within the mundane family drama *and* the transcendent cosmic drama not only facilitates an understanding of the more complex mysteries of divine love and the female mystic's access to them, but produces a language of the feminine that can, in the words of Cixous, break, "the trembling equilibrium of a deadlock" which has precluded "woman...writ[ing] woman."[58]

Conclusion

Margery Kempe's use of the child hermeneutic in her writing facilitates the construction of a self with unique status within a salvific hierarchy that has the maternal at its core. It is such an irrepressible ability to conflate the worldly, the spiritual, and the mystical that I consider offers Margery her greatest strength as a mystic—and as a writer—and that provides her with a multivalent language that can again be read in terms of Cixous's identifiably feminine tongue; in coming to writing, Margery Kempe is "living one's pregnancy...giving birth...adding to life an other."[59] Whether influenced directly by Julian or otherwise, Margery is ultimately attempting an inscription of the feminine, of herself, upon the sacred text. As a result, she draws heavily on her own lived experiences reworking them as adept hermeneutic with which to demonstrate and express spiritual and literary authority. The fourteen children to whom she gave birth, sometimes with difficulty, always with reluctance, thus provide her with one of the most insistent tools to write the book that will become her life.

It therefore comes as no surprise, indeed it is entirely appropriate, that God's final profession to Margery concerning her establishment among the chosen is articulated via a further coming together of child, text, and book toward the end of Book One. While meditating on the cross and saying her prayers, Margery is privy to the vision of an angel dressed in white who, as she insistently emphasizes, is "as it had ben a lityl childe" [as if it had been a little child].[60] The infant nature of this angel is crucial to the consolidation of the primary hermeneutic of the child in Margery's text and it is thus entirely appropriate that he bears in his arms "an howge boke beforn hym" [a huge book before him]. This book, Margery is quick to recognize, is no less than the Book of Life in whose pages has been inscribed her own name, written in gold beneath an image of the Trinity. The depiction of this small child struggling to carry and hold before him this book of such proportion remains a potent one and is another instance of the type of realism with which Margery's narrative is everywhere imbued. The primary import of this child, however, is to demonstrate the enormity of the literary and spiritual tasks that Margery herself has undertaken and that she has succeeded in achieving. Now, as earthly and divine mother, author and divine secretary, it is entirely fitting that Margery's status as such should be confirmed to her by a small child who, bringing events full circle, announces her apotheosis: "'Her is þi name at þe Trinyte foot wretyn'" [Here is your name written at the foot of the Trinity].[61] The written name of Margery Kempe thus becomes synonymous with the Trinity itself at whose feet it appears and that it serves to label; Margery and the book of her life as "very trewth schewyd in experience" [very truth revealed in experience][62] metamorphose into the sacred Book of Life itself. How fitting, then, that this truth, which has revealed itself via the experience of being female, culminates in Margery's being led by a child into the realm of the salvific hierarchy fifty or more years after the birth of the first of her own fourteen children threatened to exclude her from it forever.

Notes

1. Hélène Cixous, "Sorties," in *New French Feminisms: An Anthology*, ed. Elaine Marks and Isabelle de Courtivron (New York: Harvester Wheatsheaf, 1980), p. 93 [90–98].
2. The term "New Woman" was originally coined to refer to those late-nineteenth-century and Fin-de-Siècle women who formed part of the so-called first wave within feminist activism. These women were also closely associated with women's claim to the written word and literary productivity and much of their writing pronounced on the type of issue regarding tradition and authority as does the Wife of Bath in this extract.
3. Geoffrey Chaucer, "The Wife of Bath's Prologue and Tale," in *The Riverside Chaucer*, ed. Larry D. Benson, third edn (Oxford: Oxford University Press, 1987), p. 114, ll. 692–695 [105–122]. The translation is my own.
4. All references to Margery's text will be taken from Margery Kempe, *The Book of Margery Kempe*, ed. Kenneth Meech and Hope Emily Allen, EETS o.s. 212 (London: Oxford University Press, 1997). Again, here and elsewhere, translations are my own.
5. See, e.g., Lynn Staley who casts Margery Kempe as an acerbic socioreligious critic in her book *Margery Kempe's Dissenting Fictions* (University Park: Pennsylvania State University Press, 1994).

6. This term refers to the way in which any text is grounded in the male-identified *logos*, a philosophical rationale that underpins all meaning and therefore reproduces it as truth.
7. It is widely considered that the final scribe was responsible for the writing of the *Proem*. However, he is careful to demonstrate that Margery's input was paramount throughout the writing of the work. My argument, therefore, is made from the standpoint of Margery being a prime mover in the text's construction.
8. Kempe, *Book of Margery Kempe*, p. 3.
9. Contemporary feminist scholarship has begun to argue for the feminine nature of the mystical experience per se, whether experienced by a man or a woman. See, e.g., Caroline Walker Bynum, especially her chapter on female mystics and Eucharistic devotion in *Fragmentation and Redemption: Essays on Gender and the Human Body in Medieval Religion* (New York: Zone Books, 1992), pp. 119–150; see also Amy Hollywood, *Sensible Ecstasy: Mysticism, Sexual Difference and the Demands of History* (Chicago: University of Chicago Press, 2001), especially pp. 6–13.
10. Kempe, *Book of Margery Kempe*, p. 6.
11. Cixous, "Sorties" (see note 1 earlier) p. 91.
12. For a recent study on the life cycle of medieval women based in Yorkshire see P.J.P. Goldberg, *Women, Work and Life Cycle in a Medieval Economy: Women in York and Yorkshire c. 1300–1520* (Oxford: Oxford University Press, 1992).
13. Hélène Cixous, "The Laugh of the Medusa," in *New French Feminisms* (see note 1 earlier) p. 259 [245–264].
14. On one occasion, however, Margery admits to having greatly enjoyed sex as a young woman prior to her religious conversion: Kempe, *Book of Margery Kempe*, p. 12.
15. Ibid., pp. 23–25.
16. Margery would have been more than sixty when she first began to write.
17. The diminishing threat to society of a woman's body as she ages is corroborated by the author of *Ancrene Wisse* who advises older anchoresses be given more leeway for social interaction than their youthful counterparts. See Hugh White, ed., *Ancrene Wisse*, trans. Hugh White (Harmondsworth: Penguin, 1993), p. 38.
18. "[T]he body is not a *thing,* it is a situation" (original emphasis). Simone de Beauvoir, *The Second Sex* (London: Picador, 1988), p. 66. For a cogent analysis of de Beauvoir's theories of *situatedness*, see Toril Moi, *Sex, Gender and the Body* (Oxford: Oxford University Press, 2005), especially pp. 59–83.
19. Kempe, *Book of Margery Kempe*, p. 200.
20. Ibid., p. 210.
21. See, e.g., Liz Herbert McAvoy, *Authority and the Female Body in the Writing of Julian of Norwich and The Book of Margery Kempe* (Cambridge: D.S. Brewer, 2004).

22. See, e.g., Robert K. Stone, *Middle English Prose Style: Margery Kempe and Julian of Norwich* (The Hague: Mouton, 1970); and Wolfgang Riehle, *The Middle English Mystics* (London: Routledge, 1981).
23. Richard Lawes, "The Madness of Margery Kempe," in *The Medieval Mystical Tradition in England, Wales and Ireland: Exeter Symposium VI*, ed. Marion Glasscoe (Cambridge: D.S. Brewer, 1999), pp. 147–167; Stephen, Harper, "'So euyl to rewlen': Madness and Authority in 'The Book of Margery Kempe,'" *Neuphilologische Mitteilungen* 98:3 (1997): 53–61; Mary Hardman Farley, "Her Own Creature: Religion, Feminist Criticism, and the Functional Eccentricity of Margery Kempe," *Exemplaria* 11:1 (1999): 1–21.
24. John Boswell, *The Kindness of Strangers: the Abandonment of Children in Western Europe from Late Antiquity to the Renaissance* (Chicago: University of Chicago Press, 1988), p. 358.
25. Verena E. Neuberger, *Margery Kempe: A Study in Early English Feminism* (Berne: Lang, 1994), p. 87.
26. Kempe, *Book of Margery Kempe*, p. 94.
27. Ibid.
28. Cixous, "Sorties," p. 91.
29. This is something that, again, I have dealt with in detail in *Authority and the Female Body*, pp. 33–63.
30. Kempe, *Book of Margery Kempe*, p. 6.
31. Ibid., p. 8.
32. Ibid., p. 220.
33. Lee Edelman, *No Future: Queer Theory and the Death Drive* (Durham: Duke University Press, 2004), p. 3. I am grateful to Noreen Giffney of University College, Dublin, for alerting me to Edelman's work on the Child.
34. Ibid., p. 11.
35. Margery Kempe, *Book of Margery Kempe*, pp. 18–19.
36. Ibid., p. 19.
37. Ibid., p. 216.
38. Ibid., pp. 76–78. This episode has been examined in some depth by Kathy Lavezzo, "Sobs and Sighs between Women: The Homoerotics of Compassion in *The Book of Margery Kempe*," in *Premodern Sexualities*, ed. Louise Fradenburg and Carla Freccero, (New York and London: Routledge, 1997), pp.179–198, to which queer reading I am indebted for my own analysis both here and in *Authority and the Female Body*, pp. 55–57.
39. Bynum, *Fragmentation*, p. 198.
40. Kempe, *Book of Margery Kempe*, pp. 77–78.
41. This is a point also made by Lavezzo, "Sobs and Sighs," p. 187. See also my *Authority and the Female Body*, p. 57. This issue, in the context of women's language and agency, has been addressed by both Julia Kristeva and Luce Irigaray in their essays on the role of the Virgin and the female mystic, respectively. See Julia Kristeva, "Stabat Mater," in *The Kristeva Reader*, ed. Toril Moi (Oxford: Blackwell, 1995), pp. 160–186; and Luce Irigaray, "La Mystérique," in *Speculum of the Other Woman* (Ithaca: Cornell University Press, 1985), pp. 191–202.

42. Kempe, *Book of Margery Kempe*, pp. 221–223.
43. McAvoy, *Authority and the Female Body*, p. 33, n20.
44. Kempe, *Book of Margery Kempe*, p. 222.
45. Ibid., p. 222.
46. Clarissa Atkinson, *The Oldest Vocation: Christian Motherhood in the Middle Ages* (New York and London: Cornell University Press, 1991), p. 157 and 204.
47. See, e.g., Kempe, *Book of Margery Kempe*, p. 28, 126, and 131.
48. Ibid., p. 222.
49. McAvoy, *Authority and the Female Body*, p. 43.
50. All quotations from Julian will be taken from Julian of Norwich, *A Revelation of Love*, ed. Marion Glasscoe, second edn (Exeter: Exeter University Press, 1986). Again the translations are my own.
51. Margery Kempe, *Book of Margery Kempe*, pp. 42–43.
52. Ibid., p. 42.
53. This is a point convincingly argued for by Naoë Kukita Yoshikawa in *Margery Kempe's Meditations: The Context of Medieval Devotional Literature, Liturgy and Iconography* (Cardiff: University of Wales Press, 2007), pp. 62–63, 65–68, and 70–73.
54. Julian of Norwich, *A Revelation of Love*, pp. 72–81.
55. Ibid., pp. 72–73.
56. Ibid., pp. 81–104.
57. Ibid., p. 98.
58. Cixous, "Laugh of the Medusa," p. 247.
59. Ibid., p. 262.
60. Kempe, *Book of Margery Kempe*, p. 206.
61. Ibid., p. 207.
62. Ibid., p. 220.

CHAPTER 7

DIE GHEESTELICKE MELODY: A PROGRAM FOR THE SPIRITUAL LIFE IN A MIDDLE DUTCH SONG CYCLE

Thom Mertens

Song texts have unique possibilities to pass on experience of spiritual life. The fortnightly cycle of songs studied here has a profound effect on the singer despite its deceptive simplicity.

The Middle Dutch song cycle *Die gheestelicke melody* [The Spiritual Melody] constructs experience in a singular manner. The cycle comprises sixteen songs describing the growth of spiritual life from God-fearing through hope and love of God to acceptance of an earthly existence of suffering. Each stage in the development has a preceding crisis triggered by what at least seems to be an imposing impasse.

Venturing through each of these stages, a lyrical persona speaking from the first-person perspective ("I") undergoes development as part of the sung experience unfolded throughout the cycle. Each stage of growth is concluded by an appeal for fellow sufferers to take the same path and follow the first-person singer. In this way, the lived experience becomes a prefiguring event intended to transform disciple–singers/readers into leaders whose role it is to entice others to join in the spiritual development. Consequently, the cyclical performance of private experience to the public community of the faithful transforms an individual spiritual life into an exemplary book of life.

At the same time, the song-cycle form had greater possibilities in this regard than did contemporaneous prose works. *Die gheestelicke melody* represents an effective new mode of shaping spiritual life experience into a text and communicating it to fellow Christians. The individual songs are composed in the solidifying structure of a cycle reinforced by a division into two "books," each with its own prologue and short prose explanations accompanying almost every song. The songs of the first book are subdivided into the days of the week, suggesting that the songs are best sung systematically and repetitively, and read and meditated upon in a fixed order. The second book consists of seven songs and hence coincides numerically with the week-based structure of the first book. The songs are in themselves very simple, nevertheless describing a complete, penetrative development of spiritual life to be cyclically imprinted in a biweekly schedule of staged reading and performance.

The new mode of writing is not only manifest in the unique structure of a song cycle divided into smaller cycles of songs with prose introductions but also in the intricate manner in which textual simplicity and spiritual depth are combined. The duality of simplicity and depth is further reflected in the tensions between singing and reading, between meditation, orality, and literacy, between individual and community, and between worldly and religious life. All these dualities are expressed in the cycle—either in the songs themselves or in the accompanying prose texts—and certainly in a very natural manner. A brief examination of the text will show how the song cycle represents a very effective and straightforward way of communicating life experience to simple, illiterate people without sacrificing spiritual depth, therefore fulfilling a missionary function of propagating a community of spirituality.

The Nineteen Songs Analyzed

The cycle is written in Middle Dutch and transmitted in three manuscripts, each witnessing its own version.[1] Consisting of two books of nine and seven songs, respectively, it has a supplement of three Saints' songs.[2]

The nineteen songs are written in the first-person singular, an anonymous lyrical voice that complains, expresses her joy, or speaks to Jesus, Mary, or her fellow sisters from a personal perspective.[3] The songs in the supplement specifically address the martyrs Catherine of Alexandria (d. 307), Agnes (ca. 300), and Margaret of Antioch (d. 307). In the intervening prose pieces, the lyrical voice is referred to as "the soul," a term that I will adopt in this article for the sake of convenience, and this voice is clearly a female one in the text. In the course of the cycle, this soul undergoes a classical spiritual ascent in full keeping with other late medieval texts, especially mystical texts. Unconventionally, however, the ascent in this case is described in a series of songs and explicated in accompanying prose, which is what constitutes the uniqueness of *Die gheestelicke melody*.

The beginning and end of the progress or ascent as sketched in Book One is love. The starting point is the discovery that love of the world is unreliable and ultimately leads to nothing:

> Der werlts myn is al verloren,
> Ay want men gheen ghetrou en vijnt.
> Och lacy, wat had ic vercoren,
> Doe ic haer mit solaes ontfinck? (Song Two, ll. 1–4)[4]

> [Love of the world is entirely meaningless because nothing is found that remains true. O what did I choose when I embraced it to be comforted.]

The final point is the rapturous love of Jesus inspired by the blessings that He has performed for humanity:

> O Jhesu, uutvercoren heer,
> Na u verlanghet my so seer.
> Mijn hert end al mijn synnen
> Begheren u tontfaen. (Song Eight, ll. 1–4)

> [O Jesus, chosen Lord, I yearn for Thee so greatly. My heart and all my senses long to receive Thee.]

Book One in Two Cycles

The prologue of Book One describes the overall progress that takes place in the first book, the development from fear, through hope, to love.[5] The prologue therefore suggests that the progression is linear, but this is not the case. In fact, the ascent is cyclical, each development first reaching and then overcoming some kind of impasse. It is the breaking of the impasse that initiates spiritual growth.

Song One is a prologue song that functions as an opening prayer for the cycle and remains outside the spiritual progress that is described. The first cycle thus contains Songs Two, Three, and Four and here the soul learns to turn away from the love of the world and toward Jesus out of fear of damnation. This fear, which constitutes the point of departure, is the fear of judgment. The soul finds it difficult to break with the "world" and is afraid to assume a spiritual life. She therefore appeals to Jesus for delivery from the fear of loving Him (Song Two). In response, Jesus proceeds to comfort the soul that is then able to depart from the world (Song Three). After this initial breakthrough, the soul concludes the first stage of growth by making an appeal to her fellow sisters in the following song, beckoning them to emulate her and abandon the world.

The first cycle is followed by an impasse in which the soul is subjected to the temptation described in Prose Five, the only point in the entire cycle where the prose provides—outside the songs—important information about the soul's progress. The entire second cycle is concerned with the soul learning to concentrate on herself, forsake her own inadequate merits, and fully devote herself to Jesus. Only in this way can she outgrow fear and come to know love. Since Jesus continues to remain inaccessible to the soul throughout the second cycle, she therefore turns to Mary (Song Five). In turn, Mary teaches the soul to recognize that she can never sufficiently redeem her sins; only the suffering of Jesus is capable of providing her with salvation (Song Six). This second cycle is concluded with a joyful song, indicating that the consolation of Mary has been successful (Song Seven). In terms of content, this song also responds to what Mary taught the soul in the previous song; indeed, it makes a direct reference to it.[6] The preceding prose introduction also links Song Seven to hope, just as the prologue to Book One had done. The word "hope," however, does not appear anywhere in the song itself[7] and, while the song fits well into the spiritual progress of the soul, the division of this progress into the phases of fear, hope, and love appears to be an imposition by the prose writer of what must have been a logical and traditional sequence.

The penultimate song in Book One (Song Eight) expresses the love that the soul now feels for Jesus, and the gratitude for His suffering, concluding as follows:

> O Jhesu lief, u doot, u naem
> Is my int hert also bequaem
> Dat ic en weet te vijnden
> Gheen beter medecijn
> In my om te verwinnen
> Des viants fel venijn.
>
> Hier om bid ic u, waer ic ga
> Of waer ic bin, sit, leg of sta
> Dat gi tot allen tiden
> U naem Jhesus, u myn,
> U doot end al u liden
> Laet comen in mijn syn. (Song Eight, ll. 55–66)

[O beloved Jesus, Thy death, Thy name are so loving to my heart that I do not know how to find any better medicine to overcome the devil's fierce poison. For this reason, I pray to Thee, wherever I go or wherever I am, sit, lie or stand, that Thou always allowst Thy name Jesus, Thy love, Thy death and Thy suffering to come into my thoughts.]

Mary's admonition in Song Five therefore has its effect: the soul comes to rely on Christ's redemptive suffering. Song Eight therefore represents a transition to the third phase in the soul's ascent—her growth into love.

The second cycle is concluded by a song to fellow companions about "the sweet land" for which they are all destined (Song Nine). However, the condition that Mary expressed to the soul in Song Five is again raised here: no one enters the sweet land except those who bear the love of Jesus in their hearts (Song Nine, ll. 13–15). In the final prose passage of Book One, the desire for the heavenly kingdom is further fanned by a description of a wonderful May morning that, although of great earthly beauty, is only ever a weak reflection of the glory of the heavenly kingdom. The earth is, after all, the wasteland to which Adam and Eve are banished after the fall.

Book Two with the Third Cycle

The third cycle, which constitutes all of Book Two, recognizes and accepts the other side of love: the experience of the beloved's absence and the acceptance—and even embracing—of personal suffering as something good.[8] Therefore, *Die gheestelicke melody* is a consolation in the true sense of the word, since consolation does not remove grief but teaches us to regard it as salutary.[9]

The prologue of Book Two notes that the soul has entered into the love of God, taking patience in thought and deed as its topic under the motto "Love is patience" (1 Cor. 13:4). The first song, with its opening line "I see the day rise in the east," recalls the final prose piece of Book One, in which a marvelous May day is represented as a meager reflection of heavenly grace (Song Ten). This view increases the desire for heavenly bliss and therefore the soul desires to experience the sweetness of Jesus Christ, a desire that grows in this song into a plaint about the absence of any sign from Jesus (Song Eleven). Ultimately, this concludes by the soul retracting what it said in the joyful seventh song of Book One, the first two lines of which ("Hi troer die troeren wil, mijn troeren is gedaen" [He may grieve who wishes to grieve, my grief is over]) are echoed in the opening lines of this song:

> Och nu mach ic wel troeren.
> My dunct ic heb verloren
> Jhesum mijn suete lief.
> Ic waend hem sijn vercoren,
> Ic sprac: "en wilt nijt troeren."
> Tis al een ander brief. (Song Twelve, ll. 1–6)

> [O now I may certainly grieve. It seems to me that I have lost Jesus, my sweet love. I believed myself to be chosen by him, I said, "Do not grieve," but it is now a completely different story.]

The heart of the soul's complaint is *Mijn lief en acht my niet!* [My love does not pay me any attention!] (Song Twelve, l. 12). Repeating the initial lines of Song Five, the soul now appeals to Mary. The key portion of her answer is:

> Gi wilt mijn kijnt behaghen,
> Mer tcruys mit hem nijt draghen,
> Daer al die myn leyt aen. (Song Thirteen, ll. 4–6)[10]

> [Thou wishest to please my Child, but not bear the cross with Him, on which all love depends.]

Mary thus consoles the soul by teaching her to question her own desires, to rely on God's insight, and to be satisfied with what He predetermines. She instructs the soul not only to glorify God just when she feels a need to do so but in any and all circumstances for, even if He may appear unresponsive, He is always close by.

Attention then shifts to the encouragement of companions, who must be content in their suffering, since all those who are patient will soon receive a great reward. The key passage is:

> Mer lacy, wi sijn dic verblint.
> Wanneer ons druc of liden vijnt,
> Ons dunct dat god ons nijt en mynt. (Song Fourteen, ll. 46–48)

> [But alas, we are often dazzled. If we are touched by fear or suffering, it appears to us that God does not love us.]

The third cycle thus broadens ideas about love, showing how it not only contains joy but also its inverse: suffering. Once the soul comes to accept this duality, she crowns her assent with a request to suffer patiently:

> Hierom so laet ons trouwelijc
> Aenroepen God van hemmelrijc
> End bidden hem oetmoedelijc
> Dat hi ons liden laet hier neer,
> Verduldelic tot sijnre eer:
> O Jhesu, uutvercoren heer,
> Wi bidden, ist u wil end eer,
> Dat ghi ons liden laet hier neer
> Verduldelic, soet u behaecht,
> End daerna haelt ons onversaecht. (Song Fifteen, ll. 61–70)

[For this reason, let us steadfastly call on our God in heaven and humbly beseech Him that He allows us, who remain below, to suffer into His glory: O Jesus, chosen Lord, we beseech Thee, should it be Thy will and glory, to allow us here below to patiently suffer, if this be Thy pleasure, and then to fetch us, (we being) undaunted (by that).]

The soul consoles her companions in their suffering and now invites them to do the same for all those who are afflicted by some spiritual or material need. And on the principle of *ite* and *venite* of the Last Judgment, she recounts how those who fail to follow this counsel will have great fear, while those who follow it will know great joy. Thus, the lyrical narrator—the soul—has developed into an authoritative spiritual leader:

> O ghi die mijns raets wilt pleghen,
> Wilt die vrees doch in u weghen.
> Ghedenct den armen in haer noot.
> Coemt hem vrilic nu te baten.
> Nummermeer sel u god laten
> Van tewich leven gaen ter doot. (Song Fifteen, ll. 115–120)

[O Thou, who wishest to follow my counsel, please do consider the fear in you. Remember the poor in their need. Voluntarily come to help them. Never will God allow you to go from eternal life to (eternal) death.]

The cyclical progress from fear to love and from disciple to leader intensifies itself in the manner of a spiral, each turn of which is incorporated in the three similarly structured subcycles. The experience of fear or spiritual solitude[11] is disrupted by a dialogue in which the soul learns how she can overcome this desolation[12] culminating in a state of thankfulness for such encouragement[13] and finally enabling her to joyously beckon her fellow sisters to emulate her development.[14] At the end of the third cycle, this appeal (Song Fourteen) is extended in Songs Fifteen and Sixteen by an exhortation to her fellow sisters about the fear and hope of the Last Judgment, a plea that constitutes an invitation to undertake works of mercy in the present and to offer material as well as spiritual aid to the poor.

The circularity of the cycle is not just confined to this larger configuration. Although the spiritual development experienced by the soul occurs in three cycles of plaint, consoling dialogue, thankful joy, and the summoning of fellow sisters, there are even smaller cycles in these larger ones, some of which are crucially important. For instance, the moments of dialogue are moments when the soul learns something fundamental, resulting in a large step in her spiritual progress. In the first dialogue Jesus is the teacher; in the second and third, the soul wrestles with the problem that she cannot love Jesus in the proper manner and that He seems to be inaccessible to her. At that point, the soul refers to herself as "the miserable man" and turns to Mary, who assumes her traditional role as mediator by consoling, encouraging, and instructing the soul.

The cycle is also followed by three Saints' songs, which were added as a supplement. They do not have any accompanying prose introductions and all three songs are addressed to one of the female martyrs from late Antiquity—respectively, Catherine of Alexandria (d. 307), Agnes (ca. 300), and Margaret of Antioch (d. 307). All three died a martyr's death because of a desire to maintain their vows of chastity and refusal to marry. They were popular saints in the late Middle Ages, providing luminous examples for women wanting to lead an unmarried religious life in the cloister or a semi-religious convent, and many religious houses had one of these martyrs as their patron saint. The three songs take the form of requests for consolation in suffering, for intercession, and deliverance from sin, especially at the moment when the soul will be subject to reckoning at the end of her life.

Exemplary Life Experience

The nineteen songs of *Die gheestelicke melody* sketch an exemplary and complex spiritual development in an elegant and simple manner. It does not constitute the life story of a real person, but offers the traditional doctrine about the growth of the soul as described in other mystical literature, particularly that of the fourteenth century, but is stylized as the life experience of an anonymous, idealized first-person subject.

This stylized "life experience" is offered as a model to be emulated by companions and, more specifically, fellow sisters in the world that the text evokes: at the end of each cycle the lyrical I tells her fellow sisters about her joy and beckons them to follow. The cycle strongly invites identification with a role model. Due to the fact that the songs are written in the first-person singular, every person who sings them automatically identifies with the life experience of the I speaking in the songs. The crux is therefore that everyone who sings the songs, speaks in the persona of the I. As a result, whenever someone sings these songs, reads, or considers them, she (or he) becomes herself (or himself) the subject of the spiritual development described in the song cycle. As Fraeters notes in chapter eight of this volume, the thirteenth-century Hadewijch also formulated her mystical experiences in the form of a personal exchange of experiential wisdom, in this case between a medieval spiritual leader and her spiritual child. Similarly, the anonymous Viennese friar stylized Agnes Blanbekinn's doctrinal lessons into the *Life and Revelations* of Agnes, as Mulder-Bakker explains in chapter five. It could be argued, therefore, that the stylizing of general spiritual lessons into the life experience of a testifying first-person persona is a technique characteristic of late-medieval women's writing.

In addition, the repetitive, cyclical performance is well regulated, at least in Book One. While the prologue to the first book indicates precisely which songs should be sung or read on which day of the week, the second book consists of seven songs, a number that alone makes them well suited for equal distribution over the days of the week. Thus, the performance of the entire *Gheestelicke melody* can occur in a phased manner based on a biweekly rhythm. The goal of this preprogrammed, repeated textual or performative reception is to integrate its exemplary spiritual ascent into the daily life of the singer or reader. Complementing this evolving life experience, the cyclically renewed learning and inculcation of the text has a deepening effect, resulting in a productive interchange between the repeatedly received text and the evolving life experience. The result is a text that has a profound depth despite its deceptive simplicity.

The songs directed at fellow sisters are exceptional. Late medieval spirituality is strongly "vertically" oriented on the relationship of the individual soul with God and almost exclusively focused on individual salvation. In *Die gheestelicke melody*, the lyrical subject addresses her peers after every impasse and breakthrough in order to spur them on to the same steps in their own spiritual growth. By means of identification with the lyrical I achieved by singing and reading in the first-person singular, everyone who makes this step is invited to act as spiritual pioneer for her fellow sisters. As a consequence, this cycle has a preprogrammed social effect of constructing a fellowship of peers who share the same desire for—and make the same strenuous attempts at—spiritual development, and who maintain long-lasting mutual relationships as a result of being part of a community of singers, another example of the "community of discourse" defined in the introduction to this collection. In a number of the illustrations contained within the Leiden manuscript, this community is specified as a group of sisters in which one assumes a leading role but, like the lead singer in a choir, is otherwise indistinct from her fellow sisters.[15]

Given its varied form, which includes songs in the first-person singular, dialogues with Jesus and Mary, and songs in the second-person plural, this song cycle produces a particular effect that prose can only produce with great difficulty, even in an artless manner. Singing has an affective power to bring about identification with an exemplary lyrical subject while at the same time exhorting the fellow religious to join in the choir, so to speak. In this sense it can therefore be argued that song is more powerful than prose, both as a propagator of personal lived experience and forger of community.

Mouvance, Variance, and Movement

Up to this point my argument has been based on the text of *Die gheestelicke melody* as it appears in one particular manuscript, that is to say the Leiden manuscript, because it contains the most complete version of the cycle. However, as I intimated earlier, *Die gheestelicke melody* has been preserved in three manuscripts and has a different form in each of them.[16] Examining the textual transmission implied by the existence of these manuscripts will further clarify the constructive and integrative communal function that the songs and their prose interpretations served for their singers, readers, and listeners. The three manuscript versions are:

1. Manuscript H: The Hague, Koninklijke Bibliotheek, MS 75 H 42, fols 217r–255r, contains the prose and the songs of Book One, while the final prose of Book One is different from and much shorter than its counterparts in the other two manuscripts. The manuscript dates from 1473 and comes from Flanders.[17] An early owner was *suster Mertynken van Corcelles* (?) in Antwerp. The text in the manuscript is intended for a (primarily?) male public.[18]
2. Manuscript L: Leiden, Universiteitsbibliotheek, MS Ltk. 2058, fols 1r–72v, contains the prose and songs from Books One and Two and the supplement comprising the three Saints' songs. The manuscript is dated 1470–1480. Its provenance is unknown, although the name of an early owner, *Etheken Bernts dachter* (Etheken [an affective variant of Margaretha?]), Bernard's daughter, can be discerned in the lower margin of fol. 1r.[19]
3. Manuscript W: Vienna, Oesterreichische Nationalbibliothek, MS s.n. 12875, contains in folios 1r–17v most of the prose pieces and all the songs and melodies from Book One. Folios 32r–52v contain the songs from Book Two along with their melodies but without the prose pieces, and the three Saints' songs with their melodies.[20] The songs are not presented as a cycle in this manuscript, which some researchers date to around 1500. The literary historian Knuttel attributed it to the Tertiary Convent of Saint Margaret in Amsterdam, which was located in a place named *Gansoirde* [Goose place], but Obbema showed that this attribution was groundless in 1972.[21]

In addition, various songs have been transmitted individually outside the cycle in a number of sources.[22]

The three manuscripts exhibit remarkable differences concerning the parts of *Die gheestelicke melody* that they hand down. The Hague manuscript does not include Book Two; the Vienna manuscript is, in contrast, the only one that provides the melodies to the songs, while the prose pieces in it are very incomplete. In addition, the cycle is not well defined as such in this manuscript and the two books are not in immediate sequence. It is also not possible that the two books in this manuscript ever formed an integrated codicological whole.[23]

An effort could be made to determine what the original form of the cycle was. Book One is clearly conceived of as an autonomous whole, and it may well be that the Hague manuscript contains an earlier version. However, Book Two is so closely integrated with Book One in terms of concept, form, and textual parallels—but especially insofar as the spiritual development is concerned—that the two books together display clear conceptual unity, which of course does not exclude the possibility that Book Two was added later. Methodologically, however, it is not reasonable to regard the one form of the text as more authentic just because it is older. In previous attempts to recover or reconstruct an original "authorial text," scholars such as Paul Zumthor and Kurt Ruh have argued for accepting the inherent value of each form in which a given text is transmitted.[24] Later, this view was adopted by the "New Philology," which declared respect for textual variation to be one of its basic principles. This position is succinctly formulated by Bernard Cerquiglini in his pamphlet-like "eulogy to the variant": "Medieval writing does not produce variants, it is variance."[25]

In all three manuscripts, the texts of *Die gheestelicke melody* display some variation that is inherent to the manner of transmission, but the variations in such cases are relatively small. Much larger, more important, and more interesting are the mutual differences that are the result of choices, such as the addition or omission of Book Two, the omission of a number of prose texts in the Vienna manuscript or the addition/omission of particular melodies. These deliberate changes can be better identified using such terms as *movement, migration,* or *development* of the text. These terms have a stronger connotation with regard to coherence, intentionality, and deliberateness than *mouvance* and *variance* would seem to have.

Although we are, in principle, dealing with the relevant versions as equivalent versions here, it is still relevant to ask about the direction in which the text has "moved." It is highly likely that the Hague manuscript offers an older version of *Die gheestelicke melody* than the Leiden or Vienna manuscripts do.[26] Book One, as transmitted in the Hague, can certainly be regarded as having functioned as an autonomous whole, while Book Two is, to a certain extent, dependent on Book One, given the references and parallels that it contains. Furthermore, there is no reference at all to the second book in the prologue to Book One. Moreover, the first song, which is placed before the prologue in the Hague manuscript and after the prologue in the Leiden manuscript, is not discussed in the prologue, nor is it mentioned in the prologue contained in the Leiden manuscript. This suggests that the sequence in the Leiden manuscript is secondary, leaving me now to discuss the question of the addition or omission of the melodies.

Singing on the Threshold

We can provisionally assume that the Hague manuscript represents, in a number of respects, an older version than the ones in Vienna or Leiden, which is not to say that the Hague manuscript is a direct antecedent to the Leiden and Vienna manuscripts. The variants in the Hague manuscript cannot automatically be granted greater originality.

The Hague and Leiden manuscripts of *Die gheestelicke melody* date from the 1470s. Consequently, *Die gheestelicke melody* stands at the beginning of the tradition of devout Middle Dutch song collections, which comprises some twenty collections transmitted in manuscript and print.[27] The systematic copying of Middle Dutch religious songs came into its stride at a fairly late date. Prior to 1470, spiritual songs are only occasionally to be found in manuscripts. The only exception to this occasional transmission is the Hadewijch of Brabant cycle of forty-five songs (ca. 1250?) passed down in four manuscripts, of which three originate from the fourteenth century and the fourth from a later date.[28] Most song collections do not have any clear ordering and, while some manuscripts also transmit the melodies, others also include a number of Latin songs. Moreover, the manuscripts are, in general, very simply produced.

This raises the question of why the Middle Dutch spiritual songs were not transmitted in writing until such a late date, in contrast to secular songs.[29] We should seek an answer by examining the position of those individuals who compiled and used the collections. A notable number of manuscripts were in the private possession of women living in a religious community. In general, it was not the laity but religious and semi-religious women who constituted the most prominent audience for Middle Dutch spiritual literature.[30] They did not always live in official cloisters but frequently in communities of varying degrees of institutionalization. The tendency, which became ever stronger during the course of the fifteenth century, was the conversion of free and semi-free communities into official convents. This conversion, which took place in phases, could be a very lengthy process and, as in a number of cases, was sometimes never entirely completed.[31] Many communities did not adopt the Latin canonical hours. In a number of cases simplified vernacular imitations of the official choral prayer were used. In the last years of his life, Geert Grote (d.1384) had already compiled a Middle Dutch book of hours for free communities of women, such as the Sisters of the Common Life.[32] In the first half of the fifteenth century, there was also a "lay breviary," which consisted of a liturgically ordered book of psalms with a fully translated breviary text for a very limited number of feast days.[33] In addition, an abundance of prayer books existed, which have passed down an enormous number of prayer texts.[34] But the spirituality of women in religious communities was not only nourished by such prayer texts. They were also provided with translations of argumentative and narrative texts, such as the liturgical sermons of Bernard of Clairvaux or the *Liber apum* [Book of Bees] of Thomas of Cantimpré.[35] And above all, texts were also composed in the female convents themselves for their own use. For example, collections of biographies were composed with the aim of creating a spiritual "family" of fellow sisters who had lived exemplary lives under the same circumstances and each with her own possibilities and limitations.[36] In addition, sermons by the women's own confessor were also written down by the sisters and assembled into collections.[37] Occasionally, experimental forms were tried out, such as the *Jhesus collacien,* a cycle of sermons in which Jesus and the Holy Ghost appear as preachers to an anonymous sister, who subsequently communicates the sermons to the convent. This cycle of sermons was relatively widely circulated and was therefore not in any way a marginal phenomenon.[38]

In this sense, *Die gheestelicke melody* can also be regarded as an experiment. The idea was to transmit a program of spiritual ascent by means of a song cycle and to explain it in short accompanying prose pieces. Such material was traditionally communicated entirely in prose but, in comparison with the prose of the time, the spiritual song has a few notable characteristics of its own. For instance, Jesus and Mary frequently appear as heavenly mediators. In the contemporary prose, the figure of Mary does not have such a prominent place; and in the case of Jesus, the focus in prose is almost exclusively on his suffering. Another noteworthy characteristic of the spiritual song is the theme of abandoning the world, which forms the subject of many of the songs in this cycle, as we have seen.[39]

Written song collections appear to remain at the threshold of the cloister and frequently thematize the crossing of this threshold. Even in a material sense, the song collections remain at the doorstep. A not insignificant number of manuscripts were the private property of the women within the community. After their death, these items were passed on to another private individual, and, as a result, the collection began to grow: new texts were inserted into the margin or quires are added to the whole.[40] In other cases, items of private ownership were left directly to the community, such as the Leiden manuscript of *Die gheestelicke melody,* which bears the ownership mark on fol. 1r.

> Dit bocksen hoert Etheken Bernts dachter toe (*erased:*) ende na mijnre doet so gheve icket int ghemeen.[41]
>
> [This book belongs to Etheken Bernts' daughter, (*erased:*) and after my death I leave it to the community.]

If we recognize that song collections had a role on the margins of community life, we need to carefully distinguish between the singing and the writing of songs. It is certainly possible and even likely that spiritual songs were sung collectively, but written song collections appear to have had a function at the boundary between the private person and the community.

The primary question is of why the spiritual songs were recorded in writing (which is to say in collections) only much later than the secular song. One answer probably resides in the fact that the spiritual song was supposedly sung primarily within religious environments. Since people lived together in such communities, contact among individuals was frequent and intense. In such contexts, the distribution of songs could easily occur orally. It was unnecessary to write down songs to transmit them in such situations. So, in all likelihood, the transmission of songs to other people was not the most prevalent reason for writing them down.

A more likely explanation is to be found in the new ways in which these songs were received, in which context an investigation into the development undergone by the text in the Leiden manuscript in relation to the Hague manuscript can prove fruitful. In the Leiden manuscript, the references to singing have been systematically replaced by references to reading. The Hague manuscript discusses the melodies immediately at the beginning of the prologue to Book One:

> Dit es die gheestelike melodie tusschen Jhesum Cristum ende de minnende ziele, gheset op noetkins van weerliken liedekins om dat men die werlike worden sal moghen vergheeten, want daer niet dan ydelheit in gheleghen en es ende dicwile zijn zij een groot hinder des gheestelikens levens. (Prose One, manuscript H, fol. 217r–v)
>
> [This is the spiritual melody between Jesus Christ and the loving soul set to the notes of secular songs in order to enable the secular to be forgotten, as it only contains idleness and frequently they (the secular words) are only a great obstacle to spiritual life.]

The Leiden manuscript has abbreviated the text here and no longer mentions the melodies:

> Hier beghint dat prologus van die gheestelicke melody tusschen Jhesum Cristum ende die mynnende ziel. (Prose One, manuscript L, fol. 1^r; edition: p. 1, ll. 1–2)

[Here begins the prologue to the spiritual melody between Jesus Christ and the loving soul.]

The transition from "singing" to "reading" is extremely clear later in the prologue:

> Het es te hopene an gode als wij eenighe van desen gheestelikin liedekins zinghen, dat wij een weynich verlicht zijn sullen van des vyants temptacien. (Prose One, manuscript H, fol. 218^v)
>
> [It is the hope of God that we will be freed somewhat from the temptation of the devil when we *sing* a few of these songs.] (Emphasis added)

To be compared with:

> Het is te hopen in Gode, als enighe van desen gheestelicken hymmekijns van ons ghelesen worden of ghedacht, dat wi dan wel een weynich verlicht sellen worden van des viants temptacien. (Prose One, manuscript L, fol. 1^{r-v}; edition: p. 1, ll. 8–11)
>
> [It is the hope in God that we will be freed somewhat from the temptations of the devil when a few of these spiritual hymns are *read and contemplated* by us.][42]

It is clear that the songs cross the boundary between singing and reading here. As reading material, the cycle can better serve its function as the matter for meditation foreseen in the prologue:

> Ende want veel dinghen te samen zwaer sijn te verstaen ende verduysteren onse verstandenisse, so sijn dese ymmekijns ghescicket by ordinancie van daghe in die weecke, als aen elc ymmekijn bisonder gheteykent staet, om alle daghe wat sonderlings te nemen ende daer in te oefenen gheestelic, want elc bisonder alte veel smakelicker is alsmen die mynnentlike woerdekijns wel overdencket. (Prose One, manuscript L, fols 1^v–2^r: edition: p. 1, ll. 16–22)
>
> [And because it is difficult to understand many things at the same time and our mind is obscured as a result, these songs are therefore arranged according to the days of the week, as indicated by each song, so that a different one can be taken every day and used for spiritual exercise, since individually they have much more flavor when the sweet words are properly considered.]

According to the prologue, the songs are spread over the days of the week because they contain too much to understand at one time—even if they are rather simple in our eyes. The sequencing of the reception and the term *overdencken* [contemplate, meditate on] presupposes an intensive, meditative treatment of the text and, given the simplicity of the songs, perhaps limited spiritual experience of the readers, making an intensive, repetitive reception necessary. The manner of reception is supported by the reading of the texts, which does not exclude the possibility that they were *also* sung, although the melodies or the references to them are missing from the Hague and Leiden manuscripts.

The quotation referring to the degree of difficulty and the *overdencken* as the manner of reception also occurs in the Hague manuscript; consequently, the linking of the reading of the songs and meditation about the songs is not exclusive to the Leiden manuscript. Perhaps, reading makes for meditation, but singing does not exclude it either.[43]

Ironically, the text in the Vienna manuscript is the most closely related to the one in the Leiden manuscript. There, the Vienna manuscript, which passes down the transcribed melodies of *Die gheestelicke melody*, also displays the replacement of references to singing with references to reading. This teaches us that the creation of collections of spiritual songs is not exclusively a result of the new manner of reception. The Vienna manuscript abandons the cyclical nature of *Die gheestelicke melody*: Books One and Two are not in immediate sequence and the prose pieces associated with the cyclical character have been eliminated, in particular the prologue of Book One and the introductory prose of Song Five, which is not just concerned with the introduction of the specific song but provides crucial information about the soul's process of development. The prose pieces of Book Two have all been removed. In the Vienna manuscript, the cycle has disintegrated into a series of songs.

In general, we can observe that collections of devout songs display a certain degree of variance. Some only contain Middle Dutch songs; others contain Latin songs as well. Some collections not only contain the texts of the songs but also a number of transcribed melodies. This diversity makes us aware of the fact that the transcription of Middle Dutch spiritual songs must not purely be explained as the result of a new manner of reception coming to the fore: that is to say the reading of songs (in addition to the singing of them). For the time being, this remains an issue requiring further investigation. A new way of receiving the songs can only be a part of the explanation.

In Conclusion: Typical but Unique

Middle Dutch collections of spiritual songs were composed from around 1470 onward. *Die gheestelicke melody* was one of the first of these collections and occupies a special position in the tradition because it is a cycle, in which the songs are also explained in prose. From a material viewpoint, the collections are, in general, simply made and the ownership mark of the manuscripts makes it clear that such devout song collections were mostly used by private persons on the threshold of communal life. The theme of the songs is distinct from the contemporaneous spiritual prose as a result of the greater attention paid to the transitional problems of entering religious life. In this way, the vernacular spiritual song appears to have functioned outstandingly as "transition literature," literature that belongs to the transitional stage between the private and the communal, between the world and the cloister, between orality and literacy. Evidently, it could better serve this transitional function than prose could.

Die gheestelicke melody is typical of such collections but also a unique representative of the type because it presents a coherent and ambitious spirituality in a relatively simple manner. This combination of formal simplicity and a high level of spirituality is made possible by the singularity of the literary form: a song cycle of which the coherence is justified in the prose accounts, and in which a lyrical 'I' offering her development as a model to be imitated has her actions interpreted in the third-person prose texts. This imitation is systematized by the preprogrammed repetitive reception that allows for a two-week cycle. What *Die gheestelicke melody* expresses unsystematically in song collections is systematized and rationalized in the accompanying prose texts. As a consequence, *Die gheestelicke melody* is unique and at the same time exemplary of the genre of the spiritual song collections, which are at the same time the fruit and source of the spiritual life experience.

Appendix

Contents of Die Gheestelicke Melody

Manuscript H [1473]: The Hague, Koninklijke Bibliotheek, MS 75 H 42, fols 217r–255r (Book One).

Manuscript L [1470–1480]: Leiden, Universiteitsbibliotheek, MS Ltk. 2058, fols 1r–72v (Book One, Two; Saints' songs).

Manuscript W [ca. 1500]: Vienna, Oesterreichische Nationalbibliothek, MS s.n. 12875, fols 1r–17v (Book One with melodies, some prose lacking), fols 32r–52v (Book Two with melodies, without prose; Saints' songs).

The third column indicates the tradition in other manuscripts and printed editions up to 1600. Printed editions are indicated after a slash (e.g., 8/2 means: transmitted in eight manuscripts and two print editions).

The list is based on Martine de Bruin, Johan Oosterman, Clara Strijbosch et al., *Repertorium van het Nederlandse lied tot 1600 / Repertory of Dutch songs until 1600* (Gent: Koninklijke Academie voor Nederlandse Taal en Letterkunde, 2001) and the transmission of excerpts described by Herman Mulder, "Een nog onbekend gebedenboek uit het Amersfoortse Sint-Agnesconvent met excerpten uit geestelijke liederen," *Queeste* 8 (2001): 160–174. Some manuscripts contain the same song twice, in which case the manuscript is counted twice.

Incipits, order, and distribution over the days of the week according to Manuscript L.

P = Prose, S = Song

					H	L	W	Other
Book One								
	P01	Hier beghint dat prologus			×[a]	×		
Sunday	S01	Jhesus Cristus, Marien zoen			×[b]	×	×	
	P02	Hier beclaecht die ziel haer weerlic leven	**fear**		×	×		
	S02	Der werlts myn is al verloren			×	×	×	1
	P03	Wantet die ziel lastelic valt			×	×	×	
	S03	O Jhesu, heer, keert u tot my			×	×	×	
Monday	P04	Want die ziel nu wel ende mynlic ghetroest is			×	×	×	
	S04	Verblijt u, lieve susterkijn[c]			×	×	×	1
Tuesday	P05	Want die ziel die werrelt begheven heeft			×	×	×	
	S05	Ave Maria, maghet reyn			×	×	×	1
Wednesday	P06	Want die ziel Marie gheantwert heeft			×	×		
	S06	Maria, coninghinne			×	×	×	6/2
Thursday	P07	Want die ziel nu vulcomelic ghetroest is	**hope**		×	×	×	
	S07	Hi troer die troeren wil			×	×	×	4
Friday	P08	Want die ziel ghecomen is van anxt tot hoep	**love**		×	×	×	
	S08	O Jhesu, uutvercoren heer			×	×	×	1
Saturday	P09	Want die ziel ghecomen is tot groter mynnen	**glory**		×	×	×	
	S09	O ghi die Jhesus wijnghert plant			×	×	×	4/5
	P10a	Nota psalmus[!]: Gloriosa dicta sunt de te etc. [Ps. 87(86):3]			×			
	P10b	Een merkelicke suete verweckinghe tot hemmelrijc				×	×	

			H	L	W	Other
Book Two						
	P11	Hier beghint dat ander boecsken der gheestelicker melodien		×		
	P12	Want die ziel suete contemplacy ghehadt heeft		×		
	S10	Ic sie den dach int oest opgaen		×	×	1
	P13	Want die ziel suete contemplacy ghehadt heeft		×		
	S11	Mijn hert dat is in liden		×	×	1
	P14	Want die ziel Jhesum Cristum, haren brudegom, zeer begheret		×		
	S12	Och nu mach ic wel troeren		×	×	
	S13	O creatuer, dijn claghen		×	×	
	P15	Want die ziel nu wael ende mynnentlic ghetroest is		×		
	S14	O gi die nu ter tiden lijdt		×	×	1
	P16	Want die ziel ghetroest heeft alle die in druc ende liden sijn		×		
	S15	My verwondert boven maten		×	×	1
	P17	Hierna vertelt die ziel die vruechde		×		
	S16	O wael moech di u verhoghen		×	×	
	=S05	Ave Maria, maget reyn (text of the first strophe)			×	
Saints' songs						
	S17	Dit is een sequency van sinte Kathrijn seer scoen		×	×	
	S18	Van sint Agniet, martelaer		×	×	
	S19	Van sinte Margriet, joffrouw		×	×	

a, b S01 and P01 change places in Manuscript H.

c susterkijn: broeders mijn Manuscript H.

Notes

1. Middle Dutch spiritual song cycles are rare. Besides the songs of Hadewijch of Brabant (ca. 1250?; see note 28 later) and *Die gheestelicke melody* there is also *Den berch van Calvarien* [The Mount of Calvary] in Berlin, Staatsbibliothek zu Berlin, Preußischer Kulturbesitz, MS. germ. 8° 62 (ca. 1480, 44 fols), in which meditations on the suffering of Jesus are spread over the days of the week and the text for each day is concluded with a spiritual May song. See Johan Oosterman, "Ik breng u de mei: Meigebruiken, meitakken en meibomen in Middelnederlandse meiliederen," in *Aan de vruchten kent men de boom: De boom in tekst en beeld in de middeleeuwse Nederlanden*, ed. Barbara Baert and Veerle Fraeters, Symbolae Facultatis Litterarum Lovaniensis, series B, vol. 25 (Louvain: Universitaire Pers, 2001), pp. 177–178 [167–189]—the appendix to this

essay provides a schematic overview of the transmission of the songs and prose pieces in the three manuscripts. In this essay, I will make use of the Leiden manuscript as its basic text because it offers the most complete version. Facsimile edition: *Die gheestelicke melody: Ms. Leiden, University Library, Ltk. 2058*, ed. P.F.J. Obbema (Leiden: New Rhine Publishers, 1975). An edition of the text is provided by an Antwerp student workgroup, *Die gheestelicke melody: Kritische editie naar handschrift Leiden, Universiteitsbibliotheek, Ltk 2058* [Antwerpen: (Ufsia), 2000] [also consult www.dbnl.nl (accessed 16 December 16, 2006)].
2. The Saints' songs 17–19 in the appendix of the cycle do not have any introductory prose, neither does Song 13, merely the "direction": *Hier antwert Maria* (Mary answered); these three words are followed by an illegible word that the Antwerp edition (see note 1 earlier) indicates to be *mine* but the meaning of which is unclear. Song 13 has the same form as Song 12, and the two songs have close thematic associations. Therefore the Songs 12–13 could be considered as one song, which would explain why the introductory prose of Song 13 is lacking. Each of the songs, though, has its own melody in the Vienna manuscript, proving them to be two separate songs.
3. Self-pity (Songs 2, 11, 12a), expression of joy (Song 7), songs to Jesus (Songs 1, 8, 10, 17a), to Mary (Song 12b), to fellow sisters (Songs 4, 9, 14, 15, 16), to the martyrs Catherine of Alexandria (Song 17), Agnes (Song 18), and Margaret of Antioch (Song 19). Dialogues: with Jesus (Song 3), with Mary (Songs 5, 6, 13).
4. In the edition of the Antwerp student workgroup (see note 1 earlier), the prose pieces and the songs are unnumbered, which makes referencing a laborious task. See the appendix to this essay for the numbering method.
5. The prologue accurately indicates the songs that are attributed to each of the development phases, respectively, Song 2 (fear), Song 7 (hope), Song 8 (love). The first and last song of Book One is outside the fear–hope–love line of development, consisting of seven songs. The first song of Book One is not mentioned in the prologue (in the Hague manuscript, this is placed before the prologue). The final song about the "land of eternal glory" reached through love is an extension of the line of development but is, in fact, outside of it. As a result, we arrive at nine songs in the first book.
6. "Ic heb gezweghen stil, / Mariam verstaen" [I remained silent (and) understood Mary] (Song 7, ll. 3–4).
7. In the prose piece, hope is mentioned several times, but the only place that this word appears in the song text of Book One is in Song 8, ll. 14–15, where the soul speaks to Jesus: "Gy sijt mijn hoep / al mijn solaes" [Thou art my hope, all my solace].
8. The first two cycles consist of Song 2–4 and 5–9 in Book One; the second cycle consists of Songs 10–16 of Book Two.
9. For example, see the description of consolation provided by Johannes Gerson: "Consolatio est habitus animae quo inclinatur amplecti quodammodo et uniri sibi objectum sub ratione boni, honesti et convenientis apprehensum" [Consolation is the attitude of the soul by means

of which it is inclined to embrace misfortune, as it were, and to unite with it by recognizing that it is something good, honorable and suitable.] See J. Cornelissen, "Over consolatie-literatuur," *Mededeelingen van het Nederlandsch Historisch Instituut te Rome* 6 (1926): 149 [149–192].
10. Ll. 58–60 in the edition (in which Songs 12 and 13 are regarded as one song).
11. Song 2, Prose 5 and Song 5; Songs 11 and 12.
12. Song 3: dialogue with Jesus; Songs 5, 6, and 13: dialogue with Mary.
13. End of Song 3; Song 7 (to Mary), Song 8 (to Jesus); end of Song 13.
14. Song 4; Song 9; Song 14.
15. See the monochromatic illustrations in *Die gheestelicke melody*, ed. Obbema. The Leiden manuscript contains fourteen miniatures; a sister is portrayed in thirteen miniatures and one or (usually) more other sisters are shown in six of them, in all cases clothed in a white veil and white habit covered by an open brown (choir?) mantle. Pieter Obbema, *De middeleeuwen in handen: Over de boekcultuur in de late middeleeuwen* (Hilversum: Verloren, 1996), chapter 13, pp. 166–175. (This chapter, "Het einde van de Zuster van Gansoirde," was published first in *De Nieuwe Taalgids* 65 (1972): 181–190.) Obbema attempted to make an identification on the basis of this clothing, unfortunately to no avail, p. 168, n10.
16. For a detailed overview, see the appendix to this essay.
17. Description: *Catalogus codicum manuscriptorum Bibliothecae Regiae*, vol. 1, *Libri theologici* (The Hague: Koninklijke Bibliotheek, 1922), pp. 174–175 (no. 617); cf. Robrecht Lievens, "Een sermoen van de latere Utrechtse wijbisschop Goswinus Hex," *Spiegel der Letteren* 7 (1963–1964): 49–50 [44–50]; Obbema, *De middeleeuwen*, p. 174. For a transcription of the songs in this manuscript on cd-rom: Martine de Bruin, Johan Oosterman, and Clara Strijbosch, *Repertorium van het Nederlandse lied tot 1600/Repertory of Dutch songs until 1600*, 2 vols (Gent: Koninklijke Academie voor Nederlandse Taal en Letterkunde, 2001).
18. Song 4 (line 1.1) is addressed to "lieve broeders mijn" [my dear brothers], while the song in the MSS. L and W read "lieve susterkijn" [dear little sister].
19. Description: Obbema, *De middeleeuwen*, pp. 167–170. Editions: see note 1 earlier.
20. Description and edition of the songs with texts: *Het geestelijk lied van Noord-Nederland in de vijftiende eeuw: De Nederlandse liederen van de handschriften Amsterdam (Vienna ÖNB 12875) en Utrecht (Berlijn MG 8° 190)*, ed. E. Bruning, M. Veldhuyzen, and H. Wagenaar-Nolthenius, Monumenta Musica Neerlandica 7 (Amsterdam: Vereniging voor Nederlandse Muziekgeschiedenis, 1963), pp. xxxiii–xxxiv, 3–30, and 63–104; W. Bäumker, "Niederländische geistliche Lieder nebst ihren Singweisen: aus Handschriften des XV. Jahrhunderts," *Vierteljahrsschrift für Musikwissenschaft* 4 (1888): 153–254, and 287–350.
21. J.A.N. Knuttel, *Het geestelijk lied in de Nederlanden voor de Kerkhervorming* (1906; repr. Groningen: Bouma's boekhuis and Amsterdam: Bert Hagen, 1974), pp. 55–61; Obbema, *De middeleeuwen*, pp. 166–175.

22. See De Bruin, Oosterman, and Strijbosch, *Repertorium* and the summary based on this work in the appendix to this essay. Also see Herman Mulder, "Een nog onbekend gebedenboek uit het Amersfoortse Sint-Agnesconvent met excerpten uit geestelijke liederen," *Queeste* 8 (2001): 160–174; see 166–171 for an edition of the rhyme texts.
23. I would like to thank Patricia Stoop (University of Antwerp) who checked this point for me in the Vienna library.
24. Paul Zumthor, *Essai de poétique médiévale* (Paris: Seuil, 1972), chapter 2, pp. 64–106; Kurt Ruh, "Überlieferungsgeschichte mittelalterlicher Texte als methodischer Ansatz zu einer erweiterten Konzeption von Literaturgeschichte," in *Überlieferungsgeschichtliche Prosaforschung: Beiträge der Würzburger Forschergruppe zur Methode und Auswertung*, ed. Kurt Ruh and Hans-Jürgen Stahl (Tübingen: Niemeyer, 1985), pp. 262–272.
25. See the special issue of *Speculum* 65:1 (1990), and especially the introductory article by Stephen G. Nichols, "Introduction: Philology in a Manuscript Culture," *Speculum* 65 (1990): 1–10 [p. 1; the motto is taken from Bernard Cerquiglini, *Éloge de la variante: Historie critique de la philologie* (Paris: Seuil, 1989), p. 111]; Keith Busby, *Towards a Synthesis? Essays on the New Philology*, Faux titre: Études de langue et littérature françaises 68 (Amsterdam: Rodopi, 1993), where on pp. 29–45 there is a sharp critique by Keith Busby on the unrefined nature of Cerquiglini's eulogy. An outstanding explanation of the term "mouvance" can be found on the website of the *Wessex Parallel WebTexts*: http://www.soton.ac.uk/~wpwt/ under 'Resources'—'What is *mouvance?*' (accessed December 22, 2006).
26. This is also Obbema's view, *De middeleeuwen*, pp. 173–174.
27. Overview in Knuttel, *Het geestelijk lied*, pp. 48–69; A.M.J. van Buuren, "'Soe wie dit liedtkyn sinct of leest': De functie van de Laatmiddelnederlandse geestelijke lyriek," in *Een zoet akkoord: Middeleeuwse lyriek in de Lage Landen*, ed. Frank Willaert, Nederlandse literatuur en cultuur in de middeleeuwen 7 (Amsterdam: Prometheus, 1992), pp. 234–238 [234–254, 399–404]; Hermina Joldersma, "'Geestelijke' en 'wereldlijke' liederen: Enige aspecten van het handschrift Brussel MS II, 2631," in *Veelrehande liedekens: Studies over het Nederlandse lied tot 1600*, ed. Frank Willaert, Antwerpse Studies over Nederlandse Literatuurgeschiedenis 2 (Louvain: Peeters, 1997), pp. 61–62 [58–73]; Hermina Joldersma and Dieuwke van der Poel, "Sij singhen met soeter stemmen: Het liederenhandschrift Brussel KB II 2631," *Nederlandse Letterkunde* 5 (2000), 115 [113–137].
28. See Erik Kwakkel, "Ouderdom en genese van de veertiende-eeuwse Hadewijch-handschriften," *Queeste* 6 (1999): 23–40; edition given by J. Van Mierlo, ed., *Hadewijch, Strophische Gedichten*, 2nd edn. Leuvense Studien en Tekstuitgaven [Antwerpen: Standaard, (1942)] [both of these publications can be consulted at www.dbnl.nl (accessed December 16, 2006)]; Hadewijch of Brabant, *Hadewijch, The Complete Works*, trans. Columba Hart, The Classics of Western Spirituality (New York: Paulist Press, 1980), pp. 123–258; Kurt Ruh, *Geschichte der abendländischen Mystik*, 4 vols (Munich: Beck, 1990–1999), 2: 163–182 [158–232]; Bernard McGinn, *The*

Presence of God: A History of Western Christian Mysticism, 6 vols (New York: Crossroad, 1991–), 3: 200–222; Paul Mommaers and Elisabeth Dutton, *Hadewijch: Writer—Beguine—Love Mystic* (Louvain: Peeters, 2004). The fourth manuscript (Antwerpen, Ruusbroecgenootschap, MS. 385 II) dates from 1500 to 1510; see S.M. Murk Jansen, *The Measure of Mystic Thought: A Study of Hadewijch's Mengeldichten*, Göppinger Arbeiten zur Germanistik 536 (Göppingen: Kümmerle, 1991), pp. 211–219.

29. On the beginning and continuity of transmission for the Middle Dutch secular song, see Frank Willaert, "Een proefvlucht naar het zwarte gat: De Nederlandse liedkunst tussen Jan I van Brabant en het Gruuthuse-handschrift," in *Veelrehande liedekens*, pp. 30–46.
30. On the connection between women and song in the late-medieval period, see Hermina Joldersma, "Writing Late-Medieval Women and Song into Literary History," *Tijdschrift voor Nederlandse Taal- en Letterkunde* 117 (2001): 5–26; and also Joldersma and Van der Poel, "Sij singhen," 116–121.
31. Madelon van Luijk, *Bruiden van Christus: De tweede religieuze vrouwenbeweging in Leiden en Zwolle, 1380–1580* (Zutphen: Walburg Pers, 2004) provides a clear set of terminology to describe the institutional diversity (pp. 20–21; English summary pp. 307–308) and the process of conversion to cloistered convents (pp. 144–165; summary pp. 309–310). On the development of the extremely important Chapter of Utrecht in the fifteenth century, which was dominated by Franciscan tertiaries: Hildo van Engen, *De derde orde van Sint-Franciscus in het middeleeuwe bisdom Utrecht: Een bijdrage tot de institutionele geschiedenis van de Moderne Devotie*, Middeleeuwse Studies en Bronnen 95 (Hilversum: Verloren, 2006) (English summary pp. 426–434). This provides an important supplement to the older but still does not replace: R.R. Post, *The Modern Devotion: Confrontation with Reformation and Humanism*, Studies in Medieval and Reformation Thought 3 (Leiden: Brill, 1968). Cf. also chapter two by Goudriaan in this volume.
32. Edition: N. van Wijk, ed., *Het getijdenboek van Geert Grote naar het Haagse handschrift 133 F 21* (Leiden: Brill, 1940). [consult www.dbnl.nl (accessed December 16, 2006)]; Rudolf Th. M. van Dijk and R.A.F. Hofman, eds., *Prolegomena ad Gerardi Magni Opera Omnia*, CCCM 192 (Turnhout: Brepols, 2003), pp. 583–585.
33. Youri Desplenter, "Overgezet voor het gebed: Latijnse hymnen en sequensen in het Middelnederlands," *Tijdschrift voor Nederlandse Taal- en Letterkunde* 122 (2006): 198–207 [193–212].
34. For the rhymed prayers, see Johan B. Oosterman, *De gratie van het gebed: Overlevering en functie van Middelnederlandse berijmde gebeden*, Nederlandse literatuur en cultuur in de middeleeuwen 12 (Amsterdam, Prometheus, 1995), 2 vols. For the many prayers in prose we still have to do with the old and incomplete survey of Maria Meertens, *De Godsvrucht in de Nederlanden naar handschriften van gebedenboeken der XVe eeuw*, Historische bibliotheek van Godsdienstwetenschappen [(Antwerpen): Standaard / (Nijmegen–Utrecht): Dekker—Van de Vegt, 1930–34], 4 vols.

35. Carine Lingier, "Over de verspreiding van Sint-Bernardus' liturgische sermoenen in het Middelnederlands," *Ons Geestelijk Erf* 64 (1990): 18–40 [also: Carine Lingier, "Over de verspreiding van Sint-Bernardus' liturgische sermoenen in het Middelnederlands," in *Spiritualia Neerlandica: Opstellen voor Dr. Albert Ampe S.J.*, ed. Elly Cockx-Indestege (Antwerpen: Ruusbroecgenootschap, 1990), pp. 318–340]; Carine Lingier, "'Hongerich na den worden Godes.' Reading to the Community in Women's Convents of the Modern Devotion," in *Lesen, Schreiben, Sticken und Erinnern. Beiträge zur Kultur- und Sozialgeschichte mittelalterlicher Frauenklöster*, ed. Gabriela Signori, Religion in der Geschichte, Kirche, Kultur und Gesellschaft 7 (Bielefeld: Verlag für Regionalgeschichte, 2000), pp. 123–147; Christina M. Stutvoet-Joanknecht, *Der byen boeck: De Middelnederlandse vertalingen van Bonum universale de apibus van Thomas van Cantimpré en hun achtergrond* (Amsterdam: VU, 1990), especially pp. 129*–153*.
36. Thom Mertens, "Het Diepenveense zusterboek als exponent van gemeenschapstichtende kloosterliteratuur," in *Het ootmoedig fundament van Diepenveen: Zeshonderd jaar Maria en Sint-Agneesklooster, 1400–2000*, ed. Wybren Scheepsma, Publicaties van de IJsselacademie 152 (Kampen: IJsselacademie, 2002), pp. 77–94, 141–143, and 165–166; Annette M. Bollmann, *Frauenleben und Frauenliteratur in der Devotio moderna: Volkssprachige Schwesternbücher in literarhistorischer Perspektive* (Groningen: Rijksuniversiteit, 2004); Wybren F. Scheepsma, "'For hereby I hope to rouse some piety': Books of sisters from convents and sister-houses associated with the Devotio moderna in the Low Countries," in *Women, the Book and the Godly*, ed. Lesley Smith and Jane H.M. Taylor (Cambridge, UK: Brewer, 1995), pp. 27–40.
37. Thom Mertens, "Ghostwriting Sisters: The Preservation of Dutch Sermons of Father Confessors in the Fifteenth and the Early Sixteenth Century," in *Seeing and Knowing. Women and Learning in Medieval Europe 1200–1550*, ed. Anneke B. Mulder-Bakker, Medieval Women: Texts and Contexts 11 (Turnhout: Brepols, 2004), pp. 121–141; Thom Mertens, "Relic or Strategy: The Middle Dutch Sermon as a Literary Phenomenon," in *Speculum Sermonis: Interdisciplinary Reflections on the Medieval Sermon*, ed. Georgiana Donavin, Cary J. Nederman, and Richard Utz, Disputatio 1 (Turnhout: Brepols, 2004), pp. 293–314.
38. Anna Maria Baaij, *Jhesus collacien: Een laatmiddeleeuwse prekenbundel uit de kringen der Tertiarissen*, Zwolse drukken en herdrukken 40 (Zwolle: Tjeenk Willink, 1962). I am preparing an English-language article on the *Jhesus collacien* for the periodical *Medieval Sermon Studies*.
39. Knuttel, *Het geestelijk lied*, chapter 9, pp. 337–408.
40. See, e.g., Andreas J.M. van Seggelen, *Het liedboek van Liisbet Ghoeyuaers*, Zwolse drukken en herdrukken 56 (Zwolle: Tjeenk Willink, 1966), pp. 7–10.
41. Obbema, *De middeleeuwen*, p. 168.

42. Also compare Song 5, l. 40, manuscript H: "Wat salic van u zinghen (spreken L, denken W) meer?" [What else should I sing (speak L, contemplate W) about you?] (emphasis added).
43. See the discussion of singing of and meditation on songs in the Modern Devotion in Van Buuren, "Soe wie"; Joldersma and Van der Poel, "Sij singhen," 122–128; Ulrike Hascher-Burger, *Gesungene innigkeit: Studien zu einer Musikhandschrift der Devotio moderna (Utrecht, Universiteitsbibliotheek, MS 16 H 34, olim B 113)*, Studies in the History of Christian Thought 106 (Leiden: Brill, 2002), pp. 95–146 (pp. 141–146) gives a problematization of the terms *cantare*, *legere* and *dicere*.

CHAPTER 8

HANDING ON WISDOM AND
KNOWLEDGE IN HADEWIJCH OF
BRABANT'S *BOOK OF VISIONS*

Veerle Fraeters

In her *Book of Visions* Hadewijch provides the recipient with a model for reaching spiritual perfection as well as an experiential exegesis of God's Word.

Medieval collections of religious visions are usually ordered chronologically. They describe raptures experienced by the visionary between two given dates. The experiences are written down shortly after they occur by the visionary herself or by an amanuensis.[1] Unlike such collections, however, the *Book of Visions* of Hadewijch of Brabant (ca. 1250) has at the same time a more elliptic and a more purposeful design.[2] The Book consists of fourteen chapters, in which Hadewijch relates twelve visionary experiences that must have occurred over quite a lengthy period of time.[3] A remark in the closing chapter of the Book makes it clear that Hadewijch indeed selected a number of her visionary experiences at the explicit request of a friend who wanted to know as much as possible about Hadewijch's ecstatic encounters with the divine.[4] Hadewijch selected and arranged her visions in such a way that the Book reflects her personal growth toward spiritual perfection. Given the importance of the principle of imitation and modeling in medieval spiritual formation, we may safely assume that Hadewijch intended to provide the addressee with a mirror of how to become perfect "like" Hadewijch "through" Hadewijch.[5]

In the first part of this essay, by means of an analysis of the original communicative context within which the *Book of Visions* was born and operated, I will investigate the *Book of Visions* as a testimony of the personal exchange of experiential wisdom between a medieval visionary and her spiritual child. In the second part I will analyze one particular Vision in the Book. Visionary imagery is of necessity constructed from "texts"—in the widest semiotic sense of the word—present in the memory of the visionary. The memory of a well-read woman like Hadewijch, literate in Latin and well-versed in monastic reading, was filled with a considerable array of texts and images. By sharing with this friend her rapturous contemplations, Hadewijch not only constructed her own ascent to deiformity as "spiritual path," but also shared her theological knowledge.

The Book of Visions as Mimetic Mystagogy

Ascent to Perfection

Vision One relates how Hadewijch was rapt into the spiritual world while receiving the Eucharist on the Octave of Pentecost. The host was administered to her on her bed, since she had been struck down with excessive desire for Christ and was unable to attend Mass in church. In the vision, she is led by a throne-angel to contemplate God's face. Throne-angels occupy the lowest rank of the highest contemplative triad of the nine angelic choirs. According to medieval angelology, they embody the divine quality of "discernment."[6] Hadewijch is not led to the divine Countenance immediately, however. The throne-angel first leads her at length through an allegorical orchard where she is asked to identify seven allegorical trees. She is able to recognize and interpret the first six of them without hesitation, thus displaying the quality of discernment that makes her worthy of contemplation at the level of the throne-angels. The seventh tree, however, she is unable to name. She is then brought before the divine Countenance, which she first sees as three pillars rooted in one abyssal vortex, an image of the trinity that is three in nature and one in essence. Hadewijch then sees Christ's face, which she describes as handsome and whose head was surrounded "with curly hair, white in color."[7] Thereupon Christ addresses her in a lengthy manner, pointing out to her two shortcomings that currently hinder her similitude to him. First, she sometimes judges others, thereby wrongly assuming His place as judge. Second, she sometimes longs for rapture and ecstatic unitive experiences with God as a release from her suffering in the world; in so doing she fails to fully adopt the imitation of the passion of Christ as Man. These dissimilitudes are the reason she cannot name the seventh tree herself.

Christ then proceeds to reveal the name of this tree to her Himself: it is "knowledge of love."[8]

The last ecstatic vision rendered in the Book, Vision Thirteen, relates how Hadewijch is led to the divine Countenance by an angelic guide, which is identified as a seraph. The seraph belongs to the highest angel-choir and enjoys closest proximity to God. According to the angelology developed in the school of Saint-Victor, the writings of which had an influence upon Hadewijch, the seraph possesses "full knowledge of love."[9] In her vision Hadewijch hears the seraph cry out with a loud voice: "See here the new secret heaven, which is closed to all those who never were God's mother with perfect motherhood."[10] This new heaven is then opened and Hadewijch sees "that Countenance of God with which he will satisfy all the saints and all men for the full length of his eternity"[11]; in other words: she witnesses the eschatological beatific vision. The Countenance is sealed by six wings that are opened up for her in pairs of two. Through the two central wings, the two uppermost and the two lowermost she witnesses three types of perfect seraphic souls taking their places and praising God.[12] In the eye of the Countenance she sees Queen Love sitting on her throne, adorned magnificently. The angel then proceeds to invite Hadewijch to compare her own dress with that of Love. The appearance of Hadewijch's dress is not specified here but the reader will remember how in the previous Vision, Vision Twelve, Hadewijch saw herself as the mystical bride wearing a beautiful gown woven of the perfect possession of twelve virtues. In Vision Thirteen, Hadewijch compares her adornments to those of Queen Love and she discovers they are identical.[13]

Vision Thirteen clearly mirrors Vision One by constituting its fulfillment: while in Vision One Hadewijch could not name the tree of full knowledge of Love, in Vision Thirteen she is ready to see Love, personified as a Lady Queen, and to sit next to her. Not only does she see Love from such a close proximity that she can distinguish all the adornments (read: virtues) that belong to her, she also sees herself as being a perfectly adorned mirror image of Love. While in Vision One, she enjoyed contemplation at the level of the throne-angels, in Vision Thirteen she has reached the level of the seraph, which she defines in the closing chapter of the book as "her" choir to which she was chosen.[14] While in Vision One Christ had pointed out her remaining dissimilitude, in Vision Thirteen, she is able to witness her own similitude to Love/Christ. This brief comparison between the first and last visions in the collection, Visions One and Thirteen, makes clear that Hadewijch's *Book of Visions* reflects in its design her personal growth from someone as yet not fully grown or familiar with "the way of Love," into a perfect deiform soul who knows, and *is*, Love.

Visionary Experience as Transformational Tool

According to Hadewijch, it is the visionary experience itself that has worked this transformation from spiritual immaturity to spiritual perfection, as she points out in the closing chapter of the Book, Chapter Fourteen. This text does not report an individual vision, but contains a number of reflections by the author about her visionary encounters with the divine. Hadewijch also formulates her views about the nature and the pragmatics of visionary experiences. She says:

> I saw three times that unbearably beautiful Countenance of our Love, who is all, and each time the Countenance had a different form, corresponding to the different gifts that he bestowed on me each time. Each time then and always I received new gifts, which made known to me how far I had then advanced, and to what stages of development I had been raised.[15]

From this passage it is clear that Hadewijch perceived the visions she received as divine graces that progressively worked her transformation toward spiritual perfection. A little further on, she specifies that the visions also functioned as mirrors in which she could discover to what degree her soul had become a perfect image of God: "For each revelation, I had seen partly according to what I was myself, and partly according to my having been chosen."[16]

In Vision Thirteen she can, at last, see herself as the perfect deiform soul she was from the outset chosen to be:

> all the other revelations were nothing in comparison with the Countenance of our Beloved which I perceived on the new throne...but now I saw this and I was associated also with my choir, to which I was chosen in order that I might taste Man and God in one knowledge, what no man could do unless he were as God, and wholly such as he was who is our Love.[17]

She explains that Vision Thirteen gave her a "new power...which [she] did not possess previously," namely, "the strength of his own Being, to be God with my sufferings according to his example and in union with him, as he was for me when he lived for me as Man."[18] Like Christ, Hadewijch has come to the point where she is able to die from love to humanity [caritas]. Her *imitatio Christi* has reached completion, or, in her own terms: she has integrated Christ's "example" to the degree of "being in union with him."[19] The *Book of Visions* thus closes at the point where Hadewijch has become fully conscious of her spiritual perfection, and where, consequently, she is ready to answer and take up her salvational vocation.

Salvational Vocation

The theme of taking up the role of *exemplum* for others is an important motif throughout the *Book of Visions*. In Vision Eight, Hadewijch sees herself reaching the top of a mountain from where she contemplates the divine Countenance that then orders her "to guide those without guidance to the point they become one with us" ("us" meaning "God, Hadewijch and the perfect").[20] This salvational task as "path for others" is confirmed in Vision Ten. In this vision an evangelist addresses Hadewijch and informs her that through her immanent mystical marriage with God, those called to reach perfection but as yet lost in despair, will be saved.[21] God thereupon addresses Hadewijch as his "bride and mother."[22]

The theme is further elaborated upon in Vision Thirteen. After having witnessed the community of the perfect seraphic souls praising the six-winged divine countenance, Hadewijch is addressed by Mary. Mary invites her to use the three adornments (the three ways of being perfect at this level, corresponding to the three pairs of seraphic wings) to taste the fullness of God in his unity. Hadewijch thereupon experiences a wondrous mystical union so fulfilling that she wants to remain sitting on her throne in the seraphic choir forever contemplating God. She does not want to return to earthly life, at which point Mary reminds her of her vocation:

> "See, if you wish to have ampler fruition, as I have, you must leave your sweet body here. But for the sake of those whom you have chosen to become full-grown with you in this, but who are not yet full-grown, and above all for the sake of those whom you love most, you will yet defer it."[23]

Apart from helping her to reach spiritual perfection, the visionary experiences obviously have also been instrumental in making Hadewijch aware of her salvational vocation and one of the ways in which she responded to that vocation was to write her visions down.

In Chapter Fourteen Hadewijch describes the woman for whom she wrote down some of her visions as being "a child" who despairs of reaching spiritual perfection.[24] As we have seen, Hadewijch, in the opening lines of the Book, referred to herself as "child."[25] This allows the addressee to identify with the as yet imperfect mistress at the beginning of the *Book of Visions*. By reading through the following Visions with mimetic intention, the Book gives this woman the possibility to meditate upon and even integrate the graces her mistress received during her visionary encounters with the divine. Reading with imitative intent allows the spiritual child, through the example of her mistress, to attain the spiritual perfection of her calling. The *Book of Visions* therefore operates as a potential force propelling the child into perfection via the model of the mistress.

In this way, Hadewijch's written Visions function as an agent in a mystagogic project aimed at stimulating spiritual perfection. The pragmatics within this process mirror that of the primary visionary experience. The dynamics of love at work between Hadewijch's soul and its divine lover Christ generated the visionary experience. The exchange of words and images that took place between the two during the raptures have given the visionary the possibility to see herself reflected in the face of her Beloved. This has allowed her to gain self-knowledge and to model herself into a perfect *imago Dei*. A similar process is also at work between the mistress and the spiritual child. The dynamics of love between the two has generated the written *Book of Visions*. The words and images it contains reassure the addressee that her mistress will guide her on her way to spiritual perfection and allow her to shape herself, through the mistress's example, into a deiform soul.

The Book of Visions as Experiential Hermeneutics

Medieval religious visions are not naive renderings of spontaneous experiences. Like most thirteenth-century ecstatic visionaries, Hadewijch experienced her raptures within the sacral space of the church,[26] and "within" the words and rituals of the liturgy in which she participated with intense personal devotion.[27] The textual articulation of her ecstatic experiences will therefore reflect this liturgical setting and the practice of meditation in which she was engaged. In Hadewijch's case, the textual and thematic relation between the specific liturgical feast and the vision experienced is less literate than is the case in, for example, the revelations of the Helfta nuns.[28] Yet, deeper analysis of individual visions in Hadewijch's *Book of Visions* has disclosed revealing parallels between the liturgical setting on the one hand and the theme and imagery of the text on the other.[29]

Hadewijch's visions are contemplative in nature: in every vision she is transported to God's throne and sees, in one form or another, the Countenance of the One sitting upon that throne. God is essentially invisible and imageless. In a visionary experience he is thought to reveal himself in visual and auditory "clothing" that can be received by the inner senses of the visionary. For such a revelation to work, this clothing must be constructed from texts and images present in the *imaginatio* of the visionary. The memory of a well-read woman such as Hadewijch, literate in Latin and well-versed in monastic reading, was filled with a considerable array of texts and images. Consequently, her Visions are pregnant with intertextual references with theological bearing.

In order to illustrate this, I will now move on from the macro-level of the Book and the pragmatics of its communicative context, to the micro-level of one individual text and the concrete words and images from which it is woven, using Vision Nine to argue my case. It is a rather short text and, unlike some of the other Visions in the Book, its imagery is quite easy to convey. I have demonstrated elsewhere that Hadewijch structured her Visions in a clear and consistent way and Vision Nine is no exception.[30] It consists of three parts: first, the author briefly describes the spacio-temporal setting within which the visionary experience took place; second, the author indicates that her attention is drawn inward, following which she finds herself "in the spirit" where she perceives with the inner senses of her soul. In Hadewijch's *Book of Visions* this section is usually divided into two: she first describes what she sees and hears (*visio* and *auditio*); she then is asked by one of the heavenly inhabitants whom she has met (an angel, Christ, Mary) to interpret what she has seen and thus to reveal the spiritual meaning of the vision (*revelatio*). In Vision Nine, she sees a queen with three maidens. At the queen's request, she identifies this queen as her soul and, more particularly, her faculty of reason; the three maidens she identifies as the virtues with which her rational soul is invested: fear of the Lord, discernment, and wisdom. Finally, and this is the third part of Vision Nine, Hadewijch describes how the vision of Lady Reason fades and makes way for Lady Love who embraces her. At this very point, vision makes way for union: Hadewijch "falls out of the spirit" and she experiences an ineffable mystical union with the divine Beloved, *verdronken* [drowned], as she says, "with unspeakable wonders."[31]

Vision Nine

Vision Nine is set on the matins of the Nativity of Mary, that is, September 8. Hadewijch mentions being engaged in an affective meditation on the opening lines of the Song of Songs (Cant. 1–10), which are being read during the first nocturne of the matins of that day:

> I was at Matins on the feast *In nativitate beatae Mariae*, and after the Third Lesson something wonderful was shown me in the spirit. My heart had been moved beforehand by the words of love that were read there from the Song of Songs, by which I was led to think of a perfect kiss.[32]

This affective meditation on the Word of God causes her to be transported out of the visible world into the spiritual realm. There, "in the spirit" (cf. Apoc. 1.10: *fui in spiritu*), "something wonderful was shown" to her.³³ Hadewijch then gives an account of what she has perceived with the "senses of her soul." She sees a queen appear with three maidens in tow.

> Shortly afterwards, in the Second Nocturn, I saw in the spirit a queen come in, clad in a gold dress; and her dress was all full of eyes; and all the eyes were completely transparent, like fiery flames, and nevertheless like crystal. And the crown she wore on her head had as many crowns one above another as there were eyes in her dress; you shall hear the number when she herself declares it. Before the queen walked three maidens.³⁴

The broad outline of this image—a queen clad in golden robe, accompanied by maidens—is obviously informed by the words of the psalm read during the second nocturne of the matins of that day, that is, Psalm 44 (45):10–16:

> Adstitit regina a dextris tuis in vestitu deaurato: circumdata varietate. Audi, filia, et vide, et inclina aurem tuam: et obliviscere populum tuum et domum patris tui. Et concupiscet Rex decorem tuum: quoniam ipse est Dominus Deus tuus, et adorabunt eum. Et filiae Tyri in muneribus vultum tuum deprecabuntur omnes divites plebis. Omnis gloria ejus filiae Regis ab intus, in fimbriis aureis circumamicta varietatibus. Adducentur Regi virgines post eam: proximae ejus afferentur tibi. Afferentur in laetitia et exsultatione: adducentur in templum Regis.³⁵

> [The queen stood on thy right hand, in gilded clothing; surrounded with variety. Hearken, O daughter, and see, and incline thy ear: and forget thy people and thy father's house. And the king shall greatly desire thy beauty; for he is the Lord thy God, and him they shall adore. And the daughters of Tyre with gifts, yea, all the rich among the people, shall entreat thy countenance. All the glory of the king's daughter is within in golden borders, clothed round about with varieties. After her shall virgins be brought to the king: her neighbours shall be brought to thee. They shall be brought with gladness and rejoicing: they shall be brought into the temple of the king.]

Yet, the queen in Hadewijch's vision has several pictorial peculiarities that are not accounted for by Psalm 44. These must have been formed from other elements within the liturgical setting or from other material, textual or visual, present in Hadewijch's memory.

The golden robe of the queen is thickly studded with eyes. This image calls up the cherubim that, in medieval iconography, are represented as creatures with many-eyed wings.³⁶ As the second rank in the highest triad of contemplative angels, they specifically represent enlightened reason, or full knowledge of God.³⁷ This is, according to the allegoresis given toward the end of the Vision, exactly what the queen represents: Hadewijch's own enlightened faculty of reason.[38] Her reason being enlightened, Hadewijch can contemplate from the level of the cherubim. She has transcended the level of the thrones (discretion, cf. Vision One), and has moved one step closer toward the choir of the seraphim (burning love; Vision Thirteen) to which she essentially belongs.

The woman covered with eyes also calls up a well-known image in Hildegard of Bingen's *Scivias*.[39] There the woman covered with eyes is *Timor Dei*, Fear of God, which, in Hadewijch's text, is the name of the first maiden serving Queen Reason. Hadewijch may very well have known *Scivias*. In the *List of the perfect*, an appendix to the *Book of Visions* in which Hadewijch sums up all those who, according to her knowledge, have reached the highest degree of spiritual perfection, a "Hildegard who saw all those visions" is listed.[40] It is therefore not unlikely that the representation of the queen of Psalm 44 as someone covered with eyes was influenced by the visionary image of Hildegard that was present in Hadewijch's *imaginatio*.[41]

In Hadewijch's vision, though, the image of eyes on the golden robe of the Queen is described in more detail: they are said to be both "penetrating as fiery flames" and "clear as crystal."[42] This paradoxal imagery is likely to have been informed by the description of the court of the Heavenly Jerusalem in Revelation (Rev. 4:4–6), a passage in which the word-cluster "eyes—fiery—crystal" occurs:

> et throno procedunt fulgura et voces et tonitrua et septem lampadas *ardentes* ante thronum quae sunt septem spiritus Dei et in conspectu sedis tamquam mare vitreum simile *cristallo* et in medio sedis et in circuitu sedis quattuor animalia *plena oculis* ante et retro.[43]
>
> [And round about the throne were four and twenty seats: and upon the seats, four and twenty ancients sitting, clothed in white garments. And on their heads were crowns of gold. And from the throne proceeded lightnings and voices and thunders. And there were seven lamps burning before the throne, which are the seven Spirits of God. And in the sight of the throne was, as it were, a sea of glass like to crystal: and in the midst of the throne, and round about the throne, were four living creatures, full of eye before and behind.]

It is no surprise that this apocalyptic description of the Heavenly City was triggered in Hadewijch's mind while meditating on Psalm 44. In medieval exegesis, the queen in Psalm 44 was traditionally read as *Sapientia Dei* [God's Wisdom].[44] This divine figure, featuring in Genesis and in the Wisdom Books, was considered a type of Christ. Since the heavenly Jerusalem was the dwelling place of Christ/the Lamb, it was also named the House of Wisdom through this analogy between Wisdom and Christ.

The queen is further said to be wearing a crown that consists of many crowns, an image that may well have been informed by another passage from Revelation in which the expressions "fiery eyes" and "layered crown" occur together, namely, the description of Christ in glory on a white horse in Revelation 19:11–12:

> Et vidi caelum apertum et ecce equus albus et qui sedebat super eum vocabatur Fidelis et Verax vocatur et iustitia iudicat et pugnat *oculi autem eius sicut flamma ignis et in capite eius diademata multa habens.*[45]
>
> [And I saw heaven opened: and behold a white horse. And he that sat upon him was called faithful and true: and with justice doth knoweth but himself. And his eyes were as a flame of fire: and on his head were many diadems.]

Later on in the text, the queen herself informs Hadewijch of the exact number of the crowns as well as of the eyes: one thousand. According to medieval numerology, one thousand was a number of perfection. The adornments of the queen thus express that Hadewijch's own soul and, more particularly, the highest aspect of her soul, her reason, has complete possession of all virtues.

The motif of the maidens accompanying the queen is lifted straight from Psalm 44 where reference is made to "virgins who proceed along with the queen" [virgines post eam, proximae ejus afferentur tibi]. It is an image that inspired not only Hadewijch but other female authors too. In Mechthild of Magdeburg's *Das Fliessende Licht der Gottheit* the combination of "bride or queen with various maidservants" occurs more than once.[46] Similarly, in Mechthild the queen also refers to a quality of the soul (wisdom or love) while the girls (now three, now seven, now twelve) stand for virtues interiorized by the soul. Like the eyes and crown, the girls, therefore, point toward the realization of virtues by the queen/soul. In the allegoresis of Vision Nine Hadewijch specifies the virtues: the girl in a red dress stands for *timor Dei* [fear of God], the second in green for *discretio* [discretion], and the last in black for *sapientia* [wisdom]. These all concern virtues normally subsumed under gifts of the Holy Spirit (Isa. 11:2).

Hadewijch does more than specify the color of the girls' dresses, however; she gives each figure a detailed allegorical character with their attributes and activities. Thus the maiden in red (*timor Dei*) carries two trumpets. The trumpet is an attribute that, in line with Revelation (Rev. 1:9; 1:10; 4:1; 5:2), occurs more often in Hadewijch's Visions. It is usually blown by the angel or eagle that guides Hadewijch through the spiritual realm in order to forcefully demand attention from the spirits. Here in Vision Nine, this conventional attribute is split into two: like the double-edged sword of Revelation 1:16, the voice predicts a judgment that is formulated positively as well as negatively. The one trumpet is like a left hand striking and announces that whoever is deaf to Dame Reason will be deaf in eternity to bliss and thus never hear the highest harmony nor experience the wonders of overwhelming love. The other trumpet, a saving right hand, announces that whoever will follow Dame Reason will rule over the realm of Love. By this declaration the central mystical theme of Vision Nine is introduced: the relation between reason and love.

The second maiden in green (*discretio*) carries a palm branch in each hand "sealed" with a bookroll. With it, she dusts the days and nights, the sun and moon, from her mistress. The third young woman *(sapientia—caritas)* carries a black mantle and a "lantern of daylight" with which she can fathom the lowest depth and highest height.[47] As we saw earlier, medieval exegesis placed *Sapientia Dei* in the heart of the heavenly Jerusalem. The lamp therefore is immediately evocative of the lamp of Revelation 21:23, a text in which elements from the description of the second maiden also find echo: "et civitas non eget sole neque luna (cf. the second maiden) ut luceant in ea nam claritas Dei inluminavit eam et lucerna eius (cf. third maiden) est agnus." [And the city hath no need of the sun, nor of the moon, to shine in it. For the glory of God hath enlightened it: and the Lamb is the lamp thereof.][48] *Sapientia*, the greatest light, wears black. Medieval color symbolism linked black to death. I would suggest that image of Wisdom wearing black is rooted in Hadewijch's conviction that the birth of wisdom or enlightened reason implies the death of intellect or common reason. This theme was developed by the monastic writers Cistercian and Victorine with whose thoughts Hadewijch was familiar. In the Victorine tradition, and especially in the works of Thomas Gallus and Richard of Saint-Victor, the highest form of contemplation is "above reason" and implies "unknowing."[49] These writers, like Hadewijch, link different levels of contemplation to the different ranks of the angelic hierarchy. After having acquired the full knowledge of God belonging to the cherubim, the soul should move further by giving up reason and becoming, like Christ himself, a seraphic soul burning with love.

Revelation

In the Middle Ages a vision "in the spirit" [*visio spiritualis*], was considered to have little value in itself: it could be inspired by demons or be pure fantasies.[50] What mattered were not the images seen, but the divine message understood. The point of vision was not sight, but insight. Its function was the revelation of divine truth divulged through images. In accordance with this view, each of Hadewijch's visions contains a passage elaborating on the revelatory meaning of what was seen. In Vision Nine the passage from *visio* to *revelatio* is marked by an arresting image: that of the queen racing toward Hadewijch, putting her foot on her throat and asking "Do you know who I am?"[51]

The queen puts her foot on Hadewijch's throat. The description implies a vanquished Hadewijch, supine "beneath the feet" [*sub pedibus*] of her victor.[52] This image may well mimic the famous one of Mary, or another figure like Ecclesia, crushing the serpent (i.e., Eve, or more generally the devil) beneath her heel. The image clarifies that, in Hadewijch, all bodily impulses are subject to the highest power of the human soul, namely enlightened reason. To the direct question "Do you know who I am?" Hadewijch can answer without hesitation: "You are my soul's faculty of reason."[53] And the three maidens, too, she can identify without hesitation: they "are the officials of my own household,"[54] meaning that they are the virtues with which her rational soul is adorned.

In her translation of Hadewijch's works Columba Hart infers a textual interplay on the part of the author with Boethius' *Consolatio philosophiae* at this point. "Agnoscisne me? quid taces? pudore an stupore siluisti?" [Do you not recognize me? Why are you silent? Is it shame or is it astonishment that keeps you silent?] says Philosophia mockingly to a pitiful Boethius.[55] Here I would concur with Hart's intimation and suggest that intertextuality with Boethius is indeed at play—a link that is less surprising than one may think. The Carolingian miniaturists, looking for a model according to which they could represent the biblical *Sapientia Dei* in the miniatures opening the Books of Wisdom, resorted to the description of Philosophia in Boethius' *De consolatione philosophiae*.[56] In this intertextual play it is important that Hadewijch, illuminated by the lantern of Wisdom (unlike Boethius who does not know what to say), has a ready answer. And I suspect also a second allusion to Boethius lies in the description of the second maiden, the one symbolizing the virtue of discretion, who is described as holding a palm branch and a book with which she is said "to dust the days and nights, the sun and moon from her mistress." This description recalls the opening lines of *Consolatio Philosophiae* in which Philosophy, carrying a scepter and a book, appears to Boethius. Of her dress it is said that it is covered with dust.[57] Again, the contrast evoked by the intertextual play is telling. Boethius' powers of reason are troubled and therefore the beautiful robe of Philosophia (his rational soul) is dirty. In contrast, Hadewijch's rational faculty functions perfectly: by possessing the virtue of discretion she is able the keep the robe of Queen Reason dust-free.

At the end of Vision Nine, Queen Reason confirms the analysis Hadewijch has made and she then formulates the revelation of the vision: "It is true, with this eye-covered dress you yourself are adorned, and you have clothed me with heavenly glory."[58] The message is clear: Hadewijch's *anima rationalis* [rational soul] has fully absorbed God's Wisdom. After Queen Reason's declaration that Hadewijch is in perfect possession of Wisdom, she cedes before Love and Hadewijch is taken up, outside of the spirit/mind, into the mystical union with her Beloved where she can dwell for a while amidst "unspeakable wonders." Fully in line with Victorine thought on contemplation, the enlightenment of reason implies the transcendence of cherubic intellect by seraphic love.[59]

This analysis of Vision Nine makes clear that the *Book of Visions* is in fact an alternative form of experiential scriptural exegesis. Hadewijch's affective meditation during the reading of the opening lines of Psalm 44 brings her into rapture. In the course of that rapture the hidden sense of the scriptural text is revealed to her in a visual way. The various elements comprising the visionary images and phrases point to texts and ideas that were triggered in Hadewijch's memory and that were in one way or another connected in her mind to that liturgical text. The written report of her ecstatic experience can then function, for Hadewijch's devotee(s), as an exegetical initiation into God's truth. The colorful apparition of Queen Reason and her three ladies is a devotional image, what the Germans call an *Andachtsbild*, that was able to bring to consciousness those texts and images that Hadewijch's vision called up and that may have been latent in their own memories as well: *Sapientia*, Revelation, the House of Wisdom, Mary, Philosophia, the Consolation of Philosophy. And by meditating on the vision, the reader could, like Hadewijch during the primary visionary experience, become aware of the fact that *Sapientia Dei* resided inside their very own souls, and that it was their task to let it dwell there as queen, unhindered.

Conclusion

By handing over to her spiritual child, the *Book of Visions*, which maps her own spiritual ascent, Hadewijch provided her followers with a model for reaching perfection. Since the phrasing and imagery of each vision is rich with intertextual dialogue, the *Book of Visions* carries a plethora of intellectual knowledge as well. The transference of this experiential wisdom and intellectual knowledge is, in Hadewijch's case, distinguished by a dual immediacy. There is a direct line, first from God to Hadewijch and second, from Hadewijch to her spiritual child(ren). The first immediacy concerns the core of any visionary communication, and Hadewijch therefore shares it with all other (women) visionaries. On the other hand, the immediacy with which, in the case of Hadewijch, knowledge is transferred from a female author to her intended public, is unusual. There's no trace of clerical intervention, whether it be supportive or restrictive, unlike in the case of other female mystics such as Hildegard of Bingen, Mechthild of Magdeburg, Marguerite Porete,[60] Elisabeth of Schönau, Margery Kempe who found, or actively sought, clerical backing before spreading their writings. Women who wanted their voices to be heard outside the private circle, whether out of personal vocation or through the encouragement of a religious mentor, needed clerical authorization.[61] It would seem that Hadewijch herself abstained from preaching publicly by means of voice or text, and that she intended her texts to be consumed only within the small circle of elected souls of whom she was the mistress.[62] This allowed her to freely and directly transfer her experiential and intellectual knowledge directly to the women of her circle.

Notes

1. The *Liber visionum* of Elisabeth of Schönau and the collections of the Helfta-nuns provide good examples: F. Roth, ed., *Die Visionen der hl. Elisabeth und die Schriften der Äbte Ekbert und Emecho von Schönau* (Brünn: Verlag der Studien aus dem Benedictiner- und Cistercienser-Orden, 1884); L. Paquelin O.S.B., ed., *Revelationes Gertrudianae et Mechtildianae* (Paris/Poitiers, 1877–1885), vol. 1 and 2. A good overview of the medieval (religious) visionary literature in: Elizabeth Avilda Petroff, *Medieval Women's Visionary Literature* (New York: Oxford University Press, 1986); Peter Dinzelbacher, *Mittelalterliche Visionsliteratur: Eine Anthologie* (Darmstatt: Wissenschaftliche Buchgesellschaft, 1989).
2. Editions of the Middle Dutch text: Hadewijch of Brabant, *De visioenen van Hadewych*, ed. Jozef Van Mierlo, 2 vols (Louvain: De Vlaamsche Boekenhalle, 1924–1925). The latest edition, to which I will mostly refer, is by Frank Willaert, ed., *Visioenen*, trans. Imme Dros, Nederlandse klassieken 8 (Amsterdam: Prometheus/Bert Bakker, 1996) [Henceforth: ed. Willaert with page number]. When I quote Hadewijch, I refer to the English translation: Hadewijch of Brabant, *The Complete Works*, trans. and introd. Columba Hart, O.S.B. (New York: Paulist Press, 1980) [Henceforth: trans. with page number]. Hadewijch practised other mystagogic genres as well. She is the author of forty-five Mystical Songs, thirty-five Prose Letters, and at least sixteen Rhymed Letters (or Poems in Couplets). As a

historical figure Hadewijch has left no trace whatsoever. The contents and style of her work suggest a dating around the middle of the thirteenth century. Wybren Scheepsma has recently suggested a later date for Hadewijch, namely the early fourteenth century: Scheepsma, "Hadewijch und die 'Limburgse sermoenen'. Überlegungen zu Datierung, Identität und Authentizität," in *Deutsche Mystik im abendländischen Zusammenhang: neu erschlossene Texte, neue methodische Ansätze, neue theoretische Konzepte*, ed. Walter Haug and Wolfram Schneider-Lastin (Tübingen: Niemeyer, 2000), pp. 653–682. The arguments for his hypothesis are not convincing. I therefore stick to the *communis opinio*, i.e., "active around 1250."

3. Hadewijch, *De visioenen*, 2:50–56; Willaert, *Visioenen*, pp. 18–20.
4. Chapter 14, ll. 118–124 in Hadewijch, *De visioenen*, chap. 14.1:163–164 [154–167]; Hadewijch, *Complete works*, p. 304. Since Van Mierlo's edition in 1924–1925, Hadewijch-scholarship has entitled each of the fourteen chapters as "Vision 1, Vision 2, and so on." However, the Book contains only twelve reports of visionary experiences: "chapters/visions" 7 and 8 represent one experience and "chapter/vision" 14 is not a report of a singular ecstatic experience but rather a concluding reflection by Hadewijch on her visionary experiences as a whole. For the sake of tradition and for easy cross-referencing, in this essay I will use the conventional titles (Vision 1, Vision 2...), except for Vision 14, which I will refer to as "Chapter 14." References to a visionary experience will be rendered "vision," while references to visions within a written visionary text will appear as "Vision."
5. On the mystagogical function of Hadewijch's *Book of Visions*, see Frank Willaert, "Hadewijch und ihr Kreis in den Visionen," in *Abendländische Mystik im Mittelalter. Symposion Kloster Engelberg 1984*, ed. Kurt Ruh (Stuttgart: Metzler, 1986), pp. 368–387; Gerald Hofmann, *Hadewijch, Das Buch der Visionen*, 2 vols (Stuttgart—Bad Cannstatt: Frommann-Holzboog, 1998), 1:26–27; Veerle Fraeters, "Visioenen als literaire mystagogie. Stand van zaken en nieuwe inzichten over intentie en functie van Hadewijchs Visioenen,"*Ons Geestelijk Erf* 73 (1999): 111–130. On the importance of the principle of imitation in medieval spiritual formation, see C. Stephen Jaeger, *The Envy of Angels: Cathedral Schools and Social Identity in Medieval Europe, 950–1200* (Philadelphia: University of Pennsylvania Press, 1994), pp. 258–262; Anneke B. Mulder-Bakker, *Seeing and Knowing: Women and Learning in Medieval Europe 1200–1550* (Turnhout: Brepols, 2004), pp. 12–16.
6. Vision 1.29–30, ed Willaert, p. 32; trans., p. 263: "He who guided me was an Angel belonging to the choir of Thrones, the very ones who are charged with discernment"; Pseudo-Dionysius Areopagita, "Celestial Hierarchy," in *Pseudo-Dionysius: The Complete Works*, ed. Paul Rorem, trans. Colm Luibheid (New York: Paulist Press, 1987), pp. 143–191; medieval commentaries on Dionysius in Steven Chase, ed., *Angelic Spirituality: Medieval Perspectives on the Ways of Angels* (New York: Paulist Press, 2002), pp. 159–250.
7. Vision 1.248–50, ed. Willaert, p. 44; trans., p. 267.
8. Vision 1.405, ed. Willaert, p. 54; trans., p. 270.

9. Steven Chase, *Contemplation and Compassion: The Victorine Tradition*, Traditions of Christian Spirituality Series (Maryknoll, NY: Orbis Books, 2003), p. 92 (Richard of Saint-Victor) and p. 95 (Thomas Gallus).
10. Vision 13.16–18, ed. Willaert, p. 124; trans., p. 297.
11. Vision 13.25–28, ed. Willaert, p. 124; trans., p. 297.
12. The image of the six-winged angel is a traditional one. It goes back to Isaiah 6. In the spiritual writings of the school of Saint-Victor the six-winged cherub or seraph was a standard mnemonic symbol; see Chase, *Angelic Spirituality*, pp. 31–35; Steven Chase, *Angelic Wisdom: The Cherubim and the Grace of Contemplation in Richard of St. Victor* (Notre Dame: University of Notre Dame Press, 1995); [Alan of Lille], *On the Six Wings of the Seraph*, in *The Medieval Craft of Memory. An Anthology of Texts and Pictures*, ed. Mary Carruthers and Jan M. Ziolkowski (Philadelphia: University of Pennsylvania Press, 2002), pp. 83–102.
13. Chapter 14.109–124, ed. Willaert, p. 146; trans., p. 299: "Then he said: 'Behold, all these attributes of Love are better known to you than to me. For you, mother of Love, have looked upon these three hidden states, which you see in the Countenance of Love. We see it in the service with which we serve you, in wonder. But you see it, and you will see it, in clear reason and understanding, as a human being. Now contemplate and possess from henceforward this whole kingdom, which you see that Love possesses here. Then contemplate these three adorned states and the high song of praise that gives so much bliss. In all these three, contemplate and find yourself, but nevertheless possess yourself here wholly and adorned with the totality of the virtues with which you see Love adorned.' When I considered this, I realized it was so."
14. Chapter 14.160–162, ed. Willaert, p. 148; trans., p. 305.
15. Chapter 14.126–133, ed. Willaert, p. 146; trans., p. 304.
16. Chapter 14.158–160, ed. Willaert, p. 148; trans., p. 305.
17. Chapter 14.158–165, ed. Willaert, p. 128; trans., p. 305.
18. Chapter 14.11–16, ed. Willaert, p. 140; trans., p. 302.
19. Chapter 14.14–15, ed. Willaert, p. 140; trans., p. 302.
20. Vision 8.88–108, ed. Willaert, p. 88; trans., p. 284: "And because you have knowledge of this in the sanctity of us both, now be holy in us; and all who come to us and have knowledge of it through you shall at least be holy! Till they are so unified that they know you in this highest way above all things...Lead all the unled according to their worthiness, in which they are loved by me and with which they love and serve me according to my Nature."
21. Vision 10.45–53, ed. Willaert, p. 98; trans., p. 288: "Moreover all the living, both of heaven and earth, shall renew their life in this marriage. The dead sinners—who have come without hope, and are enlightened by the knowledge of your union, and desire grace or entrance into purgatory—cling somewhat to virtue and are not altogether naked. If only they believe in the oneness of you both, they will find full contentment through your marriage."

22. Vision 10.59, ed. Willaert, p. 98; trans., p. 288.
23. Vision 13.241–246, ed. Willaert, p. 136; trans., p. 301.
24. Chapter 14.63, ed. Willaert, p. 142; trans., p. 303.
25. Vision 1.9, ed. Willaert, p. 32; trans., p. 263: "I was still too childish."
26. If a vision occurred outside this framework, the author explicitly mentions it. The unknown author of the *Life of Beatrice*, a contemporary of Hadewijch, mentions that she had fled from the church to her cell and received a vision there: *Beatrice of Nazareth and the thirteenth-century mulieres religiosae of the Low Countries: a three volume study*, ed. and trans. Roger de Ganck, 3 vols, Cistercian Fathers series 50 (Kalamazoo, Mich.: Cistercian Publications, 1991), p. 207, ll. 35–38. Vision 1 in Hadewijch's *Book of Visions* opens with the statement that Hadewijch, because of madness of love, could not go out; she was given the host in her bed where a vision appeared to her, Vision 1.1–7, ed. Willaert, p. 32; trans., p. 263.
27. On the tight link between late-medieval visions and the liturgy, see Ernst Benz, *Die Vision: Erfahrungsformen und Bilderwelt* (Stuttgart: Klett, 1969), pp. 467–480; Peter Dinzelbacher, *Mittelalterliche Frauenmystik* (Paderborn: Schöningh, 1993); Jeffrey Hamburger, *The Rothschild Canticles: Art and Mysticism in Flanders and the Rhineland circa 1300* (New Haven, Conn: Yale University Press, 1991); Sabine B. Spitzlei, *Erfahrungsraum Herz: Zur Mystik des Zisterzienserinnenklosters Helfta im 13. Jahrhundert* (Stuttgart-Bad Cannstatt: Frommann-Holzboog, 1990), pp. 62–80; Otto Langer, "Zum Begriff der Erfahrung in der mittelalterlichen Frauenmystik," in *Religiöse Erfahrung: Historische Modelle in christlicher Tradition*, ed. Walter Haug and Dietmar Mieth (Munich: Fink, 1992), pp. 229–246; Barbara Newman, "What Did It Mean to Say 'I Saw'? The Clash between Theory and Practice in Medieval Visionary Culture," *Speculum* 80:1 (2005): 1–44. See also the contribution of Anneke Mulder-Bakker on the visionaries Juliana of Cornillon and Agnes Blannbekin, whose raptures occurred while praying the divine office.
28. For more on this topic, see Veerle Fraeters, "Gender and Genre: The Design of Hadewijch's Book of Visions," in *The Voice of Silence: Women's Literacy in a Men's Church*, ed. Thérèse de Hemptinne and Maria Eugenia Gongora, Medieval Church Studies 9 (Turnhout: Brepols, 2004), pp. 57–60 [57–81].
29. For an in-depth analysis of Vision 4 from this perspective, see Jacques Tersteeg "Met Hadewijch in de zevende hemel. Bijdrage tot een interpretatie van het vierde visioen," in *In de zevende hemel. Opstellen voor P.E.L. Verkuyl over literatuur en kosmos*, ed. H. van Dijk, M.H. Schenkeveld– van der Dussen, and J.M.J. Sicking (Groningen: Passage, 1993), pp. 137–146. In his commentary, Willaert has indicated per vision the relevant liturgical information: Willaert, *Visioenen* (see note 2 earlier), pp. 166–213.
30. Fraeters, "Gender and Genre," pp. 10–15.
31. Vision 9.70–71, ed. Willaert, p. 142; trans., p. 286.

32. Vision 9.1–6, ed. Willaert, p. 93; trans., p. 285.
33. In accordance with John of Patmos in the Apocalypse Hadewijch consistently uses the passive voice for this moment of transportation. The visionary is not the actor. It is God or his angelic assistants who pull the visionary up into their dwelling place, the invisible realm of the spirit.
34. Vision 9.6–16, ed. Willaert, p. 93; trans., p. 285.
35. *Biblia sacra vulgata*, Ps. 44.10:14; trans. Douay-Rheims English translation (www.latinvulgate.com).
36. Heinrich and Margaretha Schmidt, *Die Vergessene Bildersprache christlicher Kunst: ein Führer zum Verständnis der Tier-, Engel- und Mariensymbolik*, 2nd edn. (Munich: Beck, 1982), pp. 162–164.
37. Chase, *Contemplation and Compassion*, p. 91, 92.
38. Vision 9.39–41, ed. Willaert, p. 95; trans., p. 285: "'Do you know who I am?' And I said: 'Yes, indeed! Long enough have you caused me woe and pain! You are my soul's faculty of Reason.'"
39. Fig. in Lieselotte E. Saurma-Jeltsch, *Die Miniaturen im 'Liber Scivias' der Hildegard von Bingen: Die Wucht der Vision und die Ordnung der Bilder* (Wiesbaden: Reichert, 1998), pp. 36; CC 43, 7, p. 17. Hildegard of Bingen (1098–1179) was a renowned seer and prophetess and a prolific writer. She practised several literary genres (letters, visions, prophecies, a morality play, songs, a handbook on medicine). *Scivias* is her major visionary work. English translation: Hildegard of Bingen, *Scivias*, trans. Columba Hart and Jane Bishop, introduction Barbara J. Newman, preface Caroline Walker Bynum, *The Classics of Western Spirituality* (New York, NY: Paulist Press, 1990).
40. The List of the Perfect, ll. 191–192 in Willaert, *Visioenen*, p. 161: "Heldegaert die al de visione sach." In Hart's translation of the Complete Works (see note 2 earlier) this list is missing. The English translation of the list was published in 1980: Hadewijch of Brabant, "The List of the Perfect," trans. Helen Rolfson, *Vox Benedictina* 5 (1988): 277–287.
41. Joris Reynaert, *De beeldspraak van Hadewijch* (Tielt and Bussum: Lannoo, 1981), pp. 121–126.
42. Vision 9.10–11, ed. Willaert, p. 92; trans., p. 285.
43. *Biblia sacra vulgata*, Rev. 4:4–6; trans. Douay-Rheims English translation.
44. Barbara Newman, *God and the Goddesses: Vision, Poetry and Belief in the Middle Ages* (Philadelphia: University of Pennsylvania Press, 2003), pp. 13–14, and 248–250.
45. *Biblia sacra vulgata*, Rev. 19:11–12; trans. Douay-Rheims English translation.
46. Mechthild of Magdeburg, *Das fliessende Licht der Gottheit. Nach der Einsiedler Handschrift in kritischen Vergleich mit der gesamten Überlieferung*, ed. Hans Neumann, 2 vols (Munich: Artemis, 1990, 1993), 1:293–296 (Book 7, Chapter 48) and 1:306–308 (Book 7, Chapter 62). For an English translation, see Mechthild of Magdeburg, *The Flowing Light of the Godhead*, trans. and introd. Frank Tobin, *The Classics of Western Spirituality* (New York: Paulist Press, 1998).

47. Vision 9.33–34, ed. Willaert, p. 92; trans., p. 285.
48. *Biblia sacra vulgata* Rev. 21:23; trans. Douay-Rheims English translation.
49. Chase, *Contemplation and Compassion*, pp. 91, 92; see also pp. 95–96.
50. Rosalynn Voaden, "Women and Vision: The Devil's Gateway," in *God's Word, Women's Voices: Discernment of Spirits in the Writing of Late-Medieval Women Visionaries* (York: York Medieval Press, 1999), pp. 7–41. See also Mulder-Bakker's contribution to this volume.
51. Vision 9.39–40, ed. Willaert, p. 95; trans., p. 285.
52. In classical literature *sub pedibus* is a standard expression, see C.W.M. Verhoeven, *Symboliek van de voet* (Assen: Van Gorcum, 1957), p. 151.
53. Vision 9.41–42, ed. Willaert, p. 94; trans., p. 285.
54. Vision 9.42–43, ed. Willaert, p. 94; trans., p. 285.
55. 1Prose 2. 4 in: Ancius Manlius Severinus Boethius, *Philosophiae consolatio*, ed. L. Bieler, CCSL 94 (Turnhout: Brepols, 1957), p. 4.l.6; English translation: trans. VF; Boethius, *The Consolation of Philosophy*, trans. and introd. V.E. Watts, Penguin Classics (London, Penguin Books, 1969), p. 38 (giving a slightly less literal translation).
56. Gertrud Schiller, *Ikonographie der christlicher Kunst*, vol. 4, 1: Die Kirche (Gütersloh: Mohn, 1976), p. 72, ill. 167. Several examples in Marie-Thérèse d'Alverny, "La Sagesse et ses sept filles. Recherches sur les allegories de la philosophie et des arts libéraux du IXe au XIIe siècle," in *Mélanges dédiés à la mémoire de Félix Grat*, vol. 1 (Paris: Pecqueur-Grat, 1946), pp. 245–278.
57. Prosa 1; Prose 1.3, ed. Bieler, p. 2.14–16: "veluti fumosas imagines solet, caligo quaedam neglectae uestutatis obduxerat"; Boethius, *Consolation*, p. 36: "obscured by a kind of film as of long neglect, like statues covered in dust."
58. Vision 9.55–57, ed. Willaert, p. 95; trans., p. 286. Hadewijch, *Complete Works*, p. 286.
59. Chase, *Contemplation and Compassion*, chapter 2: "The Paths of Knowledge and Love," pp. 83–102.
60. Marguerite Porete, a beguine from Hainaut who was burnt at the stake in 1310, wrote, in Old French, *The Mirror of Simple Souls*; trans.: Marguerite Porete, *The Mirror of Simple Souls*, trans. and introd. Ellen L. Babinsky, pref. Robert E. Lerner, *Classics of Western Spirituality* (New York: Paulist Press, 1993).
61. Alcuin Blamires, "Women and Preaching: Medieval Orthodoxy, Heresy and Saint's Lives," *Viator. Medieval and Renaissance Studies* 26 (1995): 135–152. See also the contribution by Carolyn Muessig in this volume. The obligato clerical mentorship of visionary women is also addressed in the contributions of Anneke Mulder-Bakker on Juliana of Cornillon and Agnes Blannbekin, and Liz Herbert McAvoy on Margery Kempe.
62. The tradition of her oeuvre in three closely related manuscripts dating from the fourteenth century also points to a closed primary reception. Hadewijch's texts have hardly been fragmented or anthologized. On the

dating of the Hadewijch manuscripts, see Erik Kwakkel, "Ouderdom en genese van de veertiende-eeuwse Hadewijch-handschriften," *Queeste: Tijdschrift over middeleeuwse letterkunde in de Nederlanden* 6 (1999): 23–40; Kurt Ruh, *Geschichte der abendländischen Mystik*, 4 vols (Munich: Beck, 1990–1999), 2:161, dwells upon the peculiarities of the "closed" reception of Hadewijch's writings.

CHAPTER 9

AFTERWORD

Diane Watt

In a now famous letter, written around 1465, Agnes Paston granted forgiveness to her eldest son John following a period of strained relationships. This letter both follows convention and elaborates upon it. While Agnes's letters to her sons typically open with a greeting followed by a blessing, in this case the elaborate benediction is tied into an invocation of her husband William's death, and a reminder to her son of his responsibilities concerning William's salvation and the prosperity and health of John's brothers:

> Son, I greet you warmly and let you know that since your brother Clement tells me that you sincerely desire my blessing, may that blessing that I begged your father to give you the last day that he spoke and the blessing of all saints under heaven and mine come to you all days and times. And truthfully only believe that you have it, and you shall have it, provided that I find you kind and minded towards the well-being of your father's soul and for the welfare of your brothers.[1]

Agnes Paston would have been around sixty years old at the time of writing this letter. She was born Agnes Berry, the daughter of Sir Edmund Berry of Horwellbury, Hertfordshire. She had married William Paston I in 1420, when she was fifteen years old. From William's point of view the match was a good one as his own father had only been a minor Norfolk landowner, whereas Agnes's family had considerably more status and wealth. Working together Agnes and William succeeded in elevating the Paston family's position socially and in dramatically increasing its economic prosperity. Agnes brought property into the marriage and, on

Sir Edmund's death, she inherited yet more. William, a lawyer by profession, was appointed judge of the Common Bench in 1429. He added substantially to his own inherited landholdings by extensive purchases. Agnes can thus be seen as the first matriarch of this upwardly mobile East-Anglian family.

However, on William's death in 1444, their son John took his place as head of the family, while John's wife Margaret found herself in Agnes's former role. The transition was not an easy one, and Agnes's relations with her son became fraught, as the letter quoted earlier illustrates. A central area of contention, as Agnes's repeatedly redrafted wills indicate, was the provision made by William for their two youngest sons.[2] Agnes claimed that William had made oral addenda to his will, leaving more property to the younger sons, but that John had refused to honor this, and furthermore that following William's death, he had stolen various valuables and had even failed to arrange the perpetual masses for William's soul that his father had requested.

Yet, if Agnes's son John did not live up to her expectations of William's son and heir, if he proved, in her opinion at least, to be dishonest and self-seeking, and if he neglected his responsibilities to his kinsfolk, dead as well as alive, Agnes seems to have accepted her own replacement by Margaret well enough. Indeed, Agnes and Margaret remained close friends, with Margaret working hard to build bridges between Agnes and John. If Agnes's letters are anything to go by, Agnes embraced her position as widowed mother and mother-in-law, overseeing, albeit from a distance, the ongoing concerns of the Paston family. Alongside the drafts of her will, her letter of around 1465 illustrates, for example, that she saw herself as responsible not only for the financial security of John's brothers and for ensuring that her husband's wishes be honored, but also for preserving the memory of her husband. Indeed, as Elisabeth van Houts has illustrated, family memorization was a form of knowledge and history that was understood to fall to the remit of women.[3]

Older women, and especially widowed grandmothers such as Agnes, must have been an important source of information about family history and the history of family property. Consideration of Agnes's letter therefore fits clearly into the scope of this volume, undercutting as it does the opposition of experience, gendered feminine, and formal learning and intellectual endeavor, gendered masculine. In fact, in her wills, Agnes goes even further, adding to her detailed recollections of the events leading up to, and following William's death, and of conversations held, the specifics of the time and date of his passing: "On the Thursday night before the Feast of the Assumption of Our Lady, between 11 and 12 o'clock, in the year of our Lord 1444..."[4] In her will, Agnes wanted to compensate her youngest sons for the losses inflicted upon them by John, and as a consequence she also wanted to ensure that the final document could not be contested. In drafting and writing the will, she would of course have had professional advice, but, as the wife of a judge, she understood for herself the importance of precision in bearing witness and in her draft wills and elsewhere she reveals her knowledge and understanding of legal matters and intricacies.

Returning to the letter of around 1465, we find further evidence of Agnes's educated mind. The main body of the letter comprises a paragraph made up of gnomic wisdom that is at least partly ascribed to William:

> By my advice, prepare yourself as much as you can to have less to do in the world. Your father said, "In little work lies much rest." This world is but a thoroughfare and full of woe; and when we part from it, we take nothing with us except our good and bad deeds. And no one knows how soon God will call him, and therefore it is good for every creature to be ready. Whom God chastises, him He loves.[5]

In this passage, Agnes's own admonitory voice is joined by that of her late husband, and their separate but complimentary proverbial advice is reinforced by literary commonplace (an allusion to Egeus's speech in Chaucer's "Knight's Tale")[6] and New Testament reference (1 Tim. 6:7; Matt. 24:44; and Heb. 12:6). In itself, what we might think of as the *literariness* of this letter does not necessarily indicate that Agnes had received any formal education, or indeed that she was a keen reader of either poetry or Scripture. Agnes could certainly have been familiar with what we might think of as Biblical commonplaces simply from listening to sermons in Church, and she might not have read any Chaucer either (the line she apparently cites is proverbial enough). But other sources confirm that Agnes had been taught both to read and to write, and she evidently enjoyed rather more than what is often termed a "functional" literacy. She may even have been able to read Latin. We know from the evidence of a will that she would at one time have had in her possession a copy of the treatise *Stimulus Conscientiae,* a Latin version of the Middle-English *Prick of Conscience* (c. 1350).[7] The book was left in her care by a burgess of Great Yarmouth, until his son came of age. We might deduce from this that Agnes had an interest in the sort of devotional literature that was popular with a lay audience at the time, and that she was part of a community of discourse, in this case a network of pious readers who loaned books and shared ideas. Furthermore, there is compelling evidence that one of her letters is written in her own hand, and she is likely to be responsible for the composition and content of the rest even if she dictated them to a scribe or secretary.[8]

Agnes, whose responsibilities in overseeing and managing property were extensive both in her husband's lifetime and after his death, must certainly have learned a great deal from what the editors of this volume, following Hugh of Floreffe, term the "book of experience." Yet in the letter cited earlier, through the use of *communis sententia,* she establishes her authority over her son, an authority that is equally rooted in prudence, acumen, and memory.

Agnes Paston, unlike many of the women considered in this volume, was neither a visionary nor a religious, and she certainly did not write directly about matters of theology. Nevertheless, as both a reader of spiritual texts and a letter writer, she can be cited as a further example of the sort of medieval woman who was not "restricted to learning only from the book of experience."[9] The knowledge that she displays in her letters, like that of her "functionally" illiterate daughter-in-law Margaret (tellingly, the most prolific correspondent in the entire Paston collection), is in fact not dissimilar to that demonstrated by the men of the family, who benefited from a formal schooling that included education in the Inns of Court or at university. Once again the opposition of female experience and male learning and school training is undermined. In this respect, Agnes Paston, who spent much of her widowhood in Norwich, can usefully be compared to the women of authority discussed by Koen Goudriaan in the second chapter of this volume, illustrating further the point that in the fifteenth century a large proportion of women as well as men living in urban areas would have had access to some form of education.

The editors of this volume offer the image of "the woven cloth, a fabric made up of warp and weft" to describe the structure of society, arguing that "each society needs standing threads, the warp threads of laws and institutions, but also requires the connecting threads of conventions and traditions."[10] The editors observe that the warp threads were the preserve only of men in the Middle Ages, but that this was not so with regards to the weft threads. The usefulness of the metaphor is borne out to some extent by the examples of Agnes and the other Paston women to whom "conventions and traditions" did indeed offer opportunity, as Agnes's letter illustrates so vividly. Nevertheless, as we have also seen, they were not totally excluded from "laws and institutions," at least at a local level.

The editors of this volume also emphasize the importance of "communities of discourse" in the sharing of knowledge in informal contexts, including domestic settings.[11] Liz Herbert McAvoy, in the sixth chapter, picks up on this in examining the possible influence of the East Anglian mystic Julian of Norwich on her younger contemporary,

Margery Kempe. The two women met when Margery Kempe would have been forty and Julian of Norwich seventy. They spent some days together in conversation at Julian's anchorhold. Both women were evidently part of a larger community of the faithful, but their relationship is portrayed in *The Book of Margery Kempe* as one in which the elderly recluse mentors a younger protégée visionary, who is seeking reassurance about the validity of her revelations. If Julian of Norwich can be thought of as educating Margery Kempe through a sharing of experience and wisdom, while Margery Kempe herself also learned, at times literally, through a process of trial and error, a similar pattern can also be detected in Agnes Paston's relationship with her own daughter-in-law Margaret Paston.

What is particularly remarkable about the picture of family relationships and friendships that emerges from the Paston letters is the sheer depth and strength of the relationship between a mother and her son's wife. While the Paston letters provide often chilling evidence of the anger and hostility that mothers could harbor toward their grown-up daughters (and indeed vice versa), and of the resentments that might develop between mothers and sons, the relationship between mother-in-law and daughter-in-law was a surprisingly positive one. A clear example of this is found in Margaret Paston's letters to her husband concerning the secret marriage of their daughter Margery to the family servant Richard Calle. Margaret makes it clear that she had Agnes's full support when together they went to present their ultimately unsuccessful case for the annulment of the marriage to the Bishop of Norwich.[12] Here, mother-in-law and daughter-in-law join forces against the latter's recalcitrant daughter. In describing Margery's testimony to the bishop, in which Margery insisted on the validity of her wedding vows, Margaret comments "these foolish words grieve me and her grandmother as much as all the rest."[13]

It is not hard to see why the relationship between a mother-in-law and a daughter-in-law should work so well, given that the former often played a significant part in helping her son find a wife and negotiate the terms of the marriage. Furthermore, for some social classes, mother-in-law and daughter-in-law would often have spent as much, if not more, time in each other's company as did a husband and wife, and far more time together than a mother and her own daughter (at least after the daughter married). They would have worked together in the managing of the household and estate, and in caring for the children. And, crucially, the mother-in-law would effectively take upon herself the continuing education of the husband's new wife. Often the young wife would learn from assisting the older one. Again, to quote the editors of this volume "learning was effected by imitation."[14]

To extend this into a lay religious context, we even find Margaret Paston emulating Agnes in matters of piety. In a letter written in the early years of their marriage, Margaret told her husband about her concern for him after he had fallen sick while in London. She described how both she and Agnes had been deeply worried and had resolved to intercede with God on his behalf: "My mother promised another image of wax, of your weight, to Our Lady of Walsingham, and she sent 4 nobles to the four orders of friars at Norwich to pray for you; and I have promised to go on pilgrimage to Walshingham and to St Leonard's for you."[15] Here, as elsewhere in Margaret's letters, we get a strong sense of Margaret dutifully, and respectfully, following the example set by Agnes.

★ ★ ★

Reading the Book of Life invites us then to rethink the perceived dichotomy between male or masculine learning and female or feminine experience. Indeed it goes so far as to challenge its validity. In so doing it invites us to reconsider our very understanding of what constitutes education. As I hope to have shown through the example of Agnes Paston, a laywoman living and working in fifteenth-century England, the lessons that we can learn from this volume are not restricted to spiritual works, but can have a broader applicability. The editors of this volume also argue for an understanding of ways of writing that pays greater attention to collaboration, and especially (but not exclusively) collaborations between men and women. Again this can be applied to other texts, such as the letters of the Paston women, which were not only often written with the assistance of male scribes or secretaries, but which also have to be understood in terms of a much larger discursive community, a much larger network of readers and writers, and as part of a much more extended conversation.[16] As we have seen, Agnes's voice even merges at times with that of her late husband as she adds his favored aphorism to her own maxims. *Reading the Book of Life* invites us then to reevaluate the contribution of women not only to medieval religious discourse, but to medieval writing more broadly, and indeed to medieval culture as a whole. Indeed, *Reading the Book of Life* attributes to medieval women something that has been denied to them for far too long: "the power of discourse."[17]

Notes

1. *The Paston Women: Selected Letters*, ed. and trans. Diane Watt (Cambridge: D.S. Brewer, 2004), p. 34. All references to the Paston letters are to this translation.

2. Ibid., pp. 35–38.
3. Elisabeth van Houts, *Memory and Gender in Medieval Europe, 900–1200* (London: Macmillan, 1999), esp. pp. 65–92. Van Houts specifically discusses women as commissioners of chronicles and their contributions to genealogical tracts, but she also considers women's role in supplying information in relation to property disputes.
4. *Paston Women*, ed. and trans. Watt, p. 37.
5. Ibid., pp. 34–35.
6. Geoffrey Chaucer, "The Knight's Tale," in *The Riverside Chaucer*, ed. Larry D. Benson, third edn (Oxford: Oxford University Press, 1988), p. 63, l. 2847.
7. Colin Richmond, *The Paston Family in the Fifteenth Century: Endings* (Manchester: Manchester University Press, 2000), p. 64.
8. *Paston Women*, ed. and trans. Watt, pp. 23 and 135–136.
9. Mulder-Bakker in the introduction to this volume, p. 2.
10. Ibid., p. 9.
11. Ibid., p. 7.
12. *Paston Women*, ed. and trans. Watt, pp. 96–98.
13. Ibid., p. 97.
14. Mulder-Bakker in the introduction to this volume, p. 11.
15. *Paston Women*, ed. and trans. Watt, pp. 46–47.
16. See Diane Watt, *Medieval Women's Writing: Works By and For Women, 1100–1500* (Cambridge: Polity, 2007), pp. 13–16, 136–156, and 157–160.
17. Luce Irigaray, "The Power of Discourse and the Subordination of the Feminine," in *Literary Theory: An Anthology*, ed. Julia Rivkin and Michael Ryan (Oxford: Blackwell, 1998, repr. 2004), pp. 795–798.

CONTRIBUTORS

Veerle Fraeters studied Dutch language and literature at the Catholic University of Louvain. In 2002 she was appointed senior lecturer as an associate of the Ruusbroec Research Institute at the University of Antwerp. Her research is focused mainly on the area of medieval mysticism and she has published primarily on visionary literature and female mysticism. She is currently collaborating with Frank Willaert on a new edition with a modern Dutch translation of the complete works of Hadewijch (Historische Uitgeverij, Groningen).

Koen Goudriaan is professor of medieval history at the Vrije Universiteit at Amsterdam. His main field of interest is the cultural and religious history of the Low Countries in the Later Middle Ages. Under his direction a research project was executed on the tertiaries' convents in that area, within the wider context of the Modern Devotion.

Liz Herbert McAvoy is senior lecturer in gender in English studies and medieval literature within the English Department at Swansea University. Her research interests lie in the areas of anchoritic literature, medieval women's writing, and gender theory. She has published widely in these areas, including *The Book of Margery Kempe: An Abridged Translation* (Cambridge: D. S. Brewer, 2003) and *Authority and the Female Body in the Writings of Julian of Norwich and Margery Kempe* (Cambridge: D. S. Brewer, 2004). She has also edited a number of essay collections: (with Mari-Hughes Edwards) *Anchorites, Wombs and Tombs: Intersections of Gender and Enclosure in the Middle Ages* (Cardiff: University of Wales Press, 2005), *Rhetoric of the Anchorhold: Space, Place and Body within the Discourses of Enclosure* (Cardiff: University of Wales Press, 2008), *A Companion to Julian of Norwich* (Cambridge: D. S. Brewer, 2008). She is currently working on a monograph for D. S. Brewer that examines the intersections of gender and space within texts written by, for, or about medieval anchorites.

Thom Mertens is member of the Ruusbroec Society (Antwerp) and professor of the history of Dutch religious literature at the University of Antwerp. He is the editor of *Ons Geestelijk Erf*, a journal for the history of spirituality in The Netherlands. His research is mainly concerned with literary aspects of late medieval Dutch religious literature and editions of texts. He studied Dutch language and literature at the Katholieke Universiteit Nijmegen (Netherlands) and worked as a researcher at the university of Nijmegen. In 1985 he was appointed to the University of Antwerp.

Carolyn Muessig is senior lecturer in medieval theology at the University of Bristol. She is coeditor (with Veronica O'Mara) of the journal *Medieval Sermon Studies*. Her interests include medieval preaching, especially the sermons of Jacques de Vitry, female religious education, Catherine of Siena, and the theology of the stigmata. Most recently, she has published (with Beverly Kienzle) a critical edition of Hildegard of Bingen's Latin homilies.

Anneke B. Mulder-Bakker taught medieval history and medieval studies at the University of Groningen, The Netherlands. She is now Emerita at the University of Leiden. Her publications on historiography, hagiography, and gender include *Sanctity and Motherhood* (New York: Garland, 1995), *The Prime of Their Lives: Wise Old Women in Pre-Industrial Europe* (Louvain: Peeters, 2004), and *Lives of the Anchoresses: The Rise of the Urban Recluse in Medieval Europe* (Philadelphia: University of Pennsylvania Press, 2005).

Ineke van 't Spijker studied history at the university of Utrecht, The Netherlands. She is an independent scholar in Cambridge, where she is a life member of Clare Hall. She has written on hagiography, religious thought, and biblical exegesis of the High Middle Ages. *Fictions of the Inner Life: Religious Literature and Formation of the Self in the Eleventh and Twelfth Centuries* was published in 2004.

Diane Watt is professor of English at Aberystwyth University. She is the author of *Secretaries of God: Women Prophets in Late Medieval and Early Modern England* (Cambridge: D. S. Brewer, 1997), *Amoral Gower: Language, Sex, and Politics in Confessio Amantis* (Minneapolis: University of Minnesota Press, 2003), and *Medieval Women's Writing: Works By and For Women in England, 1100–1500* (Cambridge: Polity Press, 2007). She has also edited several volumes and has published widely on women's literature and spirituality in the Middle Ages and on Gower.

GENERAL INDEX

Note: Medieval names and topics are indexed here. Modern authors are indexed in a separate index.

Abelard (d. 1142, philosopher and theologian), 7, 47–64, 75 n2
   and conscience, 53–4
   and the *homo interior*, 15, 48, 55
   and intention, 49, 50–1, 52, 55
   letters to Heloise, 15, 47–64
   rule fit for women, 47, 48, 50, 52, 55, 56, 58
   and Scripture, 55–7
   sermons for the Paraclete, 47–8, 53, 54, 56, 57
   theory of *caritas*, 54–5
   see also companionship, male-female; experience (intellectual)
Aechte Eernstes (d. after c.1443, Utrecht), 10, 29, 33, 34, 37
   and the authorship of the *Devout Letters*, 32, 36
Aechte Willems (fl. 1417, Delft), 10, 27–8, 33, 35, 37
Agnes Blannbekin (d. 1315, mystic beguine, Vienna), 6, 15, 16, 83–101
   and the Book of Life, 84, 94–6
   collaborating with Franciscan scribe, 85
   experienced, 83
   experiencing her revelations (prophecies) in three stages, 91–2
   and her *Vita et Revelationes*, 15, 83, 91, 92, 95, 96
   as non-monastic religious woman, 9, 85
   as prophetess, 88–9
   stylizing her knowledge of the divine as personal revelations, 92, 130–1
   theological and Latin schooling of, 83, 85
   visions drawn from daily life of, 92
   see also authorship; religious culture; theologians, female; ways of acquiring knowledge
Agnes Paston (15th c.), 169–74
   and the community of discourse who loaned books and shared ideas, 171
   education and Latin literacy of, 171
   and experience, 170
   daughter-in-law following the example set by, 173–4
   and her personal letter to her son, 169–74
   knowledge and understanding of legal matters of, 171
   preserving the memory of husband and family history by, 170
Aleid Cluten (d. 1424, Utrecht), 10, 28–9, 33, 34, 35–6, 37–8, 39
Aleid Willem Busers (d. 1409, Delft), 10, 27, 32, 33, 35, 36, 38

GENERAL INDEX

Angela of Foligno (d. 1309, Franciscan tertiary), 6, 8, 65–70, 71
  authorial collaboration with Brother A., 15, 68–9, 74, 77 n26, 78 n29
  community of discourse of Angela and Brother A., 9, 14, 69
  experiencing the divine directly instead of reading Scripture, 12, 13, 16, 69
  and her *Memorial*, 65–70, 77 n25
  non-monastic religious widow, 9, 68–70
  and Ubertino of Casale, 69–70, 72
  see also authorship; companionship, male-female; theologians, female; ways of acquiring knowledge
Angelo Clareno (13th, Franciscan Spiritual), 70
Animarum Cibus (Juliana of Cornillon), 84
Arbor Vitae Crucifixe Jesu (Ubertino of Casale), 15, 68, 69
Aristotle
  concept of woman, 67, 76 n15
  Paris as the nest of, 70
Augustine (d. 430, church father), 28, 52, 54, 84, 85
authority, female, 17, 25–45, 103–21
  and age, 10, 32–3
  based on earthly motherhood, 10, 33, 109, 110, 111, 112, 114, 117
  based on studying books and teaching, 25, 36
  enhanced by the setting in which women operate, 25–6, 37–9, 71–4
  high status and wealth as a source of, 25–6, 32–3
  inside and outside their own convent, 27, 29, 38, 71–4
  religious knowledge as a source of, 13, 25, 35–7
  rooted in prudence, acumen, and memory, 172
  rooted in supernatural revelations, 25, 36–7, 64–74, 92
  and social background, 25, 39
  and virginity, 33
  and widowhood, 33
  see also women of authority; *compare* leaders, female spiritual
authority, male, 104
authorization, clerical, 8, 15
  absent in Hadewijch, 162
  in the works of female authors, 90
  see also individual authors
authorship, 68–9, 83–101, 133–4
  authorial male-female collaboration, 18, 68–9, 104
  reconstruction of 'authorial texts', 18
  see also individual authors: Agnes Blannbekin; Agnes Paston; Angela of Foligno; Eve of St. Martin; Juliana of Cornillon; Hadewijch of Brabant; Heloise; Margery Kempe; *compare* writers, medieval female

Bernard of Clairvaux (d. 1152, abbott), 7, 48, 49, 57, 75, 84, 85, 135
Book of Experience of, 11
Book of Experience, 11, 172
Book of Life, 4, 15, 17–18, 54, 83–101, 103–21
  Agnes Blannbekin and, 84, 94–6
  as book of wisdom or *vademecum* 83, 92, 100 n42, 123
  characterization of the genre, 84, 94–6
  combining life experience and writing, 16, 67, 94–6, 105, 118, 123
  full of exempla, 95–6
  Margery Kempe and, 16, 105, 107, 117–18

GENERAL INDEX

Mary of Oignies and, 4, 95
  as product of an experience-based thought style, 94, 107
  as validated male-female companionship in writing, 15, 18, 94–6
  see also exemplum
Book of Margery Kempe (Margery Kempe), 15–16, 104, 105–6, 110–11, 117–18
  Kempe's maternal and mystical experiences written into, 107
Book of Visions (Hadewijch), 16, 149–68
  as experiential scriptural exegesis, 149, 161
  a mystagogic project, 154
  reflecting Hadewijch's personal growth towards perfection, 149, 151
  stylized as the personal record of mystical experiences, 130, 149–50
Bridget of Sweden (d. 1373, mystic, founder of Birgittine order), 93
  role model for Margery Kempe, 108, 111
  prophetess, 93

Catharine of Naaldwijk (fl. 1400, New Devout), 29
Cecilia of Florence (13th c.), 68
Christina the Astonishing (d. 1224, holy woman, anchoress), 6
Christina of Markyate (d. after 1155, anchoress, prioress), 7
chronicles of female convents, 27, 28, 30–1, 32, 33, 37, 38
  as sources for female agency, 15, 27, 30–1
  women as commissioners of, 175
Clare of Assisi (c. 1193–1253, abbess), 68

Clare of Montefalco (d. 1308, anchoress and abbess), 10, 11, 15, 71–4, 79 n43
  debating with heretical theologians, 71–3
  education of, 72
  experiencing Christ's Passion in her body and receiving the symbols of the Passion in her heart, 11–12, 71
  486 witnesses in canonization process of, 10, 71
  giving spiritual advice inside and outside her monastery, 10, 71, 72–3
  responding to theological questions, 71–3
community of discourse, 5, 7–10, 21 n28, 65–81, 75 n4, 162
  in informal groups, clerical, monastic, and lay (m/f), 7–9, 14, 17–18, 25, 36, 68–70, 71, 74, 84–5, 94, 172, 173
  songs constructing a community of discourse, 131
  textual community and, 21 n31, 36, 87, 171
  see also thought world; *individual holy women*
companionship, male-female, 14, 27, 68–70
  authorial collaboration, 17, 18, 68–9, 90, 174
  of a mother and her son's wife, 173–4
  of an older woman and a younger protégée, 10, 84–5, 173
  partners in profession, 47–58, 90
  of a religious woman and a priest, 14, 15, 17, 25, 28, 34, 37–8
conscience (*conscientia*), 53–5
  and *fama*, 54
  female supervising of, 35–7
  experience represented in, 53

Consolatio Philosophiae (Boethius)
  in Hadewijch's Visions, 160

dialogues, 68–81
  alternative mode of theological
    debate or scholastic disputation,
    15, 70
  inner dialogues, 15, 92
  songs with dialogues, 129, 130, 131
  texts in dialogic form, 94–6
Die gheestelicke melody (The Spiritual
    Melody, c.1470), 123–47
  analysis of the cycle, 124–30
  communicating spiritual life
    experience, 123–4, 130, 131, 135
  directed at fellow sisters,
    125–30, 131
  first-person singer as spiritual
    leader in, 16, 123, 124, 129, 130
  a fortnightly cycle of songs, 16,
    123, 139–41
  interpretation of the cycle, 130–9
  intervening prose
    introductions to, 124
  Mary teaching the soul in, 126
  having a supplement with songs for
    the virgin martyrs Catherine of
    A., Agnes and Margaret of A.,
    124, 130
  textual simplicity and spiritual
    depth of, 16, 124, 138
  three manuscripts, three versions
    of, 16, 132–4, 139–41
  writing down and reading of orally
    transmitted, 134–8
Dirk van der Aar (fl. 1400), 38
documents, 30–2
  documentary evidence as a source
    for the study of female agency,
    15, 26, 27, 28, 30–1, 39
  womens' contribution to
    ordinances for female convents,
    27, 31, 34, 39

education, female school
  level of, 5–7, 67, 76n12, 86

in theology, 67, 90
Egbert of Schönau (12th c.
  theologian), 90
Elisabeth of Schönau (d. 1164, nun
  and prophetess), 89–90, 162
  collaborating with her learned
    brother, 90
  and *Liber Viarum Dei*, 90
Elisabeth van Delft (fl. 1400, Utrecht,
  prioress), 31
Eve of St. Martin (d. after 1264,
  anchoress, Liège), 6, 10, 83–5, 87
  author of French *Vie de Julienne*,
    84–5
  non-monastic religious woman, 10
  writing *exempla*, 95–6
exemplum, 11, 13, 100n44
  definition as chronotope, 95,
    100n46
  as the experience of living saints
    recorded in writing, 30, 92, 96
  as a genre to communicate
    common theology, 95–6
  Hadewijch taking up the role of,
    153–4
experience (*experientia*) general, 1–23,
    49, 60n15, 70
  and age, 10, 32–3
  and agency, 25–6, 30, 39
  as a category of analysis, 5
  definition of, 3, 48
  employed as a method of writing
    see under experience in writing
  and feeling (*affectus*), 48–9
  and hands-on training, 2, 3, 10
  including school education, 3–5, 12
  learning from the 'book of
    experience', 1, 11, 17, 67, 172
  lived, 11–12, 49, 83, 87, 105, 107,
    117, 123, 130, 131
  women of, 9, 11, 83, 94–6, 170
  see also specific types of experience; *see
    also under individual women*;
  compare knowledge; ways of
    acquiring knowledge
experience (intellectual), 47–64

and intellectual achievement,
48, 69, 70
interiority as a mode of, 15, 49
meaning knowledge,
understanding, 4
and reason, 69
of thinking, 48–9
and visions and relevations, 12–14,
15, 85, 92
see also under experience in writing;
interiority in letters of Heloise
and Abelard
experience, mystical, 13, 17, 149–62
feminine nature of, 105, 119 n9
see also religious culture;
revelations; visions
experience (practical), 25–46
acquiring knowledge by
observation, 3, 11
and managerial qualities, 3,
25–6, 31
as practical know-how, 3, 15, 31
experience (sapiential)
source of wisdom, 12, 69
type of learning, 4, 21 n40, 70
yielding true knowledge,
8, 12, 118
experience (religious), 65–81
ascetic experience, 25
and devotion, 11–12, 86–8
experiencing and embodying
salvation, 11, 71, 88, 95, 106
as a more direct source of divine
learning, 12, 15, 17, 69,
70, 85, 86
(para-) mystical and supernatural,
15, 36–7
recorded in visions, 149–68
types of religious experience, 8
see also under experience in
writing; religious culture;
individual religious women
experience in writing, 13, 16, 94,
103–21, 149–62
Book of Life as female-male, 18,
83–101

exemplary life experience in songs,
15, 123–47
fabric of: in texts by, for, and about
women, 2
general insights stylized as personal,
131, 149–68
wording prophetic imagery, 17
see also authorship; writers,
medieval female; *individual
authors*
Experiment
experimento docta, 2, 9
Eylard Schoneveld, (15th c.,
Dominican inquisitor), 29,
41 n12

Francis of Montefalco (13th c.), 72

Geert Grote (d. 1384, founder of the
New Devout), 8, 134
Gentile of Foligno (14th c.,
theologian and Spiritual
Franciscan), 70–1
Giovanna of Montefalco (d. 1291,
anchoress, abbess), 71

Hadewijch of Brabant (c. 1250, mystic
and writer), 8, 16, 134, 149–68
analysis of the *Book of Visions* of,
150–5
analysis of Vision Nine of the *Book
of Visions* of, 155–9
and the divine Countenance,
150–1, 152, 153, 154, 156
elaborating on the visions'
revelatory, prophetic
meaning, 155
exchanging experiential, visionary
wisdom with her spiritual child
and guiding her to spiritual
perfection, 16, 130, 149, 161–2,
163 n5
literate in Latin and well-versed in
monastic reading, 16, 154
non-monastic religious woman,
9, 162

Hadewijch of Brabant (c. 1250, mystic and writer)—*Continued*
  no trace of clerical intervention in the work of, 162
  and the Queen (clad in golden robe with crowns) and her maidens (*Timor Dei, Discretio* and *Sapientia*), 151, 155–9
  textual interplay with the Bible, classical authors and medieval tradition, 16, 160–1
  using the image of the woman covered with eyes as in Hildegard of Bingen's *Scivias*, 157
  using similar images as Mechthild of Magdeburg, 158
  using texts and ideas present in her memory, 16, 156–7, 161
  using visionary experience, 12, 13, 16, 130, 149–50, 152
  see also theologians, female
hagiography, 83, 95, 96
  so-called, 96, 100 n43, 101 n48
  as a source for the study of female agency, 17
Helinand of Froidmont (d. after 1229, monk and theologian), 4
  considering the book of life as the book of knowledge, 4
  experiential type of divine learning in, 4
Heloise (d. 1164, theologian and abbess), 6, 10, 47–64
  as an author, 47–58
  and *caritas*, 54–5
  and feeling, 15, 48, 49, 58
  inner experience of, 48, 49, 50, 51, 54, 55
  and integrity, 50, 54
  and intention, 49, 50–1, 52–3, 54, 55
  and interiority as a mode of experience, 15, 49, 58
  and her letters to Abelard, 15, 47–64

  and the study of Scripture, 55–7
  as a theologian, 55
Henry Mande, (d. 1431, New Devout), 22 n47, 36
Henry of Ghent (fl. 1280, scholastic theologian), 66–7, 68, 71, 74
  and woman as doctrix of theology, 66
Hugh of Floreffe (13th c., monk and hagiographer), 2–4, 18 n3, 172
  author of *Vita Juettae* (Yvette of Huy), 2
Hugh of Saint-Cher (d. 1262, scholastic theologian), 90–1, 92–3, 94, 98 n24
  author of *De Prophetia*, 90–1
  see also prophecy
Humility of Faenza (d. 1310, abbess, Florence), 73

Ida of Nivelles (d. 1231, nun), 6
intention (*intentio*), 31, 49, 50–1, 52, 53, 54, 55
  and *caritas*, 54–5
  Heloise's and Abelard's concept of, 50–1
  and inner experience, 50, 51
  and sincerity, 54
intercessory power, religious women's, 38
interiority in letters of Heloise and Abelard, 15, 47–64
  and *homo interior*, 15, 48, 55
  inner through the outer, 50–3
  Mary and Martha as a pair of inner and outer, 52
  as a mode of experience, 15, 49
inwardness, *see* interiority in letters of Heloise and Abelard

James of Vitry (d. 1239, church prelate), 19 n12, 95
  author of *exempla*, 95
  author of *Vita Mariae Oigniacensis*, 19 n12, 95
  inventing the genre of the Book of Life, 95

Jan van der Woude (fl. 1400), 27, 30
Julian of Norwich (d. after 1416, anchoress and theologian), 7, 8, 10, 20n26, 115–17, 172, 173
  and community of discourse, 8, 173
  giving good counsel to guests and visitors, 8, 115, 172
  and the motherhood of God, 115–16
Juliana of Cornillon (d. 1259, theologian and anchoress), 4, 6, 13, 16, 83–101
  and her *Animarum Cibus*, 15
  community of discourse with Eve and others, 84–5
  eucharistic theology of, 13, 85, 87, 91
  experienced, 83
  Latin learning of, 83, 84
  non-monastic religious woman, 10, 84
  as prophetess, 89
  as a theologian using visionary experience, 4, 12, 85
  and the *Vie de Julienne* (Eve of St. Martin), 85, 95–6
  and the *Vita Julianae* (anonymous), 83, 85, 91, 96

Katrijn Jacobs (fl. 1400, Leiden), 27, 33, 34, 35
Katrijn Wouters (fl. 1400, Leiden), 10, 26–7, 29, 30, 33, 34, 37, 39
knowledge
  bookish learning as a type of, 3
  formal acquisition of, 7, 66–8, 70
  life experience and, 3–4, 16, 39, 87, 109, 149–62
  type of prophetic, 3, 13, 87
  type of speculative, divine, 3
  wisdom as a type of, 1, 3, 15, 149–68
  see also ways of acquiring knowledge

language, modes of, 87, 94–6, 99n33

female linguistic idiom, 1, 8, 16, 19, 88, 103–21
leaders, female spiritual, 10, 15, 25–45, 68–74
  acting as spiritual counsellors, 23, 29, 32, 35–7, 71–4
  and discernment in religious matters, 35–7, 39
  hearing confession, 35–6
  pastoral care outside the convent by, 38, 71–4
  supervising the sisters' access to the sacrament, 35
  songs transforming the singer into, 16, 123, 124, 129, 130
  see also under authority, female; women of authority
letter writing (epistolography), 31–2
  Devout Letters, 31–2, 36
  Heloise and Abelard exchanging letters, 15, 47–64
  literariness of Agnes Paston's letters, 171
literacy, 5, 8, 11, 12–14, 16, 26, 85, 171

Machteld Cosijns (d. 1439, Gouda), 10, 28, 30, 33, 37, 38
Machteld Willems (fl. 1416, Gorinchem), 28, 33, 37
Margaret, Lame of Magdeburg (d. c.1250, anchoress), 93
  companionship of, 93
Margaret of Città di Castello (d. 1320, abbess), 68
Margaret of Faenza (d. 1330, abbess, Florence), 6, 15, 16, 65, 73–4
  reading Latin, 73
  travelling outside her monastery to give spiritual advice to men and women, 73–4
  Vitae of, 73
Margaret of Ypres (d. 1234, holy woman), 6
Margaret Paston (15th c.), 170, 172, 173–4

Margaret Paston (15th c.)—*Continued*
emulating her mother-in-law, 174
Margery Kempe (d. c. 1440, holy woman and writer, Bishop's Lynn), 7, 8, 9, 10, 11, 12, 103–21
and authority based on motherhood, 109, 110, 111, 112, 114, 117
using the child hermeneutic in her *Book*, 103–21
collaborating with scribes, 104, 119 n7
developing a language to express the mystical, 16, 107–17
experiences written into the Book of Life, 16, 105, 118
as female evangelist, 112, 116
and her *Book*, 15–16, 104, 105–6, 110–11, 117–18
and lived experience, 105, 107, 108–9, 110, 113–14, 117
mirroring the motherhood of Mary, 109–12
no education in Latin or theology, 106
and old age, 106
spiritual authority of, 103
strategy to find a personal linguistic idiom, 105, 107–13, 117–18
see also authorship; ways of acquiring knowledge
Mary, the Virgin, 7, 36, 54, 87, 135
exemplifying inwardness, 48, 53, 58
and experience, 48, 58
in Hadewijch's ninth Vision, 153, 155–60
and motherhood, 86, 87, 109, 111, 112
teaching the soul in *Die gheestelicke melody*, 124, 126–7, 128, 130, 131
Mary of Oignies (d. 1213, holy woman, anchoress), 4, 5–6, 95
reading from the book of life, 4, 95
mater, maerte (spiritual mother), 10, 27, 34, 35, 39

Martha principalis, 35
mother and *procuratrix*, 10, 29
Mechthild of Magdeburg (d. c. 1282, mystic and writer), 93, 162
companionship, 93
using similar images of the Queen and her maidens as Hadewijch, 158
Memorial, 8, 15, 68–9, 77 n25
authored by Angela of Foligo and Brother A., 69
men of letters (*litterati*), 1, 83, 84, 94–6
Modern Devotion, *see* New Devout
Motherhood
and Margery Kempe, 109–17
perfect motherhood, 151
Yvette of Huy and, 2–3

New Devout, 8, 14, 25–45, 134
non-monastic religious women, 9, 17–18
see also individual women

prophecy, 13, 88–93
and the Antichrist, 70–1
as a charism, 91
definition of, 89–91
as form of knowledge of the divine, 17, 85, 89–93
and Gregorian Reform, 90
Hadewijch's visions as forms of, 155
three stages in each, 91–2, 155
see also revelations; visions
prophetess
female theologians acting as, 89, 93
tradition of medieval prophetesses, 89–90
religious culture, 12–14, 17–18, 86–95
of conventions and traditions, 9, 14, 172
experiential character of, 11–12, 86
re-creating history of salvation in, 11, 87–8

singing and writing spiritual songs
  in, 123–47
 as a thought world, 94
 visual character of, 86–8, 94,
  99 n26
religious formation, women's role in,
  66–81
 see also individual authors; Angela of
  Foligno; Agnes Blannbekin;
  Clare of Montefalco; Hadewijch
  of Brabant; Heloise; Margaret
  of Faenza; Sisters singing *Die
  gheestelicke melody*; leaders,
  spiritual female; women of
  authority
religious knowledge, *see under* ways
  of acquiring knowledge (outside
  the schools)
religious women, non-monastic,
  17–18
 see also individual women
revelations, 115–17
 comparable to book learning, 15
 revelatory meaning of Hadewijch's
  visions, 16, 154–62
 see also Agnes Blannbekin;
  prophecy; visions
Richard of Saint-Victor
  (d. 1173, monk and
  theologian), 58, 159
Ruusbroec, John of, (d. 1381, mystic
  writer), 8, 12, 14, 36
 community of discourse in the
  Brussels of, 8, 14

sacerdotium, 12–14
 distinguished by its Latin culture,
  12, 94
 experientia cast outside, 14
 monopolizing Latin learning, 12,
  71, 90
Salome Sticken (fl. 1400, New
  Devout, Diepenveen), 31, 32
 author of *Vivendi formula*, 32
sermons: sisters composing
  collections of sermons, 135

Abelard's sermons for the Paraclete,
  47–8, 53, 54, 56, 57
sister books, genre of, 13, 30
 and collective memory of a
  convent, 30
 containing series of
  sisters' lives, 135
song cycle, the genre of the, *see Die
  gheestelicke melody*
spirituality, *see Die gheestelicke melody*;
  experience; religious culture
status, female, 32–3
 and age, 33

texts, medieval, 87, 133, 144 n25
 authority of, 96
 female use of language, 1, 103–7
 mouvance and variance, 132–4
 non-linear, non-logic forms of
  female, 94–6, 105
 non-scholastic ways of writing,
  12–15, 94–6, 103–21, 149–68
 transmission of, 133
 see also authorship; Book of Life;
  exemplum
theologians, female, 55, 68, 71–2,
  83–4, 87, 93
 acting as medieval prophetesses,
  83–4, 89
 preaching publicly, 66, 89, 162
 see individual theologians:
  Agnes Blannbekin; Angela of
  Foligno; Clare of Montefalco;
  Heloise; Juliana of Cornillon;
  Julian of Norwich
theology, vernacular, 8, 20 n16,
  65–81, 75 n3
 see also theologians, female; theology
  (*sacra pagina*)
theology (*sacra pagina*),
  65–81, 75 n2
 and experience, 70
 monastic, 65, 67–8, 71–4
 scholastic, 65, 66–7
 scholastic theology as a
  thought style, 94–6

theology *(sacra pagina)*—*Continued*
women's involvement in theological learning and teaching, 71
thinking, 47–64
  experiential quality of, 15, 47, 49
  reciprocal influence of feeling and, 47, 49
  suggested superiority of feeling over, 49
Thomas Aquinas (d. 1274, scholastic theologian), 66, 68, 71, 74
Thomas of Cantimpré (13th c. scholastic theologian and hagiographer), 6, 135
  author of *Book of Bees*, 135
thought world, 94–6
  thought style, 94–6
  see also community of discourse

Ubertino of Casale (1259–c.1328, Franciscan theologian), 68, 69–70, 71, 73
  author of *Arbor Vitae Crucifixe Jesu*, 68–9
  influenced by Angela of Foligno e.a., 69–70, 72

vademecum for the spiritual life, *see* Book of Life
vernacular literature, 13, 17
  and experience, 8
vernacular theology, *see* theology, vernacular
Vie de Julienne (Eve of St. Martin), 85, 95–6
visions, 11, 12, 13, 16, 29, 74, 83–101, 130, 149–68
visions as an alternative form of experiential scriptural exegesis, 149–68
  collections of, 215–16
  creating experiential knowledge, 13, 36–7, 85, 86, 94–6, 99 n29
  received in church, 86, 87, 92
  see also revelations; *individual mystics*; *compare* prophecy
Vita et Revelationes (Agnes Blannbekin), 15, 83, 91, 92, 95, 96
  recorded by Franciscan scribe, 85
  stylized as the personal record of mystical visions, 92, 130–1
Vita Julianae (anonymous), 83, 85, 91, 96

ways of acquiring knowledge (outside the schools), 6–7, 10–12
  by dialogues of love of God, 92
  experiential, 1, 3, 87
  by imitation, 30–2, 150, 161–2
  learning by experience, 3, 18, 39
  receiving visions and revelations, 36–7, 85–7
  re-creating the history of salvation, 86–8
  prophetic knowledge as, 3, 87, 88–93
  by studying books, 3
  supernatural, religious, 36–7
ways of recording knowledge (outside the tradition of the schools), *see* Book of Life; texts, medieval; writers, medieval female; *individual authors*
Wermboud van Boskoop (d. 1413, Chapter of Utrecht), 28–9, 34, 36, 37–8
William of Saint-Thierry (d. 1148, abbot and mystic), 48, 49, 57
women of authority, 6, 10, 18, 25–45, 68–81, 169–74
  addressing theological matters, 55–7, 68, 71–3, 74, 83–6, 87, 89, 91–3, 95–6, 154–61
  advising people inside and outside their convent, 10, 38, 71, 72–3
  and agency, 25–6, 30, 39
  and eloquence, 34–5
  by experience, 10, 25, 31, 92
  founding convents, 25–9, 33, 34

having discernment in religious matters, 35–7
having managerial qualities, 25–6, 34–5
hearing confessions, 35–6
preaching publicly, 66, 162
taking legal action, 30
spiritual woman (*geestelike vrouwe*), 29, 92
supervising elections, 27, 29, 37
see also under authority, female; experience (religious); leaders, female spiritual; status, female
writers, medieval female *see individual writers*: Aechte Eernstes; Agnes Blannbekin; Agnes Paston; Angela of Foligno; Elisabeth of Schönau; Eve of St. Martin; Hadewijch of Brabant; Heloise; Humility of Faenza; Juliana of Cornillon; Julian of Norwich; Margery Kempe; Mechthild of Magdeburg; Paston women; Salome Sticken; (religious sisters composing collections of); sermons (sisters compiling and writing); sister books, genre of
writers, medieval male, *see* Abelard; Angela of Foligno's Brother A.; Agnes Blannbekin's Franciscan scribe; Margery Kempe's scribe

Yvette of Huy (1158–1228, mother and anchoress), 2–4, 6, 18 n3
learned from the book of experience, 2–4
possessing fivefold knowledge, 3–4
well-versed in sacred learning, 4

INDEX OF MODERN AUTHORS

Note: All names of modern authors, mentioned in the texts and the notes are indexed by page number or by page number plus note.

Aelst, José van, 42n22, 98n12
Allen, Hope Emily, 118n4
Allen, Prudence, 67, 76nn13, 15
Alphandéry, Paul, 98n22
Arendt, Hanna, 60n15
Armstrong, Timothy J., 64n71
Atkinson, Clarissa, 121n46

Baaij, Anna Maria, 146n38
Babinsky, Ellen L., 167n60
Baert, Barbara, 141n1
Barrat, Alexandra, 98n14
Barshack, Lior, 22n46
Basserman, Lawrence, 22n46
Beauvoir, Simone de, 106, 107, 119n18
Benson, Larry D., 118n3, 175n6
Benz, Ernst, 165n27
Berndt, Rainer, 61n16
Blamires, Alcuin, 76n11, 167n61
Blasucci, Antonio, 78n27
Bocquet, Damien, 60n10
Bollmann, Annette M., 41n17, 42n25, 146n36
Boswell, John, 120n24
Brémond, Claude, 100n44
Brinkerink, D.A., 41n13, 42n22
Brown, Catherine, 61n24, 62n30
Bruin, Martine, 140, 143n17, 144n22
Bruning, E., 143n20
Bürkle, Susanne, 21n41
Burr, David, 77n18, 78n36, 81n68

Busby, Keith, 144n25
Buuren, A.M.J. van, 144n27, 147n43
Buytaert, Eligius M., 63n65
Bynum, Caroline Walker, 17, 22n50, 112, 119n9, 120n39, 166n39

Carasso-Kok, Marijke, 41n18
Carruthers, Mary, 164n12
Cerquiglini, Bernard, 133, 144n25
Chase, Steven, 163n6, 164nn9, 12, 166n37, 167nn49, 59
Chenu, M.-D., 50, 61n19
Cixous, Hélène, 103, 105, 107, 109, 117, 118n1, 119nn11, 13, 120n28, 121n58
Clanchy, Michael T., 59nn1, 3, 60n13, 61n23, 62n56
Clark, Anne L., 98n23
Coakley, John, 13, 22nn42, 49, 51, 78n26
Constable, Giles, 19n13, 59n3
Cornelissen, J., 143n9

Dahan, Gilbert, 63n67
Dalarun, Jacques, 78n28
D'Alverny, Marie-Thérèse, 167n56
Damiata, Marino, 77nn18, 19, 78nn33, 34, 79nn47, 50
Davis, Charles, 77nn18, 24
Delville, Jean-Pierre, 97n1
De Santis, Paola, 61n18
Desplenter, Youri, 145n33

Diehl, Peter D., 21 n39
Dijk, Hans van, 165 n29
Dijk, Mathilde van, 43 n38, 45 n77
Dijk, Rudolf Th. M. van, 145 n32
Dinzelbacher, Peter, 97 nn2, 8, 100 n43, 162 n1, 165 n27
Donavin, Georgiana, 147 n37
Douglas, Mary, 94, 100 n39
Dronke, Peter, 59 nn1, 3, 61 n24
Dutton, Elisabeth, 145 n28

Edelman, Lee, 111, 120 n33
Elder, E. Rozanne, 63 n63
Engen, Hildo van, 40 n1, 145 n31
Erler, Mary C., 21 n28

Farley, Mary Hardman, 120 n23
Fradenburg, Louise, 120 n38
Fraeters, Veerle, 6, 16, 130, 141 n1, 149–68, 163 n5, 165 nn28, 30, 179
Fredericq, Paul, 41 n12

Gabriel, Astrik L., 75 n5
Ganck, Roger de, 165 n26
Georgianna, Linda, 47, 48, 60 nn5, 11, 61 n24
Glasscoe, Marion, 120 n23, 121 n50
Goldberg, P.J.P., 119 n12
Goudriaan, Koen, 6, 15, 25–45, 44 n65, 145 n31, 172, 177
Griffith, Fiona J., 21 n33, 59 n2, 61 n17, 63 n64
Grube, Karl, 41 n13
Gunn, Gate, 20 n16, 98 n14
Gurjewitsch [Gurevic], Aaron, 95, 99 n31, 100 n44

Hadot, Pierre, 64 n71
Hamburger, Jeffrey, 98 n19, 165 n27
Harbison, Craig, 98 n19
Hart, Columba, 144 n28, 160, 162 n2, 166 nn39, 40
Hascher-Burger, Ulrike, 147 n43
Haug, Walter, 20 n24, 163 n2, 165 n27
Heijden, Maarten van den, 77 n18, 80 n59

Hemptinne, Thérèse de, 19 n11, 165 n28
Hendrikman, Anton J., 40 n2
Hollywood, Amy, 21 n40, 100 n45, 101 n48, 119 n9
Houts, Elisabeth van, 170, 175 n3
Hutchison, Ann M., 20 n26

Irigaray, Luce, 1, 2, 9, 11, 12, 14, 18 n1, 20 n25, 21 nn32, 35, 37, 22 nn45, 53, 120 n41, 175 n17

Jaeger, C. Stephen, 60 n3, 163 n5
Jay, Martin, 60 n15
Johnson, Penelope D., 76 n12
Joldersma, Hermina, 144 n27, 145 n30, 147 n43
Jolivet, Jean, 61 n24
Jordan, Mark D., 76 n8

Kaup, Matthias, 78 n38, 79 n40
Kearney, Eileen, 63 n63
Kienzle, Beverly Mayne, 75 n7, 178
King, Margot, 20 n12, 97 n8, 100 n41
Klotz, Margaret E., 75 n3, 79 nn43, 44, 80 n55
Knuttel, J.A.N., 143 n21, 144 n27, 146 n39
Koorn, Florence W.J., 40 n2, 41 n12
Kors, M.M., 44 n60
Kristeva, Julia, 120 n41
Kühler, W.J., 42 n25
Kurath, Hans, 19 n5
Kwakkel, Erik, 144 n28, 168 n62

LaCapra, Dominick, 17, 19 n6, 22 n48
Lachance, Paul, 78 nn29, 31
Langer, Otto, 165 n27
Largier, Niklaus, 20 n24, 21 n31
Lavezzo, Kathy, 120 nn38, 41
Lawes, Richard, 120 n23
Leclercq, Jean, 21 n34
Leonardi, Claudio, 79 nn43, 46
Lerner, Robert E., 61 n22, 78 n38, 79 n40, 167 n60
Lesser, Bertram, 41 n16

INDEX OF MODERN AUTHORS

Levin, Carole, 63 n63
Lievens, Robrecht, 143 n17
Ligtenberg, Christina, 27, 40 n4, 43 n46, 44 n74
Lingier, Carine, 146 n35
Louis, René, 60 n6
Luijk, Madelon van, 40 nn4, 6, 45 n79, 145 n31
Luscombe, David, 61 nn22, 24

Makowski, Elizabeth, 80 n68
Marenbon, John, 50, 52, 59 n1, 61 nn20, 25, 62 nn34, 50, 63 nn58, 68, 64 nn74, 75
Marks, Elaine, 118 n1
Martin, John Jeffries, 62 n54
Matter, E. Ann, 78 n26
McAvoy, Liz Herbert, 1–23, 11, 15, 20 n26, 98 n14, 103–21, 121 nn43, 49, 167 n61, 172, 177
McGinn, Bernard, 7, 19 n7, 20 n24, 21 n40, 75 nn3, 4, 77 n17, 96, 99 n29, 101 n48, 144 n28
McGuire, Brian Patrick, 44 n73, 77 n16
McLaughlin, Mary, 47, 50, 60 n6, 61 n20
McLaughlin, T.P., 59 n3
McNamara, Jo Ann, 18 n3
Meertens, Maria, 145 n34
Menestò, Enrico, 79 nn43, 46
Mertens, Thom, 16, 19 n14, 22 n47, 44 n61, 123–47, 146 n36, 146 n37, 177
Mews, Constant J., 59 nn1, 3, 61 n18, 63 nn58, 64, 70
Mierlo, J. van, 144 n28, 162 n2, 163 n4
Minnis, Alistair J., 22 n52, 76 nn9, 10
Moi, Toril, 119 n18, 120 n41
Moll, W., 44 n61
Mommaers, Paul, 145 n28
Mooney, Catherine M., 77 n26, 78 nn27, 30, 31
Moore, Robert I., 13, 21 n39, 22 n44
Morawski, J., 75 n5
Muckle, J.T., 59 n3

Muessig, Carolyn, 6, 8, 15, 65–81, 100 nn36, 40, 167 n61, 178
Mulder, Herman, 140, 144 n22
Mulder-Bakker, Anneke B., 1–21, 15, 18 n3, 19 nn11, 12, 25, 26, 33, 43 nn36, 37, 44 n73, 75 n4, 76 n12, 78 n37, 83–101, 97 nn1, 3,7, 98 n16, 99 nn24, 26, 100 nn36, 41, 45, 131, 140, 144 n22, 146 n37, 163 n5, 165 n27, 167 nn50, 61, 175 nn9, 14, 178
Murk Jansen, Saskia, 145 n28

Nessi, Silvestro, 79 nn46, 47, 80 n53
Newman, Barbara, 97 n1, 165 n27, 166 nn39, 44
Nichols, John A., 77 n16
Nichols, Stephen G., 144 n25

Obbema, Pieter, 132, 142 n1, 143 nn15, 17, 19, 21, 144 n26, 146 n41
Olson, Linda, 20 n23, 60 n3
Oosterman, Johan, 140, 141, 143 n17, 144 n22, 145 n34
Orlandi, Giovanni, 59 n3

Paquelin, L., 162 n1
Peppermüller, Rolf, 64 n72
Petroff, Elizabeth Avilda, 162 n1
Poel, Dieuwke van der, 144 n27, 145 n30, 147 n43
Post, R.R., 145 n31
Potestà, Gian Luca, 77 n18
Pranger, M. Burcht, 60 n9
Pryds, Darleen, 75 n7

Ranft, Patricia, 61 n17
Renna, Thomas, 75 n2
Reynaert, Joris, 166 n41
Rice, Nicole R., 22 n47
Richmond, Colin, 175 n7
Riddy, Felicity, 20 n26
Riedl, Matthias, 21 n40
Roest, Bert, 77 n18, 78 n28, 80 n59
Roren, Paul, 163 n6

Roth, F., 162 n1
Ruh, Kurt, 85, 97 n2, 133, 144 nn24, 28, 163 n5, 168 n62

Saurma-Jeltsch, Lieselotte E., 166 n39
Scheepsma, Wybren, 31, 32, 40 n1, 41 n17, 42 nn22, 23, 25, 44 n59, 146 n36, 163 n2
Schiller, Gertrud, 167 n56
Schmidt, Heinrich, 166 n36
Schmidt, Margaretha, 166 n36
Schmitt, Clément, 78 n27
Scott, Joan Wallach, 19 n6
Seggelen, Andreas J.M. van, 146 n40
Sensi, Mario, 79 n45
Signori, Gabriela, 146 n35
Simonetti, Adele, 80 n57
Simons, Walter, 19 n11
Smith, Lesley, 76 n11, 147 n36
Smits, Edmé Renno, 59 n3
Sommerfeldt, John R., 75 n2
Spijker, Ineke van 't, 15, 47–64, 178
Staley, Lynn, 118 n5
Stoklaska, Anneliese, 97 n2
Stutvoet-Joanknecht, Christina M., 20 n21, 146 n35
Summit, Jennifer, 22 n52
Suydam, Mary, 99 n34

Tersteeg, Jaques, 165 n29
Thier, Ludger, 77 n25
Tobin, Frank, 166 n26
Torrel, Jean-Pierre, 98 n24

Van Engen, John, 7, 20 n23, 40 n1, 42 n25
Verger, Jacques, 76 n12
Verhoeven, C.W.M., 167 n52
Verhoeven, Gerrit, 40 n6
Vermeulen, P.J. 41 n12
Voaden, Rosalynn, 98 n22, 100 n35, 167 n50
Von Moos, Peter, 59 n3

Waddell, Chrysogonus, 61 n26
Warnar, Geert, 8, 20 n27, 21 n29, 44 n60
Watson, Jeanie, 63 n63
Watson, Nicholas, 20 n26
Watt, Diane, 19 n14, 20 nn22, 26, 78 n30, 169–75, 174 n1, 175 nn4, 8, 12, 16, 178
Waugh, Scott L., 21 n36
Wehrli-Johns, Martina, 22 n43
Wetherbee, Wintrop, 60 n8
Wheeler, Bonnie, 59 n1
White, Hugh, 119 n17
Wiethaus, Ulrike, 92, 97 n2, 99 n34, 101 n48
Wijk, N. van, 145 n32
Willaert, Frank, 144 n27, 145 n29, 162 n2, 165 n29, 177

Yoshikawa, Naoë Kukita, 121 n53

Ziolkowski, Jan M., 59 n3, 164 n12
Zumthor, Paul, 133, 144 n24